84 Inspiring Women

The Lives of Influential Sheroes that Rebelled, Made a Difference, and Inspire (Feminist Book)

By History Activist Readers

Introduction

This book is a must read for all women, from middle schoolers to retirees.

The 84 powerful stories in this Feminist book will inspire you and make your life more colorful. It's perfect for anyone looking to learn more about feminism as well as gain insight into how these female heroes shaped our world today.

Enjoy short biographies of some of the most inspiring women in history and alive today. It is a great way to get inspired and learn more about the greatness of women.

Including:

- 19 women in science
- 15 female artists
- 18 female freedom fighters
- 16 influential women
- 16 Black women

Though much progress has been made in the fight for gender equality, there is still a long way to go. This inspiring book tells the stories of 84 remarkable women who have made a difference in the world. From early suffragettes to modern-day politicians, these women have rebelled against the status quo and fought for change. In doing so, they have paved the way for future generations of women.

These female heroes come from all walks of life and their stories are sure to resonate with readers of all ages. This book is an essential read for anyone who wants to learn more about the powerful women who have shaped history. It is sure to inspire readers to follow in their footsteps and make a difference in the world.

You will be amazed by the courage, strength, and resilience of these sheroes. They are an inspiration to us all and prove that anything is possible if you put your mind to it. Don't miss out on this amazing opportunity to get inspired by some of the most powerful women in history and today.

Purchase your copy now!

Table of Content

1. Stephanie Kwolek (1923 - 2014)

American chemist best known for her role in inventing Kevlar

"I hope I'm saving lives. There are very few people in their careers that have the opportunity to do something to benefit mankind."

Stephanie Louise Kwolek (New Kensington, July 31, 1923 - Wilmington, June 18, 2014) was a Polish-American chemist whose main interest was in polymer chemistry. She is the discoverer of poly-p-phenylene terephthalamide or *para-aramid*, better known by the brand name *Kevlar*.

Biography

Kwolek was the daughter of Polish immigrants Jan Kwolek and Nellie Zajdel Kwolek, who had settled in New Kensington in 1923. Her father died when she was ten years old. Kwolek earned her bachelor's degree in chemistry in 1946 from Margaret Morrison Carnegie College of Carnegie Mellon University. Her plans were to earn money to continue her studies in medicine.

In 1946 Hale Charch offered Kwolek a job with the DuPont chemical company. She liked that work so much that she ended up working there until her retirement. In 1950 she moved to Wilmington for her work. Here Kwolek discovered Kevlar in 1965. Kwolek retired in 1986, but was still associated with DuPont as a consultant. During her career she was credited with about twenty patents, including that for the production of Kevlar.

She died at 90 in a Delaware hospital.

Highlights

- DuPont had introduced nylon just before World War II, and in the postwar years the company resumed its drive into the highly competitive market of synthetic fibres.
- DuPont moved with the company's Pioneering Research Laboratory to Wilmington, Delaware, in 1950 and retired with the rank of research associate in 1986.
- Kwolek is best known for her work during the 1950s and '60s with aramids, or "aromatic polyamides," a type of polymer that can be made into strong, stiff, and flame-resistant fibres.
- Her laboratory work in aramids was conducted under the supervision of research fellow Paul W. Morgan, who calculated that the aramids would form stiff fibres owing to the presence of bulky benzene (or "aromatic") rings in their molecular chains but that they would have to be prepared from solution because they melt only at very high temperatures.

2. Rachel Carson (1907 - 1964)

American marine biologist and nature writer

"One way to open your eyes is to ask yourself, "What if I had never seen this before? What if I knew I would never see it again?"

Rachel Louise Carson (Springdale (Pennsylvania), May 27, 1907 - Silver Spring (Maryland), April 14, 1964) was a biologist who grew up in Springdale, Pennsylvania. She became best known for her books and her fight to protect the environment.

Lifecycle

Rachel's love of nature was encouraged by her mother. From an early age she wrote about it and this also determined her later choice of study at the Pennsylvania College for Women (now Chatham College). In 1929 she graduated and in 1932 she received her doctorate in zoology from Johns Hopkins University. She later taught at this university and at the University of Maryland.

She wrote radio scripts for the U.S. Bureau of Fisheries during the depression years and a number of articles on natural history for the Baltimore Sun. Then she also began a fifteen-year career as a scientist and publisher in federal service. Eventually she was promoted to chief editor for all publications for the U.S. Fish and Wildlife Service.

The main line in all her works is the idea that the human race is only a part of nature, while on the other hand it possesses the capacity to alter the environment, in some cases irreparably. Rachel Carson was so alarmed by the abundant use of synthetic chemical insecticides after World War II that she focused on them from then on. She wanted to warn the public about the effects of pesticide abuse. She became world-famous with her book *Silent Spring* (1962), in which environmental issues take a central place. The title is a reference to the apocalyptic spring when the birds stopped singing because they were exterminated due to the use of pesticides. Despite the backlash and criticism, her book greatly stimulated research into non-toxic pesticides. In 1963 she gave a speech to the U.S. Congress demanding new human health and environmental protection.

Rachel Louise Carson died in 1964 after a long battle with breast cancer. Her ideas about the beauty and protection of life continue to inspire new generations to protect the world and all living things.

Silent Spring

As her last book, Rachel Carson wrote her seminal work on environmental issues, *Silent Spring*. The book is still timely and based on anecdotal, systematic and literature review of the use of various pesticides. It was widely supported by scientists, including John F. Kennedy's scientific advisory committee. Initial criticism came mainly from the chemical industry. Starting in the 2000s, libertarian think tanks also attacked the book, falsely claiming that agricultural restrictions on DDT would lead to more deaths from malaria.

Highlights

- Rachel Carson early developed a deep interest in the natural world.
- She entered Pennsylvania College for Women with the intention of becoming a writer but soon changed her major field of study from English to biology.
- An article in The Atlantic Monthly in 1937 served as the basis for her first book, Under the Sea-Wind, published in 1941. The Sea Around Us (1951) became a national best seller, won a National Book Award, and was eventually translated into 30 languages.
- The outlook of the environmental movement of the 1960s and early '70s was generally pessimistic, reflecting a pervasive sense of "civilization malaise" and a conviction that Earth's long-term prospects were bleak.

3. Maria Goeppert Mayer (1906 - 1972)

German-born American theoretical physicist and 1963 Nobel Prize winner

"Winning the prize wasn't half as exciting as doing the work itself."

Maria Gertrud Goeppert-Mayer (Katowice, June 28, 1906 - San Diego, February 20, 1972) was a German-born American theoretical physicist. In 1963 she received the Nobel Prize in Physics at the same time as Eugene Wigner and together with Hans Jensen "for their discoveries concerning the shell structure of the atomic nucleus." She was the second female winner of the Nobel Prize in Physics, after Marie Curie in 1903.

Biography

Maria Gertrud Göppert was born in Katowice, Upper Silesia, the only child of Friedrich Göppert and Maria Wolff. The family moved to Göttingen in 1910 when her father was offered an appointment as professor of

paediatrics at the university there. Her father was for that time a
progressive person who believed in equal opportunities for boys and girls.

Göppert attended private and public schools in Göttingen and received an
excellent education. All the more so because she was surrounded by
students and teachers from her father's university, including the later
Nobel laureates Enrico Fermi, Werner Heisenberg, Paul Dirac and
Wolfgang Pauli, while mathematician David Hilbert was her closest
neighbor. Her father placed her at a private *Frauenstudium* run by
suffragettes, which prepared girls for the *Abitur*, the university entrance
examination. Although this school closed in the 1920s due to the
hyperinflation of the Weimar Republic, the teachers continued to teach
their pupils.

In 1924 Göppert passed her entrance exam and was able to enter
university with the intention of becoming a mathematician. But after taking
a seminar from Max Born, she switched to physics. Among her professors
were three future Nobel laureates: Born, James Franck and Adolf
Windaus. She spent a year in Cambridge, studying English at Ginton
College but also met Ernest Rutherford. In 1930 Mayer completed her
scientific doctorate (on two-photon excitation). That same year she
married physical chemist Joseph Edward Mayer (1904-1983), James
Franck's assistant. The following year the couple moved to the United
States, Mayer's native country.

For the next several years Goeppert-Mayer worked unofficially or as an
unpaid assistant at the universities where her husband was a professor.
First at Johns Hopkins University in Baltimore (1931-39), then at Columbia
University (1940-46) and finally at the University of Chicago. It was the
time of the Great Depression and no university wanted to hire the wife of a
professor because of the anti-nepotism policy. In America she also had
her two children, in 1933 daughter Maria-Ann was born and five years
later son Peter Conrad.

Nevertheless, she was able to do research on energy transfer from solid
surfaces, together with the physicist Karl Herzfeld with whom she wrote
some papers. At Columbia she worked together with chemists and
physicists like Harold Urey, Willard Libby and Enrico Fermi. During the war
she became friends with Edward Teller, a Hungarian refugee who would
play an important role in the development of the hydrogen bomb, and with
whom she would work on the Mantattan Project.

Chicago was the first university where she was not seen as a nuisance
(because of the prevailing discrimination against women) but was

welcomed with open arms, but again they could not offer her a permanent position. She was appointed volunteer professor at the faculty of physics and at the *Institute for Nuclear Studies*. She also got a position at the *Argonne National Laboratory*, despite her little knowledge of nuclear physics. It was during her time at Chicago and Argonne that she developed the mathematical model concerning the structure of atomic shells, the work for which - together with Jensen - she received the Nobel Prize.

In 1960, Goeppert-Mayer was appointed (full time) professor of physics at the University of California at San Diego, although her salary was only three quarters of that of her husband. Although she suffered a stroke shortly after arrival, she was able to continue her research and teaching for several years. She died of a heart attack in February 1972.

Magic numbers

It was Teller who asked Mayer to further investigate his theory of the origin of elements. They discovered that certain elements, such as tin and lead, were much more stable than could be explained by current theory. This was also true for other elements. When Mayer looked at the number of neutrons and protons in the nucleus of these elements, she saw that certain numbers recurred. She called these numbers "magic numbers" and identified seven of them: 2, 8, 20, 28, 50, 82 and 126. Any element that has any of these numbers of protons or neutrons is very stable. Nuclei in which both the number of protons and the number of neutrons are a magic number are called 'double magic' and are extra stable. These include ^{4}He$_2$, ^{16}O$_8$, ^{40}Ca$_{20}$, ^{48}Ca$_{20}$, ^{48}Ni$_{28}$ and ^{208}Pb$_{82}$.

Based on this theory she developed the shell model of the atomic nucleus, in which the nucleus is composed of shell-shaped layers in which the nucleons move. She published her hypothesis in the journal *Physical Review*. The German physicist Hans Jensen reached the same conclusion independently, but submitted his article to the same journal two months after her. The journal published his work one issue before Mayer's, however. After an exchange of letters they decided to write a book together: *Elementary Theory of Nuclear Shell Structure* (1955).

Highlights

- Maria Goeppert studied physics at the University of Göttingen (Ph.D., 1930) under a committee of three Nobel Prize winners.

- In 1930 she married the American chemical physicist Joseph E. Mayer, and a short time later she accompanied him to Johns Hopkins University in Baltimore, Maryland.
- In 1939 she and her husband both received appointments in chemistry at Columbia University, where Maria Mayer worked on the separation of uranium isotopes for the atomic bomb project.
- Maria Goeppert received a regular appointment as full professor in 1959.

4. Rosalind Franklin (1920 - 1958)

English chemist and X-ray crystallographer

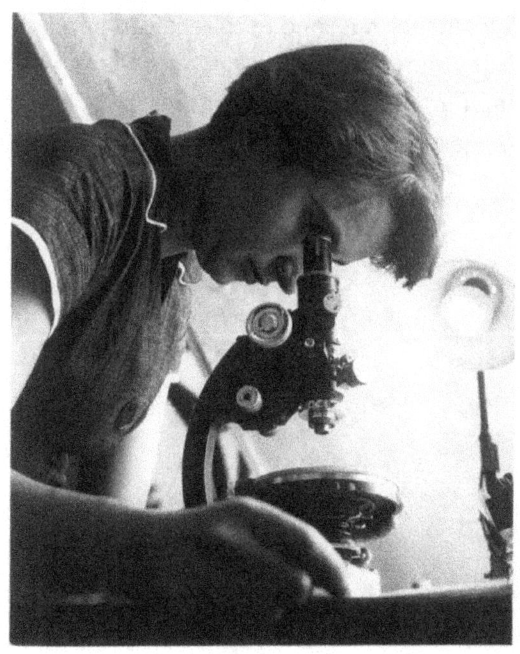

"Science and everyday life cannot and should not be separated."

Rosalind Elsie Franklin (London, 25 July 1920 - there, 16 April 1958) was a British chemist known primarily for her contributions to the discovery of the structure of DNA using X-ray diffraction.

Youth

Franklin was a daughter of banker Ellis Franklin and his wife Muriel Frances Waley (1894-1976). She attended St. Paul's Girls School, one of the few girls' schools with physics and chemistry classes, at the age of twelve. At fifteen, she decided she wanted to become a researcher. However, her father was against higher education for women and wanted her to become a social worker. He therefore refused to pay for her university education, although she had already passed the entrance

16

examination to Cambridge University. He only relented when an aunt agreed to pay for her studies and his wife appeared to support their daughter.

Scientific career

In 1938 Franklin was admitted to Newnham College at Cambridge University, where she graduated in natural sciences in 1941, specializing in physical chemistry. After another year at the university she became a researcher at the British Coal Utilisation Research Association in 1942, during the Second World War. There she investigated the porosity of coal with helium in order to use coal as economically as possible due to the scarcity of coal in the war period, and to make good gas masks with coal powder. This work formed the basis for her doctorate in physical chemistry with the thesis *The physical chemistry of solid organic colloids with special reference to coal* at Cambridge University in 1945.

Paris

Her period at Cambridge was followed by three years of study in Paris at the "Laboratoire Central des Services Chimiques de l'Etat". Here she learned the X-ray diffraction techniques of crystallography that would contribute to the discovery of the structure of DNA.

London

In 1948 she returned to the United Kingdom as a researcher in the field of molecular X-ray diffraction at King's College London under the direction of Sir John Randall.

Unclear responsibilities for the DNA testing caused friction between Franklin and Maurice Wilkins, a longtime Randall researcher. Franklin was secretive about her results and also behaved strangely: despite the fact that her research showed that DNA showed a helix structure, she declared to everyone that this was not the case, and in the summer of 1952 she posted in her research institute a message saying: "It is with great regret that we have to announce the death, on Friday 18th July 1952 of D.N.A. helix ... It is hoped that Dr. M. H. F. Wilkins will speak in memory of the late helix". Wilkins showed X-ray diffraction pictures of DNA to James Watson, the Cambridge competitor, who got the idea that the structure of DNA must look like a double helix, after Linus Pauling had come up with a similar but wrong model (he assumed a triple helix instead of a double helix). This resulted in an article by Watson and Francis Crick in the

scientific weekly Nature. Immediately preceding in the same issue of
Nature also an article by Franklin appeared in support of his conclusions.

Whether Franklin herself would have found the structure of DNA and to
what extent her name should be mentioned in connection with the
discovery of the structure of DNA remains a matter of discussion to this
day. The fact remains that without her high quality X-ray diffraction photos
of DNA it would have taken longer before the structure would have been
found.

Birbeck College

After the DNA publications, she left for Birkbeck College where she got her
own research group and concentrated on viruses - she was only allowed
to leave King's College if she stopped working on DNA - particularly
tobacco mosaic virus and polio virus.

During a visit to the United States in 1956, she fell ill and was diagnosed
with ovarian cancer. She died two years later at the age of 37 as a result
of this illness, which was most likely caused by her nonchalant handling of
X-rays during her research: she rarely wore a lead apron and frequently
exposed herself to an X-ray beam.

In 1962, Watson, Crick and Wilkins received the Nobel Prize. It is possible
that Rosalind Franklin would have shared in this honour had she still been
alive. However, the prize is not awarded posthumously, nor is it awarded
to more than three people.

Highlights

- Rosalind Franklin attended St. Paul's Girls' School before studying
  physical chemistry at Newnham College, University of Cambridge.
- After graduating in 1941, she received a fellowship to conduct
  research in physical chemistry at Cambridge.
- When she began her research at King's College, very little was known
  about the chemical makeup or structure of DNA.
- Her work to make clearer X-ray patterns of DNA molecules laid the
  foundation for James Watson and Francis Crick to suggest in 1953
  that the structure of DNA is a double-helix polymer, a spiral
  consisting of two DNA strands wound around each other.

5. Rosalyn S. Yalow (1921 - 2011)

American medical physicist, and the second woman to ever win the Nobel Prize in medicine

"We must believe in ourselves as no one else will believe in us, we must match our expectations with the competence, courage and determination to succeed."

Rosalyn Sussman Yalow, born *Rosalyn Sussman*, (New York, July 19, 1921 - there, May 30, 2011) was an American medical physicist and Nobel laureate. In 1977, she won the Nobel Prize in medicine for developing the Yalow-Berson method. She shared the prize with Roger Guillemin and Andrew Schally who received the prize for other research.

Biography

Yalow was born the daughter of Simon Sussman and Clara Zipper, Jewish immigrants. She was educated at Walton High School in New York. In the late 1930s she began her studies at Hunter College, a college attached to the City University of New York for female students. Here she developed her interest in physics and chemistry.

Yalow began her career as secretary to Dr. Rudolf Schoenheimer, a prominent biochemist with the College of Physicians and Surgeons at Columbia University. She trained in stenography and served as secretary to Michael Heidelberger. Because of World War II many men were drafted, she received an offer to assist with physics classes at the University of Illinois at Urbana-Champaign. She was the first female staff member since 1917. In 1943, she married Aaron Yalow. In 1945 she became the first woman at that university to receive her doctorate in nuclear physics.

After college, she joined the Bronx Veterans Administration Hospital to assist in setting up a radioisotopic service. Here she met Solomon Berson, a New York physician researching diabetes, with whom she subsequently worked until his death in 1972. Together they developed radioimmunoassay (RIA), a technique by which - by means of radioactive tracers - minute quantities of a biological substance can be measured in the blood. Originally this method was used to measure insulin levels in diabetes mellitus patients. Later the technique was also applied to many other substances such as hormones, toxins, vitamins and enzymes, as well as measuring concentrations of narcotics in the blood. Despite the great commercial potential of the method, Yalow and Berson refused to patent it because they wanted humanity to benefit from this technique.

In 1968, Yallow was appointed research professor at Mount Sinai Hospital, New York. She later held the position of Solomon Berson Distinguished Professor at Large there.

In 1975, Yalow and Berson received the AMA Scientific Achievement Award. The following year, Yalow became the first female winner of the Albert Lasker Award for Basic Medical Research, and in 1988 she received the National Medal of Science.

Highlights

- Rosalyn S. Yalow graduated with honors from Hunter College of the City University of New York in 1941 and four years later received her Ph.D. in physics from the University of Illinois.

- From 1946 to 1950 she lectured on physics at Hunter, and in 1947 she became a consultant in nuclear physics to the Bronx Veterans Administration Hospital, where from 1950 to 1970 she was physicist and assistant chief of the radioisotope service.
- With a colleague, the American physician Solomon A. Berson, Yalow began using radioactive isotopes to examine and diagnose various disease conditions.
- Yalow and Berson's investigations into the mechanism underlying type II diabetes led to their development of RIA.
- In 1976 she was the first female recipient of the Albert Lasker Basic Medical Research Award.

6. Rita Levi-Montalcini (1909 - 2012)

Italian Nobel laureate, honored for her work in neurobiology

"Above all, don't fear difficult moments. The best comes from them"

Rita Levi-Montalcini (Turin, 22 April 1909 - Rome, 30 December 2012) was an Italian neurologist who in 1986, along with her colleague Stanley Cohen, received the Nobel Prize in Physiology or Medicine for their discovery of growth factors. She was appointed for life in the Italian Senate in 2001 and until her death was the oldest living Nobel Prize winner, and also the first to live to be at least 100. She was also, until her death, the oldest active politician in the world. In Italy she was awarded the title *"Cavaliere di Gran Croce Ordine al Merito della Repubblica Italiana"* (Knight of the Grand Cross of Merit of the Republic of Italy).

Lifecycle

Rita Levi-Montalcini, like her twin sister Paola, was born in 1909 in Turin to a Sephardic Jewish family. The twin sisters were the youngest of four children. Their father, Adamo Levi, was an electrician and a gifted mathematician. Their mother, Adele Montalcini, was a talented painter and, according to Levi-Montalcini, 'an outstanding human being'.

After a friend of her family died of cancer, Levi-Montalcini decided to study medicine. Despite the objections of her father, who felt that a professional career would interfere with her duties as a wife and mother, she studied medicine in Turin from 1930. After graduating *summa cum laude* in 1936, she became assistant to Giuseppe Levi, with whom she had worked during her studies. In 1938, however, Benito Mussolini introduced anti-Semitic laws which, among other things, prohibited Jews from holding academic positions. During World War II, she conducted her experiments in a home laboratory dealing with the growth of axons (nerves) in chicken embryos. For this she needed large fertilized eggs, which she collected by bicycle from local farmers. These experiments formed the basis for her later research. This first genetic laboratory was in her bedroom, and when her family later fled to Florence, she installed a home laboratory there as well. Her family returned to Turin in 1945.

In September 1946, Levi-Montalcini accepted an invitation to continue her research for one semester at Washington University in Saint Louis, under the supervision of Professor Viktor Hamburger. In 1952 she achieved her most important scientific breakthrough; the isolation of the growth factor of nerve cells, the protein NGF, in the brains of embryos.

In 1958 she was promoted to professor. In 1962 she established a research unit in Rome, and from then on she spent her time partly in St. Louis, and partly in Rome. From 1961 to 1969 she headed the Research Center for Neurobiology (*Consiglio Nazionale delle Ricerche*) in Rome, and from 1969 to 1978 she headed the Laboratory of Cellular Biology there.

Rita Levi-Montalcini and her research group discovered in the period 1993-1996 the mechanism of action of the anti-inflammatory and analgesic substance palmitoylethanolamide. They discovered that this endogenous substance acts as a natural modulator of hyperactive mast cells, counteracting the pro-inflammatory action of NGF. Since their first publication on this subject, scientific interest in palmitoylethanolamide has increased dramatically.

On August 1, 2001, she was appointed senator for life by the then President of Italy, Carlo Azeglio Ciampi. When not engrossed in her global academic activities, she actively participated in Senate discussions.

Highlights

- Levi-Montalcini studied medicine at the University of Turin and did research there on the effects that peripheral tissues have on nerve cell growth.
- In 1947 she accepted a post at Washington University, St. Louis, Missouri, with the zoologist Viktor Hamburger, who was studying the growth of nerve tissue in chick embryos.
- In 1948 it was discovered in Hamburger's laboratory that a variety of mouse tumour spurred nerve growth when implanted into chick embryos.
- Levi-Montalcini and Hamburger traced the effect to a substance in the tumour that they named nerve-growth factor (NGF).

7. Chien-Shiung Wu (1912 - 1997)
Chinese-American particle and experimental physicist

*"There is only one thing worse than coming home from
the lab to a sink full of dirty dishes, and that is not going
to the lab at all!"*

Chien-Shiung Wu (Shanghai, May 31, 1912 - New York, February 16,
1997) was a Chinese-American physicist who demonstrated the violation
of parity symmetry. Her work included the Manhattan Project (for enriching
uranium) and she received the Wolf Prize in 1978.

China

Although her family is from Taicang in Jiangsu province, Wu was born in
Shanghai. Her father, Wu Zhongyi, was an advocate of equal rights for
women, and was the founder of the Mingde Vocational Continuing School
for Women, where Chien-Shiung went to school until she entered Suzhou

Teacher Training School for Women Number Two at age eleven. Wu's mother was Fan Fuhua.

In 1929 she was admitted to the National Central University in Nanjing. At that time it was regulation that students from normal school who wanted to go to university had to teach for a year first. This she did at the Shanghai *Public School of China* founded by Hu Shi. From 1930 to 1934 she studied at the physics department of the Central University (called Nanjing University after 1949). For two years after graduation, she worked with another female researcher, Jing Weijing, at this university.

United States

In 1936, Wu Chien-Shiung Wu moved to the U.S. with a friend, Dong Ruofen, a chemist from Taicang. Wu studied at the University of California at Berkeley, where she received her Ph.D. in 1940. Two years later she married Luke Chia-Liu Yuan, also a physicist. They had a son, Vincent, who later also became a physicist. The family moved to the eastern United States, where Wu taught at Smith College, Princeton University and Columbia University (1957). At the NIST Institute in the US, she then set up the Wu experiment. She won the National Medal of Science in 1975, and the first Wolf Prize in Physics in 1978.

Furthermore, Wu was the first woman to:

- Taught in the physics department at Princeton University.
- Got an honorary doctorate from Princeton.
- Became president of The American Physical Society (in 1975).

Discovery of pariteic weak nuclear force

Wu discovered the parity violation in the weak nuclear force in 1956. At that time it was generally assumed that parity was preserved. However, Chen Ning Yang and Tsung-Dao Lee suspected on theoretical grounds that it was possible that parity was not conserved in the weak interaction (which plays a role in beta decay), and Wu proposed to Lee a method to test this experimentally, with the so-called Wu experiment. With this experiment Wu indeed succeeded in showing that parity conservation was violated in beta decay of cobalt-60, and thus that parity was not a conserved feature in nature. This earned Yang and Lee the Nobel Prize in Physics in 1957. Wu did not share in the prize, unjustly according to many. Her book *Beta Decay* (1965) is still a standard work for nuclear physicists.

Commemoration

In 1990, the Chinese Academy of Sciences named an asteroid after Wu Chien-shiung: the Wu Jianxiong Xing. In 1995, four Taiwanese/Chinese Nobel laureates (Tsung-Dao Lee, Chen Ning Yang, Samuel Ting, and Yuan Lee) established the Wu Chien-Shiung Education Foundation in Taiwan to provide scholarships for young scientists.

Wu died of a stroke in Manhattan in 1997. Her ashes were buried at Mingde Senior High School (the successor to Mingde Women's School). Her husband, who died in 2003, is buried next to her. The headstone is inscribed with calligraphy by Tsung-Dao Lee and Chen Ning Yang (for Wu), and Samuel Ting and Yuan T. Lee (for Yuan).

Name

Chien-Shiungs Wu generation name, Chien, is the same as that of her brothers, and not a typical woman's name. Moreover, Shiung, her personal name, means "hero, victor. Hence, many Chinese who first hear her name initially assume that Wu was a man.

Highlights

- Chien-Shiung Wu graduated from the National Central University in Nanking, China, in 1936 and then traveled to the United States to pursue graduate studies in physics at the University of California at Berkeley, studying under Ernest O. Lawrence.
- After receiving a Ph.D. in 1940, Wu taught at Smith College and at Princeton University.
- In 1944 she undertook work on radiation detection in the Division of War Research at Columbia University.
- She observed that there is a preferred direction of emission and that, therefore, parity is not conserved for this weak interaction.
- Wu, who received the National Medal of Science in 1975 and served as president of the American Physical Society that year as well, was considered one of the premier experimental physicists in the world.

8. Katherine Johnson (1918 - 2020)

American mathematician for NASA

"Like what you do, and then you will do your best."

Katherine Johnson (White Sulphur Springs (West Virginia), August 26, 1918 - Newport News (Virginia), February 24, 2020) was an American mathematician who contributed to the United States' aerospace programs through early use of digital computers at NASA. Known for her accuracy in computerized celestial mechanics, she did orbit calculations for the Mercury program and the 1969 flight of Apollo 11 to the moon.

Biography

Katherine Coleman was born in 1918 to Joshua and Joylette Coleman in White Sulphur Springs in Greenbrier County, West Virginia.She had three siblings. Her father worked as a carpenter, farmer and handyman. Her mother was a teacher. Since she was young, Katherine had a great talent for mathematics. Her parents stressed the importance of education. Because in Greenbrier County black students could not attend school after the end of elementary school ("*eighth grade*") Katherine and her brother(s) and sister(s) attended high school in Institute, Kanawha County, West

Virginia. The family lived alternately in Institute during the school year and in White Sulphur Springs during the summer.

Johnson attended West Virginia State College after high school and took mathematics courses with several professors, including chemist and mathematician Angie Turner King (who was also her mentor during high school) and W.W. Schiefflin Claytor (the third African-American to receive a doctorate in mathematics). Johnson graduated summa cum laude in mathematics and French in 1937 at the age of eighteen. Johnson then moved to Marion, Virgina, to teach mathematics, French, and music.

In 1938, Johnson was the first African-American woman to be admitted to West Virginia University in Morgantown, West Virginia, following the United States Supreme Court ruling in the Missouri ex rel. Gaines v. Canada.

Mathematical career

Johnson heard that the National Advisory Committee for Aeronautics (NACA), later NASA was looking for new people, especially African-American women for the *Guidance and Navigation Department*. Johnson joined the staff in 1953.

From 1958 until her retirement in 1983, she worked as an aerospace technologist. She later joined the Spacecraft Controls Branch. There she calculated the orbit for the 1959 space flight of Alan Shepard, the first American in space. She also calculated the launch window for his Mercury program in 1961. She also prepared navigation tables for astronauts in case of electronic problems.

When NASA first used electronic computers to calculate John Glenn's orbit around the earth in 1962, Johnson was asked to calculate the results. Johnson later worked with digital computers herself. She also calculated the orbit for the Apollo 11 flight to the moon in 1969. During the moon landing Johnson was at a meeting in the Pocono Mountains. She and a few others watched the first steps on the moon seated around a television.

In 1970, Johnson worked on the Apollo 13 mission to the moon. Once this mission was aborted, Johnson worked on alternative procedures and tables that allowed the crew to return safely to Earth four days later. Later in her career, Johnson worked on the space shuttle program, the Earth Resources Satellite, and on plans for a mission to Mars.

Inheritance

Johnson co-authored a total of twenty-six scientific papers. NASA maintains a list of Johnson's major articles.

Johnson's social influence as a pioneer in space science and computers can easily be gauged from the accolades she has received and the numbers of times her story has been told. As a result, she can be seen as a role model.

Since 1979 (before she retired) Johnson's biography had had a place of honor in surveys of African Americans in science and technology.

On November 16, 2015, U.S. President Barack Obama nominated Johnson as one of 17 Americans to receive the 2015 Presidential Medal of Freedom. She received the award on November 24, 2015 and was cited as an example of African-American women in STEM fields.

In 2017, the film *Hidden Figures* was released, a film about Johnson and her African-American colleagues at NASA.

Private life

In 1939 Johnson married James Francis Goble; together they had three daughters. After Goble's death in 1956, she remarried Lt. Colonel James A. Johnson in 1959, after which she continued her career at NASA.

Highlights

- Katherine Johnson's intelligence and skill with numbers became apparent when she was a child; by the time she was 10 years old, she had started attending high school.
- In 1937, at age 18, Coleman graduated with highest honors from West Virginia State College (now West Virginia State University), earning bachelor's degrees in mathematics and French.
- Johnson received numerous awards and honors for her work, including the Presidential Medal of Freedom (2015).
- Margot Lee Shetterly published Hidden Figures: The American Dream and the Untold Story of the Black Women Mathematicians Who

Helped Win the Space Race, about the West Computers, including Johnson, Dorothy Vaughan, and Mary Jackson.
- A film based on the book was also released in 2016.

9. Florence Rena Sabin (1871-1953)

American anatomist and investigator of the lymphatic system

"It's dishonest to simplify anything that isn't simple"

Florence Rena Sabin (Central City (Colorado), November 9, 1871 - Denver, October 3, 1953) was an American medical scientist. She was a pioneer for women in science; she was the first woman to obtain a full professorship at Johns Hopkins School of Medicine, the first woman to be admitted to the National Academy of Sciences, and the first woman to become department head at the Rockefeller Institute for Medical Research.

Biography

Florence Sabin was born in Central City, Colorado Territory, the youngest daughter of Serena Miner and George Kimball Sabin. Her father was a mining engineer so the Sabin family spent several years in various mining communities. When Florence was seven years old, her mother died of maternal fever. After this, she and her sister Mary went to live with her uncle Albert Sabin in Chicago and then with her father's grandparents in Vermont.

She received her bachelor's degree from Smith College in 1893, after which she wanted to study medicine. Because her family did not have sufficient funds for a college education, she taught mathematics at her old high school in Denver for two years and zoology at Smith College for a year until she saved up enough tuition for a first year of college. Sabin entered the Johns Hopkins School of Medicine as one of fourteen female students in a class of forty-five. This school had opened in 1893 and was open to both men and women from the beginning.

In 1900, Sabin and her classmate Dorothy Reed Mendenhall won a prestigious apprenticeship to study under William Osler. However, both Sabin and Mendenhall found the school atmosphere under him very unpleasant for women. For a while, she doubted whether medical school would have been a good career move for her. A year later, in 1901, she was awarded a fellowship to work with Professor Franklin P. Mall on the anatomy faculty at Johns Hopkins. In 1905 she was promoted to associate professor and eventually to full professor of embryology and histology in 1917 - making her the first woman to become a professor at a medical university. In 1921, she was named the first woman president of the "*American Association of Anatomists*".

Sabin transferred to the Rockefeller Institute in 1925, where she took charge of the department of cellular immunology; she thus became the first woman to be a full member of the faculty staff. In 1926, she became the first woman to be admitted to the National Academy of Sciences.

When she retired at age 67 in 1938, she remained an active participant in the scientific community through her correspondence, memberships, and various advisory boards. In 1944 she was asked by Governor John Vivian to become health advisor to a post-war planning committee in Colorado. The goal was to improve the then very poor health laws and establish more health facilities. Sabin died of a heart attack in Denver at the age of 81.

Research

During her long scientific career, Sabin built an impressive reputation for her work in embryology and histology. In 1900 she published her first book "*An Atlas of the Medulla and Midbrain*" on the development of the nervous system in infants. She also overturned the traditional explanation of the development of the lymphatic system by proving that the system develops from the vessels in the embryo and grows into tissue, not the other way around.

At the Rockefeller Institute, she focused her attention on the role of white blood cells (monocytes) that ward off infectious bacteria, such as *Mycobacterium tuberculosis*, the organism that causes the highly contagious tuberculosis. Although the TB bacteria had already been discovered by Robert Koch in the previous century, the disease was still a feared health threat in the twentieth century. To support her research work, she received a substantial grant from the National Turbeculosis Association in 1924.

She also trained a large team of modern scientists in solving medical problems, as well as training the next generation of scientists.

Highlights

- After teaching in Denver and at Smith to earn tuition money, Florence Rena Sabin entered the Johns Hopkins University Medical School in Baltimore, Maryland, in 1896.
- After graduation in 1900 she interned at Johns Hopkins Hospital for a year and then returned to the medical school to conduct research under a fellowship awarded by the Baltimore Association for the Advancement of University Education of Women.
- In 1901 she published An Atlas of the Medulla and Midbrain, which became a popular medical text.
- In 1902, when Johns Hopkins finally abandoned its policy of not appointing women to its medical faculty, Sabin was named an assistant in anatomy, and she became in 1917 the school's first female full professor.
- She then turned to the study of blood, blood vessels, and blood cells and made numerous discoveries regarding their origin and development.

10.　　　Françoise Barré-Sinoussi (born 1947)

French virologist who was awarded the 2008 Nobel Prize in Physiology or Medicine

"When you work in HIV, it's not only working in HIV, it's working far, far beyond. "

Françoise Barré-Sinoussi (Paris, July 30, 1947) is a French virologist. She and Luc Montagnier won the 2008 Nobel Prize in Physiology or Medicine for their discovery of human immunodeficiency virus (HIV). They share the Nobel Prize with Harald zur Hausen for his discovery of human papillomaviruses (HPV) that can cause cervical cancer.

Biography

Barré-Sinoussi was born in Paris, the daughter of Roger Sinoussi and Jeanine Fau. She graduated from the Lycée Bergson. She went on to study biomedical sciences, but broke off her studies prematurely because she found the university far too theoretical. In the early 1970s, she joined Jean-Claude Chermann, a French virologist at the Pasteur Institute at Marnes-la-Coquette. In 1975 she obtained her doctorate in virology from

the Faculty of Science. In 1978 she married the French scientist Jean
Claude Barré.

Working at the Pasteur Institute, she researched retroviruses. Together
with Montagnier, Barré-Sinoussi isolated lymph node cells from patients
whose immune system had been completely paralysed - a disease that
would later be given the name AIDS. In these cells they found the enzyme
reverse transcriptase - an enzyme that retroviruses need to replicate
themselves in the cells of a host. Later, their discovery of these first
human retroviruses was given the name HIV. After this discovery, they
actively participated in research for a cure and vaccine against HIV.

In 1986 Barré-Sinoussi became laboratory head, in 1992 department head
and in 1996 professor and head of the research group on the biology of
retroviruses at the Pasteur Institute. In 2009, she wrote an open letter to
Pope Benedict XVI about his statement that condoms are ineffective in the
AIDS crisis at best. In July 2012, she was appointed president of the
International AIDS Society (IAS), the organization for HIV professionals
and HIV patients.

Recognition

In 2006, Barré-Sinoussi was appointed an Officer of the Order of the
Legion of Honour and elevated to Commander in 2009 and Grand Officer
in 2013. She received an honorary doctorate from Tulane University in
2009 and one from the University of New South Wales in 2014.

Barré-Sinoussi contributed actively to several scientific societies and
committees at both the Pasteur Institute and other AIDS organizations,
such as the National Agency for AIDS Research in France. She has also
been active internationally, for the World Health Organization (WHO) and
the UN organization UNAIDS/HIV, among others.

Highlights

- Françoise Barré-Sinoussi earned a Ph.D. (1975) at the Pasteur
  Institute in Garches, France, and did postdoctoral work in the United
  States at the National Cancer Institute in Bethesda, Maryland.
- In 1975 she joined the Pasteur Institute in Paris, and in 1996 she
  became head of the Retrovirus Biology Unit (later called Regulation
  of Retroviral Infections Unit) there.

- From 2012 to 2014 Barré-Sinoussi was president of the International AIDS Society.
- When Montagnier led efforts at the Pasteur Institute in 1982 to determine a cause for AIDS, Barré-Sinoussi was a member of his team.

11.　Margaret Hamilton (born 1936)

American computer scientist, lead Apollo flight software engineer

"*Software eventually and necessarily gained the same respect as any other discipline.*"

Margaret Heafield Hamilton (Paoli (Indiana), August 17, 1936) is an American computer scientist and systems engineer. She was director of the software engineering department at MIT that developed Colossus, the on-board software for the Apollo program. In 1986, she founded Hamilton Technologies. On November 22, 2016, Hamilton received the Presidential Medal of Freedom from U.S. President Barack Obama for the Apollo on-board software.

Biography

Margaret Heafield was born in Paoli, Indiana. She attended the University of Michigan to study mathematics in 1954 and received her bachelor's degree with a minor in philosophy in 1958. For a short time she taught high school mathematics and French while her husband studied at Harvard. Hamilton moved to Boston, Massachusetts, to continue her studies in pure mathematics at Brandeis University.

In 1960 she worked at MIT developing weather forecasting software for meteorologist Edward Lorenz on Marvin Minsky's computers. Hamilton wrote that computer science and its application software engineering were not then independent disciplines and that programmers learned on the job.

From 1961 to 1963, Hamilton co-programmed the software for the first AN/FSQ-7 computer (the XD-1) to search for hostile aircraft in Lincoln Lab's (MIT) Semi-Automatic Ground Environment project. This SAGE project was an extension of MIT's Whirlwind project to develop a computer system that could predict and track weather systems with simulators. SAGE was soon further developed for air defense against possible Soviet attacks during the Cold War.

NASA

After the SAGE project, Hamilton joined MIT's Charles Stark Draper Laboratory, which was then working on the Apollo program. Eventually, Hamilton led the group that wrote the software for Apollo and Skylab. Hamilton's team was responsible for the *in-flight* software, with algorithms from the senior programmers for the Apollo main module, lunar lander, and Skylab. Another part of the team designed and developed error detection and data recovery software that included Hamilton's own *Priority Displays*.

Business

From 1976 to 1984 Hamilton was director of Higher Order Software (HOS), which she co-founded. With HOS Hamilton wanted to further develop ideas on fault tolerance and fault prevention based on her experiences at MIT. Hamilton left the company in 1985. In March 1986 she founded Hamilton Technologies to apply her Universal Systems Language (USL) with the 001 Tool suite.

Influence

When Hamilton introduced the term "software engineering," this discipline was not considered a science and was not taken as seriously as other types of applied science. Hamilton used the term "software engineering"

39

during the first Apollo missions to give software the same status as other disciplines such as hardware engineering.

Highlights

- Margaret Hamilton helped write the computer code for the command and lunar modules used on the Apollo missions to the Moon in the late 1960s and early '70s.
- Although Margaret planned to study abstract mathematics at Brandeis University, she accepted a job at the Massachusetts Institute of Technology (MIT) while her husband attended Harvard Law School.
- At MIT she began programming software to predict the weather and did postgraduate work in meteorology.
- In the early 1960s Hamilton joined MIT's Lincoln Laboratory, where she was involved in the Semi-Automatic Ground Environment (SAGE) project, the first U.S. air defense system.

12.　Emmy Noether (1882 - 1935)

German mathematician known for her landmark contributions to abstract algebra and theoretical physics

"My [algebraic] methods are really methods of working and thinking; this is why they have crept in everywhere anonymously."

Amalie Emmy Noether (Erlangen (Germany), March 23, 1882 - Bryn Mawr (United States), April 14, 1935) was a German mathematician of Jewish descent. Her work in the field of abstract algebra has given new prestige to the whole of algebra. She is counted among the best female mathematicians and also Albert Einstein praised her.

Introduction

Noether is known for her pioneering contributions to abstract algebra and theoretical physics. She was considered the most important woman in the history of mathematics by David Hilbert, Albert Einstein, and others. Noether revolutionized the theories of rings, bodies or fields, and algebra and is considered the founder of abstract algebra. In theoretical physics, Noether's theorem explains the fundamental connection between symmetry and conservation laws.

Noether was born into a Jewish family. Her father was the prominent mathematician Max Noether. Emmy originally planned to become a teacher of French and English. She also passed her exams to be allowed to teach in Bavarian high schools. She then decided to study mathematics at the University of Erlangen, where her father was also a professor. After completing her dissertation in 1907 under the supervision of Paul Gordan, she worked at the Erlangen Mathematical Institute for seven years without pay. With few exceptions, women were still forbidden to hold academic positions at the beginning of the 20th century. In 1915, Noether was invited by David Hilbert and Felix Klein to join the faculty of mathematics at the University of Göttingen, then a world-renowned center of mathematical research. The philosophy faculty, however, objected. For four years, Noether gave lectures under Hilbert's name. Her habilitation was approved in 1919. Afterwards she obtained the title *Privatdozent*.

Until Hitler's seizure of power in 1933, Noether would remain a leading member of the Göttingen mathematics faculty; her students were sometimes called the "Noether boys". In 1924 the Dutch mathematician B.L. van der Waerden joined her *inner circle*. He soon became the main expounder of Noether's ideas: her work was the basis for the second part of his influential 1931 book, *Modern Algebra*. By the time of Noether's plenary address at the International Mathematical Congress in Zurich in 1932, her algebraic insight was recognized throughout the world. The following year, the incoming Nazi government decided to dismiss all Jews working at German universities. Noether now moved to the United States, where she was appointed to Bryn Mawr College in Pennsylvania. Two years later she had to undergo a risky operation for an ovarian cyst. She died four days after the operation on 14 April 1935 at the age of 53.

Noether's mathematical work has been divided into three 'periods'. In the first period (1908-1919) she made important contributions to the theories of algebraic invariants and number bodies. Her work on differential invariants in the calculus of variations, Noether's Theorem, has been called "one of the most important mathematical theorems ever proved to guide the development of modern physics". In the second period (1920-1926) she began the work that "changed the face of [abstract] algebra". In her classic article *Idealtheorie in Ringbereichen* (*Theory of ideals in ring domains*, 1921) Noether developed the theory of ideals in commutative rings into a powerful tool with enriching applications. She made an elegant use of the ascending chain condition. Objects satisfying this condition are called Noethers in her honor. In the third period (1927-1935) she published important works on noncommutative algebra and hypercomplex numbers. She united the representation theory of groups with the theory of modules and ideals. In addition to her own publications, she was generous in sharing her ideas. She is credited with several lines of research published by other mathematicians, including in areas far removed from her main work, such as algebraic topology.

Biography

Emmy's father Max Noether was born in Mannheim in 1844. When he was fourteen he contracted infantile paralysis, and as a result would remain disabled on one leg for the rest of his life. He studied mathematics at the renowned University of Heidelberg. He worked as a private lecturer in Heidelberg for several more years, before going to the University of Erlangen, near Nuremberg in Bavaria, in 1875 to work as an assistant professor. Finally, in 1888, he received a full professorship. He was one of the leading figures in algebraic geometry of the time; he did much research on invariants of algebraic varieties under the action of birational transformations, building on the work of Bernhard Riemann and Luigi Cremona, among others.

Youth

Emmy was born in Erlangen on March 23, 1882. She was the first child of Max and his wife Ida Kaufman, both of Jewish origin. Emmy had three more brothers: Alfred, Fritz, and Gustav Robert. From 1889 to 1897 Emmy went to the Höhere Töchter Schule in Erlangen, where she studied German, English and French as well as arithmetic. At home she learned to play the piano, but unlike her mother, she did not excel at it. She did love dancing and parties with the children of her father's colleagues. After school she decided to continue her studies as a foreign language teacher. She studied English and French for three more years and in April 1900 she successfully passed the Bavarian state examination for both languages, after which she was allowed to teach in the Bavarian girls' schools.

Mathematics study

Before she started working as a teacher, however, Emmy decided to study mathematics. This was not a common choice for a woman in 1900's Germany: in most other European countries, women had been allowed to study at universities for several decades, but in Germany, a woman had to get permission from the professor to attend each class, and this permission was not always given. Emmy, however, was allowed to attend lectures in Erlangen, probably thanks to the influence of her father.

However, she had to take her exams at the Realgymnasium in Nuremberg.

In 1903 she went to Göttingen, where she attended lectures by famous mathematicians such as Hermann Minkowski, Felix Klein and David Hilbert. The following year, however, Noether returned to Erlangen, because there it had now become possible for female students to sit exams. Three years later, in 1907, she obtained her doctorate under Paul Gordan.

Period 1907-1915

After her doctorate, Noether continued to work at the University of Erlangen. She supported her father, who began to suffer more and more from his physical infirmities, and replaced him regularly at lectures. During this period in Erlangen she also did a lot of research in invariant theory. She also supervised two PhD students with their theses.

Period in Göttingen

In 1915, after her mother had died, Noether went to Göttingen. In Erlangen, she had worked unpaid all that time, but in Göttingen Klein and Hilbert, the two most prominent mathematicians in Göttingen, tried to arrange something better for her. She had to give a lecture so that she could be appointed as a private lecturer. But the university put a stop to this: according to a law from 1908 women were not allowed to become private professors. It was mainly the philosophy and history faculties that opposed Noether's appointment. Hilbert entered the discussion by saying: "I don't see why someone's gender should be an argument against her appointment. After all, we are a university here and not a bathhouse." Nevertheless, Noether continued to work and teach at Göttingen. The classes she taught were taught under Hilbert's name. This wasn't even that far from the truth: Noether and Hilbert worked together a lot during this period, and besides, it would be many years before Noether had developed into the great mathematician she would become.

From the middle of the twenties a group of mathematicians arose in Göttingen who also did a lot together outside mathematics, like music evenings or boat excursions. They often had long discussions on both mathematical and non-mathematical topics at Fritz Klie's swimming pool. Besides Noether, Richard Courant, the director of the mathematical faculty was the most important person in the group. Also people like the topologists Alexandrov, Heinz Hopf and in a later stage Hermann Weyl belonged to this group.

Noether was a remarkable person within this group and not only because she was the only woman besides Courant's wife. She was certainly not slim and had a very loud voice. However, she was also a very social person and knew how to stimulate many other mathematicians. Much of her own research was published under the names of her colleagues and students.

Visiting Moscow

In the winter of 1928-1929, Noether accepted an invitation from Moscow State University, where she continued her work with Pavel Alexandrov. In addition to her research, she gave lectures in abstract algebra and algebraic geometry. Among others, she worked there with the topologists Lev Pontryagin and Nikolai Chebotaryov, who later praised her contributions to the development of *Galois theory*.

Although politics was not central to her life, Noether had a keen interest in political affairs. According to Alexandrov, Noether demonstrated considerable support for the Russian Revolution (1917). She was particularly taken with the Soviet advances in natural science and mathematics. She saw this as an indication of the new opportunities made possible by the Bolshevik project. This attitude caused her problems in Germany, however, culminating in her eviction from a boarding house after student leaders complained that they did not want to live in the same building as "a Marxist-oriented Jewess."

Noether planned to return to Moscow, receiving support from Alexandrov. After she left Germany in 1933, Alexandrov tried to help her get a chair at Moscow State University. He pleaded for this with the Soviet Ministry of Education. Although this attempt was unsuccessful, they corresponded regularly during the 1930s. In 1935, Noether made plans to visit the Soviet Union. After losing his job in Germany, her brother, Fritz Noether, accepted a position at the Institute of Mathematics and Mechanics in Tomsk, in the Siberian part of Russia.

Last years in Bryn Mawr

In January 1933 Adolf Hitler came to power in Germany. This soon had major consequences for Jewish employees of the universities. Some, such as Courant, were dismissed, others were made difficult to teach by pro-

45

Nazi students. Among these students was Werner Weber, who had graduated with Noether. They believed that 'Aryan students wanted Aryan mathematics and not Jewish mathematics'. Noether tried to ignore the situation and continue with mathematics, but in the summer of 1933 her appointment, like that of all other Jewish staff, was terminated.

She received offers from Somerville College, Oxford and the University of Moscow, among others, but chose to go to Bryn Mawr College, a university only for women, in Pennsylvania in the United States. This was a completely new situation for Noether: not only were her colleagues and students all women, but for the first time she had an official, permanent position. This was in contrast to Göttingen, where she was only an 'extraordinary assistant professor'. The new situation suited Noether extremely well, as she became very good friends with some of her colleagues from Bryn Mawr.

In the summer of 1934 she returned once more to Germany, where she discovered that the situation in Göttingen had changed completely since her departure a year earlier, partly due to the racism made into government policy by the Nazis. Almost all her former friends and colleagues here had left, with the great exception of David Hilbert, who was also unhappy with the new situation. She also visited Artin in Berlin. With Artin she often made long walks, during which Noether told Artin her mathematical insights. Because Noether spoke very fast, she had to explain it several times before Artin understood. Not long after her return to America, she became a member of the American Mathematical Society and lecturer at the later world famous Institute for Advanced Study in Princeton.

Death

In April 1935 doctors discovered a tumor in Noether's pelvis. She urgently needed an operation. Concerned about the possible complications of an operation, they first prescribed two days of bed rest. During surgery on April 10, the surgeon discovered an ovarian cyst "the size of a melon." Two smaller tumors in her uterus appeared benign and were not removed, also to avoid prolonging the surgery. At first, Noether seemed to recover normally. However, four days later, on April 14, she became unconscious, her temperature rising rapidly to nearly 43°C. Soon after, Emmy Noether died. "It is not easy to say exactly what happened in Dr. Noether," one of the doctors wrote. "It is possible that there was a common and virulent infection affecting the base of the brain, where the heat centers are located."

The mathematical world reacted with shock, especially since Noether had told only a few friends of her illness. A few days after Noether's death, her friends and colleagues at Bryn Mawr held a small memorial service at the home of College President Park. Hermann Weyl and Richard Brauer came from Princeton and spoke with Wheeler and Taussky about their late colleague. In the months that followed, a number of obituaries appeared in various places around the world. Albert Einstein, Bartel van der Waerden, Hermann Weyl and Pavel Aleksandrov, among others, paid their respects to Emmy Noether. Her body was cremated and her ashes were buried under the walkway that extended around the cloister of the M. Carey Thomas Library on Bryn Mawr.

Contributions to mathematics and physics

First of all mathematicians remember Noether as an abstract algebraist and because of her work in topology. Physicists know her best for her famous theorem; this because of its far-reaching consequences for theoretical physics and dynamical systems. Noether had a great talent for abstract thinking which enabled her to approach mathematical problems in new and original ways. Her friend and colleague Hermann Weyl divided her scientific output into three eras:

"Emmy Noether's scholarly output can be divided into three distinctly different periods:

1. the period of relative dependence (1907-1919);
2. research grouped around the general theory of ideals (1920-1926);
3. the study of noncommutative algebras, their representations by linear transformations, and their application to the study of commutative number bodies and their arithmetic operations (1927-1935)."

During the first period (1907-1919), Noether was primarily concerned with differential and algebraic invariants. This interest began with her dissertation under the supervision of Paul Gordan. As a result of close collaboration with Gordan's successor, Ernst Sigismund Fischer, she became acquainted with the work of David Hilbert. Under his influence, her mathematical horizon broadened in a more general and abstract direction. After moving to Göttingen in 1915 she produced there her pioneering work in the field of theoretical physics, the two theorems of Noether.

In the second period (1920-1926) Noether devoted himself to the development of the theory of mathematical rings.

In the third period (1927-1935), Noether focused on noncommutative algebra, linear transformations, and commutative number bodies.

Historical context

In the century from 1832 until Noether's death in 1935, mathematics - and more specifically algebra - underwent a profound revolution, the reverberations of which can still be felt today. In previous centuries, mathematicians were limited to research into practical methods for solving specific types of equations, such as third-, fourth- and fifth-degree equations, as well as the related problem of constructing regular polygons using compasses and rulers, beginning with Carl Friedrich Gauss' 1829 proof that prime numbers such as five can be decomposed into Gaussian integers, Evariste Galois' introduction of permutation groups in 1832, William Rowan Hamilton's discovery of quaternions in 1843, and Arthur Cayley's more modern definition of groups in 1854, research increasingly focused on determining the properties of increasingly abstract systems defined by increasingly universal rules. Noether's major contributions to mathematics were to the development of this new field, abstract algebra.

Abstract algebra and conceptual mathematics

Two of the most elementary objects in abstract algebra are groups and rings.

The structures of groups and rings are very general and can be applied to many real and abstract situations. Any set with one or two operations defined on it that satisfy all the rules for a group or a ring, thus obeys all the theorems about groups or rings. Integers, and the operations of addition and multiplication, are just one example. The elements can be, for example, computer data words, where the first combining operation is an exclusive disjunction and the second is a logical conjunction. Theorems from abstract algebra are powerful because they are general; they govern a large number of systems. One might think that one cannot learn much about objects defined with so few properties, but therein lay Noether's gift: to *discover the maximum that can be inferred from a given set of properties, or conversely, to identify the minimal set, the essential properties, responsible for a given observation*. Van der Waerden recalled in his obituary that unlike most mathematicians, who arrive at abstractions by generalizing known examples, Noether rather worked directly with the abstractions.

The maxim by which Emmy Noether was guided in her work can be formulated as follows: "All relations between numbers, functions, and operations become transparent, generalizable, and fully productive only after they have been isolated from their specific objects and formulated as universally valid concepts.

This is conceptual mathematics, which was characteristic of Noether. This style of mathematics was later adopted by other mathematicians and flourished after her death in new forms, such as category theory.

First period - period 1908-19

In 1907, Noether received her doctorate from Paul Gordan with her thesis *Über die Bildung des Formensystems der ternären biquadratischen Form*. Gordan was a friend of Max Noether and one of the founders of invariant theory, a field in which Emmy Noether was to play a prominent role. Emmy was his only doctoral student. Two parts of her dissertation became her first two publications. After her doctorate, Noether continued to work at the University of Erlangen. During this period in Erlangen she did a lot of research in invariant theory, especially under the influence of Gordan, Hilbert and Fischer.

Galois Theory

Galois theory relates to transformations of number bodies that permute the roots of an equation.

In 1918, Noether published a seminal paper on the inverse Galois problem. Instead of determining the Galois group of transformations of a given field and its extensions, Noether asked whether, given a field and a group, it is always possible to find an extension of the field which has the given group as its Galois group. She reduced this research question to the so-called "Noether's problem". This asks whether the fixed field of a subgroup G of the permutation group S_n , acting on that field $k(x_1 , ..., x_n)$ is always a pure transcendental extension of the field k. (She first mentioned this problem in her 1913 paper, where she attributed the problem to her colleague Ernst Fischer.) She showed that this is the case for $n=2$, 3 or 4. In 1969, however, R.G. Swan found a counterexample to Noether's problem, with $n=47$ and G a cyclic group of order 47, although this group can be realized as a Galois group over the rational numbers in other ways. The inverse Galois problem is unsolved to date (2012).

Theorem of Noether

Noether was asked by David Hilbert and Felix Klein to come to Göttingen in 1915. They needed her expertise in invariant theory to help them understand the then brand new general theory of relativity, a geometric theory of gravity that had been developed primarily by Albert Einstein. Hilbert had noted that in the general theory of relativity the law of conservation of energy seemed to be violated. This was due to the fact that gravitational energy was in turn also attracted by gravity. Noether came up with the solution to this paradox. In 1915 she proved Noether's first theorem. Although not published until 1918, this theorem became a fundamental tool for modern theoretical physics. Noether solved the problem not only for the general theory of relativity, but determined that "conserved" quantities for *all* systems of physical laws, which possess some continuous symmetry.

After receiving her work, Einstein wrote to Hilbert: "Yesterday I received from Miss Noether a very interesting paper on invariants. I am impressed that such things can be understood in such a general way. The old guard at Göttingen should take a few lessons from Miss Noether. She seems to know what she is talking about."

To illustrate: If a physical system behaves the same no matter how this system is oriented in space, the physical laws governing this space are said to be rotationally symmetric; Noether's theorem then shows that the angular momentum of the system must be preserved. The physical system itself need not be symmetrical; an uneven asteroid spinning through space retains its angular momentum despite its asymmetry. The very symmetry in the physical laws governing this system is responsible for the conservation law. Another example: if a physical experiment has the same outcome at any place and time, then its laws of physics are symmetric under continuous translations in space and time; by Noether's theorem, these symmetries within this system are responsible for the conservation laws of momentum and energy, respectively.

Noether's theorem has become a fundamental tool within modern theoretical physics, both as a result of the insight it provides into the conservation laws, and also as a practical computational tool. Her theorem enables researchers to determine the quantities to be conserved via the observed symmetries of a physical system. Conversely, the theorem facilitates the description of a physical system based on classes of the hypothetical laws of nature. To illustrate, suppose a new physical phenomenon has been discovered. Noether's theorem provides a test for theoretical models of this new phenomenon: if the theory has a continuous symmetry, then Noether's theorem guarantees that the theory also has a conserved quantity, and for the theory to be correct a conservation law must be observable in experiments.

Second period - period 1920-26

Noether's main research, however, focused on algebra, which she approached with such abstraction and generality that she was later nicknamed the "founder of modern abstract algebra. In a 1921 paper she looked at a certain chain condition of ideals, which led to the definition of Noether's rings.

After the First World War had ended in 1918, much had changed politically and socially in Germany, which meant, among other things, that the position of women had improved considerably, with the result that women were allowed to become private tutors. Emmy Noether was also appointed as a private tutor.

During the twenties Noether became more and more known in mathematics and several foreign mathematicians came to Göttingen to visit her. One of them was Bartel van der Waerden, a 21-year-old Dutchman, who had studied under Brouwer in Amsterdam and went to Göttingen in 1924 to follow Noether's lectures. Van der Waerden would write his famous book *Modern Algebra* in 1931, which was largely based on the work of Noether and some of her colleagues, such as Hilbert and Artin.In 1925 Noether spent Christmas in Blaricum in the Netherlands. There she met Brouwer and became interested in abstract topology. She created a row of Abelian groups in a topological space, which we now call homology groups. According to the Russian topologist Pavel Aleksandrov, who would become Noether's colleague in Göttingen a year later, the mathematical world was initially sceptical, but soon realised that the homology groups had many interesting applications.

Rising and falling chain conditions

During this period, Noether became famous for her deft use of ascending or descending chain conditions.Ascending and descending chain conditions can be formulated very generally for all sorts of mathematical objects that can be partitioned. Although superficially not very powerful,

51

Noether showed how such conditions can be used to maximum effect to show, for example, that each collection of partial objects has a maximum/minimum element or that a complex object can be generated from a smaller number of elements. Such conclusions are often crucial steps in a proof.

Commutative rings, ideals, and modules

Noether's article, *Idealtheorie in Ringbereichen* (*Theory of ideals in ring domains*, 1921), is the foundation of general commutative ring theory and provides one of the first general definitions of a commutative ring. Before Noether's article, most results in commutative algebra were limited to special examples of commutative rings, such as polynomial rings over fields, rings or algebraic integers. Noether proved that in a ring satisfying the increasing chain condition on ideals, every ideal is finitely generated. To describe this property, French mathematician Claude Chevalley formulated the term, *Noether's ring* in 1943. A further important result in Noether's 1921 paper is the Lasker-Noether theorem. This theorem extends Lasker's theorem about the primary decomposition of ideals of polynomial rings to all Noetherian rings. The Lasker-Noether theorem can be seen as a generalization of the main theorem of arithmetic, which states that every positive integer can be expressed as a product of prime numbers and that this decomposition is unique.

Noether's work *Abstrakter Aufbau der Idealtheorie in algebraischen Zahl- und Funktionenkörpern* (*Abstract structure of the theory of ideals in algebraic number bodies and function fields*, 1927) characterizes rings, in which the ideals can be uniquely decomposed into prime ideals, as Dedekind domains: integral domains that are Noetherian, 0 or 1-dimensional and that are integral closed in their quotient fields. This article also contains what are now called isomorphism theorems. These describe some fundamental natural isomorphisms and some other fundamental results with respect to Noetherian and Artinian modules.

Contributions to topology

As noted by both Pavel Alexandrov and Hermann Weyl in their obituaries, Noether's contributions to topology illustrate her generosity of ideas and also how her insights proved capable of transforming entire subfields within mathematics. In topology, mathematicians study the properties of mathematical objects that remain invariant under deformation, properties such as their coherence.

Noether is credited with the fundamental ideas that initiated the development of algebraic topology from the earlier combinatorial topology, specifically the idea of homology groups. According to Aleksandrov's description, Noether attended lectures with Heinz Hopf and Aleksandrov in the summers of 1926 and 1927, where "she constantly made remarks, which were often deep and subtle." Alexandrov continues by stating:

When ... she first became familiar with a systematic construction of combinatorial topology, she immediately remarked that it would be worthwhile to study directly groups of algebraic complexes and cycles of a given polyhedron and the subgroup of the cycle group consisting of cycles homologous to zero; rather than the usual definition of Betti numbers. She immediately proposed to define the Betti group as a complementary (quotient) group of the group of all cycles by the subgroup of cycles homologous to zero. This observation now seems obvious. But in those years (1925-1928) this was an entirely new point of view.

Third period - period 1927-35

In the nineteenth and early twentieth centuries much work had been done on hypercomplex numbers and group representations. But the results were varied. Noether unified the results and gave the first general representation theory of groups and algebra. In the short article she classified the structure theory of associative algebra and the representation theory of groups into a single arithmetic theory of moduli and ideals in rings, which satisfied ascending chain conditions. This single work by Noether was fundamental to the development of modern algebra.

Noncommutative algebra

Noether was also responsible for a number of other developments in the field of abstract algebra. Together with Emil Artin, Richard Brauer and Helmut Hasse, she was at the forefront of the theory of central singular algebras.

A seminal paper by Noether, Helmut Hasse and Richard Brauer concerned division algebras. These are algebraic systems in which division is possible. They proved two important theorems: a local-global theorem, which states that if a finite dimensional central division algebra over a number body splits locally everywhere, it will also split globally (and thus is trivial). From this they deduced their main theorem: any finite dimensional central division algebra over an algebraic number body F splits over a cyclic cyclotomic expansion.

These theorems allow us to classify all finite-dimensional central division algebras into a given number body. A subsequent article by Noether showed, as a special case of a more general theorem, that all subspaces of a division algebra D are splitting bodies. This article also included the Skolem-Noether theorem, which states that any two embeddings of an extension of a field k in a finite dimensional central singular algebra over k are conjugate. Brauer-Noether's theorem gives a characterization of the splitting bodies of a central division algebra over a field.

Posthumous recognition

Over the years Noether would gain increasing recognition for her work as a mathematician, many scientific biographies would be published about her. Although the fact that she was a woman often worked against her, it earned her quite a lot of interest posthumously.

Highlights

- Emmy Noether was certified to teach English and French in schools for girls in 1900, but she instead chose to study mathematics at the University of Erlangen (now University of Erlangen-Nuremberg). At that time, women were only allowed to audit classes with the permission of the instructor.
- Noether received a Ph.D. degree from Erlangen in 1907, with a dissertation on algebraic invariants.
- From 1927 Emmy Noether concentrated on noncommutative algebras (algebras in which the order in which numbers are multiplied affects the answer), their linear transformations, and their application to commutative number fields.
- In collaboration with Helmut Hasse and Richard Brauer, Noether investigated the structure of noncommutative algebras and their application to commutative fields by means of cross product (a form of multiplication used between two vectors).

13.   Valentina Tereshkova (born 1937)

Soviet cosmonaut, engineer and the first woman in space

"Hey sky, take off your hat, I'm on my way!"

Valentina Vladimirovna Tereshkova (Russian: Валентина Владимировна Терешкова) (Maslennikovo, Yaroslavl Oblast, March 6, 1937) is a member of the Russian Duma and a former Russian cosmonaut. She flew as a Russian astronaut aboard the Vostok 6, becoming the first woman in space.

Training and space travel

After school, Tereshkova worked in a tire factory and then went on to study engineering. She learned to parachute at the local flying club.

From more than 400 applicants, she and four other women were selected for the female cosmonaut group. Of this group, only Tereshkova has flown in space. Tereshkova was launched aboard the Vostok 6 on June 16, 1963, becoming the first woman and also the first civilian in space. Two days earlier the Vostok 5 had been launched. During the flight, Vostok 5 and 6 approached each other to within five kilometers and had radio contact with each other. Tereshkova landed on Earth after a flight of nearly three days. Plans for further flights by women were cancelled. For 19 years Tereshkova remained the only woman who had flown in space, until on August 19, 1982, Russia's Svetlana Savitskaya followed her in the Soyuz T-7.

Other work

After her space flight, Tereshkova studied at the Shukowski Air Force Academy, where she graduated as a cosmonaut engineer in 1969. In 1977 she received her doctorate in engineering sciences. Tereshkova held various political positions. From 1966 to 1974 she was a member of the Supreme Soviet, from 1974 to 1989 she was a member of the Presidium of the Supreme Soviet, from 1969 to 1991 she was in the Central Committee of the Communist Party. In 2011 she was elected to the State Duma on behalf of the United Russia party; in 2016 she was re-elected. On March 10, 2020, she came to the fore during the discussion of President Putin's constitutional proposals. She proposed, when amending the constitution, to start counting presidential terms again, so that Putin could serve another two six-year terms. In doing so, she presumably revealed the true intent of the whole operation. Her proposal was approved by unanimous vote.

Private

On November 3, 1963, Tereshkova married spaceman Andrian Nikolaev. They had one daughter and divorced in 1982. Tereshkova later remarried and became a widow in 1999.

Highlights

- Although Valentina Tereshkova had no pilot training, she was an accomplished amateur parachutist and on this basis was accepted for the cosmonaut program when she volunteered in 1961.
- From 1966 until 1991 Tereshkova was an active member in the U.S.S.R. Supreme Soviet. She directed the Soviet Women's Committee in 1968, and from 1974 to 1991 Tereshkova served as a member of the Supreme Soviet Presidium.

- In 2008 Tereshkova became the deputy chair of the parliament of Yaroslavl province as a member of the United Russia party.
- Tereshkova was named a Hero of the Soviet Union and was twice awarded the Order of Lenin.

14.   Lynn Margulis (1938 - 2011)

American evolutionary theorist, biologist, science author, educator, and science popularizer

"For all the accomplishments of molecular biology, we still can't tell a live cat from a dead cat."

Lynn Margulis (Chicago, March 5, 1938 - Amherst (Massachusetts), November 22, 2011) was an American biologist known for her "symbiogenetic theory" or *Serial Endosymbiosis Theory* (SET) for the origin of eukaryotic cells. Margulis was, together with the British chemist James Lovelock, the co-developer of the Gaia hypothesis, which implies that on Earth the biosphere interacts with the inorganic environment so that a self-regulating system arises.

Biography

Lynn Margulis was born Lynn Alexander, eldest daughter of Morris Alexander (lawyer and businessman) and Leone Wise (tour guide). She attended Hyde Park High School and by the age of fourteen attended the University of Chicago, where she received her degree in 1957. The same

58

year she married the later famous astronomer Carl Sagan. She then
studied genetics and zoology at the University of Wisconsin, graduating in
1960. In 1963 she divorced Sagan. She received her PhD in 1965 and that
same year she married the chemist Thomas Margulis, from whom she
divorced in 1978, but she continued her work under his surname. She died
on 22 November 2011, a few days after suffering a brain haemorrhage.

Along with Tony Swain, Margulis was the founder of the *Planetary Biology
Internship* in 1979, which allows advanced students to participate in NASA
biological research.

In 1998, the *American Institute of Biological Sciences* awarded her the
AIBS Distinguished Scientist Award. In 2008, she received the *Darwin-
Wallace Medal* from the *Linnean Society of London* .

Scientific work

In her 1965 dissertation, sixty years after the Russian botanist Konstantin
Merezhkovsky published the thesis that chloroplasts could be traced back
to symbiotic single-celled algae, she demonstrated an "endosymbiont
hypothesis": eukaryotic cells would have evolved from symbiosis of
various types of bacteria. Margulis argued that complex cell organelles
would contain evolutionary evidence for this. In 1967, her paper *Origins of
Mitosing Cells* was published in the *Journal of Theoretical Biology*.

In 1983 she was elected a member of the National Academy of Sciences.
Her *SET-theory* is now widely accepted in scientific circles as the
endosymbiont theory.

Gaia hypothesis

When Margulis expressed doubts about the inorganic origin of gases in
the atmosphere, because she investigated many bacteria that emitted
gases, she was advised to go to Lovelock. From that moment on there
was an intense collaboration between Margulis and Lovelock. She
proposed that bacteria in particular contribute to homeostasis. Another
important contribution of hers was the idea that the Earth should not be
viewed as an organism, but as a system. She summarized this in the
statement: *"No organism eats its own waste"*.

Highlights

- In addition to Lynn Margulis's scholarly publications, she wrote numerous books interpreting scientific concepts and quandaries for a popular audience.
- Among them were Mystery Dance: On the Evolution of Human Sexuality (1991), What Is Life? (1995), What Is Sex? (1997), and Dazzle Gradually: Reflections on Nature in Nature (2007), all cowritten with her son.
- Margulis also wrote a book of stories, Luminous Fish (2007).
- She was elected to the National Academy of Sciences in 1983 and was one of three American members of the Russian Academy of Natural Sciences.

15.   Cecilia Payne-Gaposchkin (1900 - 1979)

British-born American astronomer and astrophysicist

"Your reward will be the widening of the horizon as you climb. And if you achieve that reward, you will ask no other."

Cecilia Helena Payne-Gaposchkin (Wendover, May 10, 1900 - Cambridge (Massachusetts), December 7, 1979) was an Anglo-American astronomer who in 1925 showed in her doctoral dissertation, using spectroscopy, that hydrogen and helium are the principal elements (99% of the mass) of stars.

Early life

Cecilia Helena Payne was one of three children of Emma Leonora Helena (born Pertz) and Edward John Payne, a London lawyer, historian and gifted musician. Her mother was of Prussian descent and had two well-known uncles, the historian Georg Heinrich Pertz and the writer James John Garth Wilkinson, a supporter of Swedenborg's teachings. Cecilia

61

Payne's father died when she was four years old and her mother had to bring up the children alone.

Cecilia attended St Paul's Girls' School and in 1919 she received a scholarship to study botany, physics and chemistry at Newnham College of the University of Cambridge. Here she attended a lecture by Arthur Eddington about his expedition to Principe in the Gulf of Guinea. Eddington went there during the solar eclipse of 29 May 1919 to photograph stars in order to test Albert Einstein's general theory of relativity. This lecture sparked her interest in astronomy. She completed her studies, but did not obtain an academic degree because the University of Cambridge did not grant it to women until 1948.

Cecilia Payne realized that her only career opportunity in the United Kingdom lay in teaching, so she sought grants that would allow her to move to the United States. After being introduced to Harlow Shapley, the director of the Harvard College Observatory, who had just started a PhD program in astronomy, she left England in 1923. This was made possible by a scholarship that encouraged women to study at the observatory. The first recipient of this was Adelaide Ames (1922) and Payne became the second.

Promotion

Shapley convinced Payne to write a dissertation and so in 1925 she became the first person to receive a PhD in astronomy from Radcliffe College (now part of Harvard). The title of the dissertation was "Stellar Atmospheres, A Contribution to the Observational Study of High Temperature in the Reversing Layers of Stars". At the time, astronomers Otto Struve and Velta Zeberg called it "undoubtedly the most brilliant astronomical dissertation ever written".

Payne was able to accurately relate the spectral class of stars to their temperature by applying the ionization theory of Indian physicist Meghnad Saha. She showed that the large variation in absorption lines in star spectra was caused by different ionization rates at different temperatures, and not by different amounts of the elements. She found that silicon, carbon and other common metals visible in the solar spectrum had the same relative abundance as on Earth, which was consistent with the then accepted theory that stars had about the same elemental composition as Earth. However, she found that especially hydrogen and to a lesser extent helium were much more abundant in stars than on Earth (hydrogen about a million times more). Her thesis proved that hydrogen was the main element in stars and thus the most abundant element in the universe.

When Payne's thesis was reviewed, the astronomer Henry Norris Russell advised her against presenting the conclusion that the sun was composed mainly of hydrogen and thus the composition of the sun was very different from that of the Earth, because that contradicted the then current theory. She therefore described the result in her thesis as "incorrect". However, Russell changed his mind four years later after having obtained and published the same result in a different way. Although he briefly mentions her work in his article, Russell is often credited with the discovery even after Payne's work was accepted.

Career

After her PhD, Payne studied stars of high luminosity to investigate the structure of the Milky Way. She later studied all stars brighter than the tenth magnitude. She and her collaborators made more than 1,250,000 observations of variable stars. This work was later expanded to include 3,000,000 measurements of variable stars in the Magellanic clouds. These measurements were used to study star evolution. Her conclusions were published in her second book, *Stars of High Luminosity* (1930). These measurements and their analysis, which she did with her husband (the astronomer Sergei I. Gaposchkin), laid the basis for all subsequent work on variable stars.

Payne-Gaposchkin remained academically active and spent her entire academic career at Harvard. At first she had no official position, serving only as Shapley's technical assistant from 1927 to 1938. Because of this low status and salary, she considered resigning, but Shapley intervened on her behalf and in 1938 she was granted the title "Astronomer", later changed at her request to Phillips Astronomer. She was elected to the American Academy of Arts and Sciences in 1943.

When Donald Menzel became Director of the Harvard College Observatory in 1954, he sought to further enhance her appointment, and in 1956 she became the first woman to be promoted to Professor (Phillips Professor of Astronomy) at Harvard's Faculty of Arts and Sciences. She was later appointed head of the Faculty of Astronomy, making her the first woman in such a position at Harvard.

Her students included Helen Sawyer Hogg, Joseph Ashbrook, Frank Drake, and Paul W. Hodge, all of whom made significant contributions to astronomy.

Payne-Gaposchkin retired in 1966 and was then named Emeritus Professor of Harvard. She continued her research as a staff member of the Harvard-Smithsonian Center for Astrophysics, and was editor for 20 years for Harvard Observatory published journals and books.

Influence on female scientists

According to G. Kass-Simon and Patricia Farnes, Payne's career marked a turning point at Harvard College Observatory. Under Harlow Shapley and E. J. Sheridan (whom Payne-Gaposchkin described as a mentor), Harvard Observatory had already offered more opportunities in astronomy than other institutions, and noteworthy contributions had been made earlier in the twentieth century by Williamina Fleming, Antonia Maury, Annie Jump Cannon, and Henrietta Swan Leavitt. But the promotion of Payne-Gaposchkin normalized the position of women. Payne inspired many women, such as astrophysicist Joan Feynman (Richard Feynman's younger sister). Feynman's mother and grandmother had advised her against science because they believed that women could not understand scientific concepts.

Highlights

- In 1933 Payne traveled to Europe to meet Russian astronomer Boris Gerasimovich, who had previously worked at the Harvard College Observatory and with whom she planned to write a book about variable stars.
- Payne met Sergey Gaposchkin, a Russian astronomer who could not return to the Soviet Union because of his politics. They married in 1934 and often collaborated on studies of variable stars.
- She was named a lecturer in astronomy in 1938, but even though she taught courses, they were not listed in the Harvard catalog until after World War II.
- In 1956 Payne was appointed a full professor at Harvard and became chairman of the astronomy department.

16.   Jocelyn Bell Burnell (born 1943)

British astronomer who discovered the first radio pulsars

"There is stardust in your veins. We are literally, ultimately children of the stars."

Dame **Susan Jocelyn Bell Burnell** (Belfast, July 15, 1943) is a British astrophysicist who as a PhD student discovered the first pulsar, and thus the first neutron star. Her thesis supervisor was Antony Hewish, who received a Nobel Prize for this discovery along with Martin Ryle. Burnell was president of the Institute of Physics (IoP) in London for two years. She was the first woman ever to be appointed president of the *Royal Society of Edinburgh* in 2014. In 2018, she received the Special Breakthrough Prize worth three million US dollars for her 1967 discovery.

Biography

Jocelyn Bell was born in the Northern Irish city of Belfast. Her father was an architect for the nearby Armagh Planetarium. As a child she read many books on astronomy, including the *Frontiers of Astronomy* by British astronomer Fred Hoyle. She was one of the first girls allowed to study science at a college in Lurgan.

In 1965 she received her bachelor (B.Sc.) degree from the University of Glasgow. For her PhD she went to Cambridge University where Professor of Astrophysics Hewish became her PhD supervisor. With other students she was involved in the construction of Hewish *Interplanetary Scintillation Array*, a radio telescope with the intention of investigating quasars. In July 1967 Bell discovered something strange in the graph that rolled out of the paper-scanner. Peaks packed up that did not belong in it and which she called *scruff*. With a faster writer she could measure the interval between the peaks: 1.3 seconds. After ruling out a terrestrial origin, Hewish raised the possibility of the *Little Green Men hypothesis* - an extraterrestrial race of 'Little Green Men' seeking contact with Earth. Just before her Christmas break, she also discovered *scruff* at another radio source, but this time with a regularity of 1.25 seconds. After the discovery of two more pulsating sources from space, Hewish and Bell concluded - via an exhaustive process of elimination - that the signals had to come from rapidly rotating neutron stars. In all, Bell analyzed some thirty meters of graph paper a day, for a total of nearly five kilometers of graphs. Bell herself attributed her thoroughness to her imposter syndrome: the feeling of being inferior to one's (work) environment, in which one systematically questions one's own talents, achievements and successes.

In 1969 Bell completed her PhD on radio astronomy and the discovery of the pulsar. The year before, she married (divorced 1993) and had a son, who also became a physicist.

Following her PhD, Bell Burnell worked at the University of Southampton (1968-1973), University College London (1974-1982) and the *Royal Observatory* in Edinburgh (1982-1991). After working as a teacher, consultant, examiner and lecturer, she was appointed Professor of Physics at The Open University in 1991, a position she held for ten years.

Recognition

Despite being the first to discover a pulsar she did not share in the glory of the 1974 Nobel Prize in Physics when it was awarded to Antony Hewish and Martin Ryle. She herself showed no bitterness about this fact. In an interview she stated, "It is the supervisor [Hewish] who bears the ultimate responsibility for the success or failure of the project. It only seems reasonable to me that he should also benefit from the successes".

She did receive several honors and awards, including:

- 1973 - *Michelson Medal*, Franklin Institute
- 1978 - *J. Robert Oppenheimer Prize*
- 1978 - *Rennie Taylor Award*
- 1987 - *Beatrice M. Tinsley Prize*, American Astronomical Society
- 1989 - *Herschel Medal*, Royal Astronomical Society
- 1995 - *Karl G. Jansky Prize*

In 2007 she was appointed Dame Commander of the Order of the British Empire by Queen Elizabeth. She was also President of the *Royal Astronomical Society* from 2002 to 2004 and President of the *Institute of Physics* from 2008 to 2010. In 2014, she became President of the *Royal Society of Edinburgh*.

In November 2018, Burnell still received recognition for her discovery through the $3 million Special Breakthrough Prize awarded to her in San Francisco.

Highlights

- Jocelyn Bell Burnell attended the University of Glasgow, where she received a bachelor's degree (1965) in physics. She proceeded to the University of Cambridge, where she was awarded a doctorate (1969) in radio astronomy.
- As a research assistant at Cambridge, Bell Burnell aided in constructing a large radio telescope and in 1967, while reviewing the printouts of her experiments monitoring quasars, discovered a series of extremely regular radio pulses.
- After monitoring the pulses using more sensitive equipment, the team discovered several more regular patterns of radio waves and determined that they were in fact emanating from rapidly spinning neutron stars, which were later called pulsars by the press.
- Bell Burnell also served as president of the Royal Astronomical Society (2002-2004) and was elected to a two-year term as president of the Institute of Physics in 2008.

17.   Lise Meitner (1878 - 1968)

Austrian physicist who discovered the radioactive isotope protactinium-231

"Science makes people reach for truth and objectivity; it teaches people to accept reality, with wonder and admiration, not to mention the deep awe and joy that the natural order of things brings to the true scientist."

Lise Meitner (Vienna, 7 November 1878 - Cambridge, 27 October 1968) was an Austrian-Swedish physicist who, together with Otto Hahn and Fritz Strassmann, discovered atomic fission, the fundamental mechanism responsible not only for nuclear energy but also for nuclear weapons. She is cited as a typical example of a woman whose exceptional scientific achievement was overshadowed by a male colleague when she was awarded the Nobel Prize.

Meitner worked together with Otto Hahn and his assistant Fritz Strassmann, but as a Jew had to flee Germany because of Nazism. Their collaboration continued by letter. A few months after her flight, on 17 December 1938, Hahn and Strassmann succeeded in the experiment: for the first time they had split an atomic nucleus. In January 1939, together with Otto Frisch, Meitner provided the first physical theoretical explanation of nuclear fission. Her colleague Otto Hahn was awarded the Nobel Prize in Chemistry in 1944 for their discovery. The element meitnerium was named after Meitner.

Biography

The split was discovered in 1938 by Otto Hahn, Fritz Strassmann and Lise Meitner in Berlin. Lise Meitner, birth name Elise, was born in Vienna and was the third of eight children from a liberal Jewish family. She grew up in Leopoldstadt, the second district of Vienna, which together with Budapest formed the capital of Austria-Hungary. The register of births of the Vienna Jewish Community gives 17 November 1878 as her date of birth. All other official sources give November 7, 1878, the date used by Lise Meitner. Her father, Philipp Meitner, was one of the first lawyers of Jewish descent in Austria. Her mother was Hedwig Meitner-Skovran. Lise did not receive a Jewish but a secular, or according to another source, a Protestant upbringing. Later she converted to Lutheranism and was baptized. After five years of primary school, she went to a Viennese *Mädchen-Bürgerschule*, a middle school for girls, because the grammar school that prepared her for university was not open to girls. After the girls' middle school, her education was declared complete ("vom weiteren Schulbesuch befreit"). The only possibility for women to continue studying was to attend a private school, the *hohere Tochterschule*, and to choose a teaching profession in a limited number of subjects. A degree in science required a university education. She decided to study French, but never really had a passion for the subject. After this training she taught French at a secondary school for a year. With this she earned some money for the advanced music lessons of her sister Auguste (Gusti), who later became a concert pianist.

University of Vienna

Meitner was given the opportunity to pursue a scientific education in 1897. In this year the law that forbade women in Austria-Hungary to study at a university was repealed. On the advice of her father, she first completed her training as a French teacher to ensure that she could support herself. With the help of a local private tutor, through hard work she managed to complete the eight-year course at the Akademisches Gymnasium Wien to prepare for the university entrance examination in two years. Here she indicated that she saw philosophy as a realistic continuation study. Shortly before her 23rd birthday, she entered the University of Vienna as one of the few female students. Inspired by her professor, Ludwig Boltzmann, Meitner decided to focus entirely on physics after her first year. He was the only physics professor at the time, and accepted women as a matter of course. He was married to the mathematics and physics teacher Henriette von Aigentler who was allowed to take classes at the university with a great deal of effort and help from Boltzmann. Meitner received her doctorate summa cum laude on February 1, 1906 with a dissertation on heat conduction in non-homogeneous bodies. This made her the second woman to obtain a doctorate in physics at that university, but as a female researcher she hardly got any work. Eventually she wrote to Marie Curie, but it turned out that she had no position available for Meitner.

To earn money, she decided to return to teaching French at a secondary school. After Boltzmann's suicide, she became Stefan Meyer's assistant, who took over Boltzmann's work. She worked for Meyer for a year, during which she learned a lot about nuclear physics. She also published several papers on radioactivity: "Über Absorption von α- und β-Strahlen" and "Über die Zerstreuung von α-Strahlen".

However, there were no further career opportunities in Vienna, and after meeting the physicist Max Planck, a professor at the University of Berlin, she decided to try her luck in Berlin. Her plan was to stay there for one or a few semesters. She was allowed to attend Planck's lectures on theoretical physics, a remarkable gesture on Planck's part, who until then had admitted only one other woman, Elsa Neumann. In Berlin she also made the acquaintance of Otto Hahn.

Scientific career

The early twentieth century was the time of the great discoveries in the field of radioactivity. During the thirty years in Berlin Meitner worked intensively with Hahn, first at the Chemical Institute of the University of Berlin headed by Emil Fischer and from 1912 at the newly founded Kaiser-Wilhelm-Institut für Chemie in Berlin-Dahlem. The work in Berlin was not easy for Meitner. As a "guest" of Hahn, she was allowed to work without pay in a converted laboratory in the basement of the Chemical Institute, provided she never entered the upper floors of the building. To use a toilet she had to go to a nearby café. Hahn and Meitner complemented each other well: while Hahn worked more intuitively, Meitner was the analyst of the two. Their laboratory in the basement of the Chemical Institute quickly became radioactive and the partners often suffered from dizziness and nausea. A year later, women were admitted to the lectures and Meitner was allowed to enter the building freely.

Only in 1913 did Meitner get a permanent position at the Kaiser-Wilhelm-Institut. The same Fischer who tolerated her only as a guest in 1907 supported her more and more, until in 1916 she was paid the same salary as Hahn. An offer from Prague in 1914, a low academic position with the prospect of a better job, gave her more prestige, and a doubled salary.

She interrupted her work in 1915 to work as a nurse and x-ray technician in the Austrian army during the First World War. She returned to Berlin in 1916. Otto Hahn served as a soldier throughout the war and was only occasionally at work in the laboratory. In 1918 Hahn and Meitner were the first to isolate a long half-life isotope of the chemical element protactinium ($^{231}_{91}Pa$) and in 1921 the isotope uranium-Z ($^{234}_{92}U$). Although Lise Meitner had done almost all the work for the discovery of $^{231}_{91}Pa$, Hahn was the first author of the paper they published on it. For this discovery she was awarded a silver Leibniz Medal of the Prussian Academy of Sciences in 1924. Meitner also received her own department in the Kaiser-Wilhelm-Institut, the *Physikalisch-radioaktive Abteilung,* in 1917, and was allowed to manage her own personnel and finances. With this she also earned enough to leave her student room and move into a house for herself. Although she now had her own department, she continued her daily contact with Hahn. In 1919 she received the title of professor.

Meitner obtained her habilitation in October 1922 with the *Habilitation thesis* "Die Bedeutung der Radioaktivität für kosmische Prozesse" (The significance of radioactivity for cosmic processes), after which she was allowed to lecture on radioactivity. This step on the academic ladder had only been open to women since 1920. Shortly afterwards, she discovered the Auger effect in 1922. In 1926 Meitner became the first woman in Germany to be officially appointed extraordinary professor at the University of Berlin - at a greatly reduced salary and without her own laboratory. Meitner began a study of the properties of gamma and beta radiation, correctly assuming that the particles of beta radiation were electrons from the nucleus.Hahn remained on the faculty of chemistry. A long series of experiments by Charles Drummond Ellis and Lise Meitner led to the hypothesis of the existence of the neutrino in 1930. Other pioneering work on radioactivity included the discovery of positron-electron pairs, her work on artificial nuclear reactions and her mass determinations of neutrons. Albert Einstein often called her "our Marie Curie" during this period.

Search for transurans

Lise renewed the collaboration with Otto Hahn in 1934 after the Italian physicist Enrico Fermi had published about transuranium elements. By

71

bombarding elements with slow neutrons he and his group had produced elements with a higher atomic number, each time emitting a β-particle. Fermi supposed that by bombarding uranium with neutrons, he had produced elements with an atomic number higher than 92.

There were two assumptions within physics and chemistry that led to the wrong conclusion from the experiments. The first was that the nucleus behaved like a stable liquid droplet, and could only change in steps of one or two atomic numbers. The other assumption was that the transurans would behave like transition metals. Since the products of nuclear fission, which actually took place here, were transition metals, they thought they had found transuranics. In the years that followed, Hahn and Meitner published frequently about the transuranium metals they thought they had made. Meitner could not give a theoretical explanation of the "discovery" of the transuraniums.

Nazi Germany and flight

Due to the rise of National Socialism in Germany, Meitner experienced increasing inconvenience at the university. Many Jewish researchers, such as Fritz Haber, Leó Szilárd and her cousin Otto Frisch, were forced to give up their positions and decided to leave the country. Although Meitner lost her position as a professor in 1933, she decided to stay in Germany. Four things protected her from the anti-Jewish law that was declared in 1933: her Austrian nationality, the fact that the Kaiser-Wilhelm-Institut was not a government agency, her friendship with prominent researchers, such as Max Planck and Otto Hahn, and the fact that she was a prominent researcher.

Nevertheless, her protected status could not completely exempt her from the public fate that Jews had to endure. She was forced to wear the yellow Jewish star and was regularly the target of coarse remarks and even physical violence. After the annexation (*Anschluss*) of Austria in March 1938 by Germany, Meitner also decided to flee the Nazi regime. Her Austrian passport was invalidated by the Nazi regime, and she was forbidden to carry more than ten Reichmarks. Hahn gave Meitner his mother's diamond ring on her flight so that she could bribe a border guard. In the end she did not use it: with the help of the Dutch physicists Dirk Coster, Peter Debye and Adriaan Fokker, she narrowly escaped to the Netherlands on 13 July, from where she travelled via Denmark to Sweden. In the weeks before, Fokker and Coster had been busy collecting money to be able to offer Meitner a position at the University of Groningen, where foreigners were not allowed to have paid positions. Although they had collected only a fifth of the required amount, they decided to bring her from

Germany with the permission of the Dutch government. No visa was required for a holiday. To give the appearance of a vacation, she packed very lightly: some clothes, the ten rijksmark, and the diamond ring. (The latter she would eventually give to her cousin's fiancé).

In Denmark she worked with Niels Bohr for a short time, but decided to accept the offer from Stockholm and left for Sweden at the end of August. At Manne Siegbahn's Nobel Institute in Stockholm, Meitner continued her research in nuclear physics with the few resources at her disposal. She received little support from Siegbahn because of his prejudices about women in science.

Discovery of nuclear fission

The breakthrough came in 1938 in the laboratory of Irène Joliot-Curie, who after a bombardment with neutrons found an element with properties she could not explain. Hahn and Strassmann thought it was an isotope of radium. Lise, who after her flight continued to contribute to research on transuranium elements through intensive correspondence, could not explain the origin of this element. In November 1938, at a clandestine, secret meeting in Copenhagen, Meitner and Hahn discussed progress at the Berlin laboratory. She insisted that Hahn and Strassmann verify the results from Paris. Hahn kept this correspondence with the Jew secret, claiming that Strassman and he did their research alone. However, Hahn and Strassmann immediately upon their return from Copenhagen began to carry out the suggested experiments.

Meitner spent the Christmas holidays of 1938 in the Swedish town of Kungälv, where her cousin Otto Frisch, who had come over from Copenhagen, was also present. Shortly before, she had received a message from Berlin. In the letter Hahn reported that during the bombardment of uranium nuclei with slow neutrons, he and Strassmann had produced the lighter element barium, with atomic number 56, as one of the by-products, a result which he could not explain, however, partly because the disintegration of an atomic nucleus was considered unthinkable on theoretical grounds.

On the basis of the droplet model of Niels Bohr and others, Meitner and Frisch concluded that the nucleus is so violently disturbed by the incident neutron that the original droplet splits into two smaller droplets, making them the first to explain how an atomic nucleus could split: uranium nuclei disintegrated into barium and krypton and various neutrons with a lot of energy.

It also became clear that no naturally stable atoms can exist with an atomic number greater than 92 (uranium): the electrical repulsion of the many protons there overcomes the strong nuclear force, which holds the other nuclei together.

Meitner was the first to understand that the small amount of lost mass was converted into the large kinetic energy of the decay products, according to Einstein's equation for the mass-energy relation $E = m c^2$. Frisch used the term "*fission*" for this process. Thus the principle of nuclear fission was discovered.

When Ida Noddack first came up with the (theoretically unsubstantiated) idea of nuclear fission in 1934, after studying Fermi's experiments, it was met with skepticism and even hostility by Hahn and Meitner, partly because of the outcry after she claimed the discovery of the element masurium.Because of the political situation in Nazi Germany, Hahn and Meitner had to publish their results separately. Hahn's article in the German *Die Naturwissenschaften* (January 6) described the experiment and the finding of barium as a byproduct. The article by Meitner and Frisch entitled *"Disintegration of Uranium by Neutrons: a New Type of Nuclear Reaction"* described the physics behind the phenomenon of nuclear fission, extended by the article *"Products of Fission of the Uranium Nucleus"* (*Nature*, March 18, 1939). It was only after these two publications that Hahn and Strassman began a subsequent series of experiments, which included verification of her predictions of the presence of krypton as a fission product, and its subsequent decay into rubidium, strontium, and yttrium. After the war Meitner's name was rarely mentioned in connection with the experimental research, although even from Sweden she steered the research in the right direction by means of an intensive correspondence with Hahn, and had been a member of the experimental group in the four preceding years.

Later career

Before World War II broke out, she was offered a position at the Cavendish laboratory in Cambridge. However, she delayed accepting this because of the promise of an assistant in Stockholm and because her passport application went unanswered. She did not want to immigrate illegally a second time. In 1943 she was asked to collaborate on the American Manhattan Project, but as a convinced pacifist, Meitner refused to contribute to an atomic bomb. Nevertheless, she was regularly approached by intelligence officers from Great Britain and the United States for information about the ongoing nuclear weapons research in Germany, because of her correspondence with Otto Hahn. Meitner knew

74

nothing about the progress of atomic bomb development until the bombing of Hiroshima.

After the war she refused to return to Germany, bitter about the fact that leading German scientists such as Planck, Heisenberg and Von Laue before and during the war were more concerned with their own scientific careers than with the rights of their Jewish colleagues. She also turned down a personal request from Hahn and Strassmann to help rebuild the Kaiser Wilhelm Institute in Mainz. Here she was offered the entire physics department. Only in 1948 did she return to German soil for the first time, to attend a memorial ceremony for Max Planck.

Karl Herzfeld offered her a visiting professorship at the Catholic University of America for the winter season 1945-1946, which she accepted. She received several offers of professorships during her stay in the United States, but decided to return to Sweden. Although her role in technical development was marginal, after the war she was portrayed in the American press as the "Jewish mother of the atomic bomb" and as the fugitive Jew who had snatched the secret of the atomic bomb from under Adolf Hitler's nose. She was even asked to star in a feature film, but resolutely refused, "I'd rather walk naked down Broadway," she told Otto Frisch. In the year she stayed in the United States, she was proclaimed "Woman of the Year".

In 1947 she was appointed professor at Stockholm University, was given assistants and a decent income. In 1949 she became a Swedish citizen and a few years later she decided to retire at the age of 75.

To live near her cousin Otto Frisch, Meitner settled in the United Kingdom in 1960, where she died in Cambridge in 1968 - shortly before her 90th birthday. Otto Frisch's inscription on her gravestone reads: A scientist who never lost her humanity

Private life

Lise Meitner looked back on her childhood in Vienna as an extremely stimulating environment and was grateful for the incredible kindness of her parents. Although Leopoldtstad was a largely Jewish district, religion did not play a major role in her upbringing. Otto Frisch later firmly believed that all the children in the family were raised Protestant and were all baptized. Idealism was important in the family; her father was a passionate politician. Thus, while studying French, she did volunteer work, as well as tutoring to raise money for her sister Auguste's education. During her private lessons in preparation for the Matura (final exam), her sisters and brothers teased her about her industriousness: "You're not going to make it: just now you walked around the room without a textbook."

Her personality was often described as shy when she wasn't doing physics. Nevertheless, she could make friends very easily. For example, she had a close friendship with Otto Hahn and his wife Edith, and they often spent weekends together. She was the godmother of both their son and grandson, and she called Hahn *colleague brother*. Their friendship made Hahn's distortion of the story about the discovery of nuclear fission, and his failure to correct it after the war, all the more painful.How much she valued her Viennese ancestry was shown by the fact that she did not apply for Swedish citizenship until it became possible to retain her Austrian passport.

Recognition

Hahn received the 1944 Nobel Prize in Chemistry (awarded in 1945), while Meitner was ignored by the Nobel Committee, in part because Hahn minimized her role in the discovery process after her forced escape from Germany. He defended himself by claiming that the discovery of nuclear fission had taken place after Meitner's forced escape and was entirely due to his and Strassmann's chemical research. He gave her part of the prize money, but did not disclose it.

The Nobel Committee was under the impression that Bohr was the first to provide a theoretical explanation for nuclear fission. Bohr's letter stating that this was not so arrived too late for the 1944 Nobel Prize. Why it did not revise its decision in subsequent years remains unclear. Possibly personal reasons played a role.Over the years Meitner has been nominated at least 46 times for a Nobel Prize, both for Chemistry, and for Physics. A number of times together with Otto Hahn, a few times together with Otto Frisch, and she has also been nominated for an undivided Nobel Prize. Among the nominators were James Franck and Max Planck.

Failure to obtain the prize probably brought her more notoriety than any award, partly because her exclusion was perceived by the community as disadvantaging women in science, turning her into a feminist icon. This was partially corrected in 1966 when she was awarded the Enrico Fermi Prize along with Hahn and Strassmann. Furthermore, in 1949 she received (together with Hahn) the Max Planck Medal and in 1955 she was the first winner of the *Otto-Hahn-Preis für Chemie und Physik*, which she shared with Heinrich Wieland.

The prestigious Deutsches Museum has an exhibition on the discovery of nuclear fission. A work table with Lise Meitner's physical apparatus, used for the discovery of nuclear fission, was referred to as Otto Hahn's work table, and Meitner herself described as his collaborator instead of colleague. The text was changed around 1990 after protests.

In 1945 she was elected a foreign member in the Royal Swedish Academy of Sciences; in 1951 this was converted to normal membership.

In 1997, the element meitnerium, discovered in 1982 by the group of Peter Armbruster and Gottfried Münzenberg, was officially named after her by the IUPAC. Two craters on the Moon and Venus are also named after her.

Highlights

- After receiving her doctorate at the University of Vienna (1906), Lise Meitner attended Max Planck's lectures at Berlin in 1907 and joined Hahn in research on radioactivity.
- During three decades of association, she and Hahn were among the first to isolate the isotope protactinium-231 (which they named), studied nuclear isomerism and beta decay, and in the 1930s (along with Strassmann) investigated the products of neutron bombardment of uranium.
- In 1944 Hahn received the Nobel Prize for Chemistry for discovering nuclear fission, though some have argued that Meitner merited a share of the award.
- During this time, Meitner was invited to work on the Manhattan Project (1942-1945) in the United States. She opposed the atomic bomb, however, and rejected the offer.

18.   Christiane Nüsslein-Volhard (born 1942)

German developmental biologist and Nobel Prize-winner

*"I immediately loved working with flies. They fascinated
me, and followed me around in my dreams. "*

Christiane Nüsslein-Volhard (Magdeburg, October 20, 1942) is a
German biologist and Nobel laureate. In 1995 she won the Nobel Prize in
Physiology or Medicine together with Edward B. Lewis and Eric
Wieschaus for the discovery of the genes involved in early embryonic
development of the fruit fly, the homeobox genes. She also won the Albert
Lasker Award for Basic Medical Research in 1991.

Biography

Christiane Nüsslein-Volhard was born as the second of five children of
Rolf Volhard, an architect, and Brigitte Hass. In 1964 she studied
biochemistry at the Eberhard-Karls-University of Tübingen. She completed
her studies in 1968 and obtained her PhD in molecular biology in 1973.
She worked at the universities of Basel and Freiburg and the European

Molecular Biology Laboratory in Heidelberg before being appointed
Professor of Genetics at the Max Planck Institute in Tübingen in 1981.

Christiane Nüsslein-Volhard has been the director of the Max Planck
Institute for Developmental Biology in Tübingen since 1985. She also
heads the genetics department here. In 1986 she received the Gottfried
Wilhelm Leibniz Prize of the Deutsche Forschungsgemeinschaft.

Work

Together with Wieschaus, she introduced "Big Science" into biology by
carrying out a successful mutagenesis project on a large scale. This
investigated the embryonic development of the fruit fly *Drosophila
melanogaster*. At the time of her research, most molecular biology
experiments were small-scale. The genes responsible for embryonic
development were identified by inducing random mutations in the genes of
the fruit flies. The result was a comprehensive catalogue of mutations
leading to physiological deficiencies. This research led to important
discoveries about evolution. The homeobox gene was found to play an
essential role in early embryonic development in fruit flies; it was later
shown to occur in all species.

Nüsslein-Volhard is also credited with the discovery of the toll gene, which
led to the identification of toll-like receptors and which play an important
role in our immune system.

Since 2001 she has been a member of the *National Ethics Council* for the
ethical assessment of new life sciences and their impact on the
community. In 2004 she founded the Christiane Nüsslein-Volhardstichting,
named after her, which offers, among other things, childcare and domestic
help to talented young women with children so that they can still develop
their scientific careers.

In June 2005 she received an honorary doctorate from Oxford University.

Highlights

- At Eberhard-Karl University of Tübingen, Christiane Nüsslein-Volhard
  received a diploma in biochemistry in 1968 and a doctorate in
  genetics in 1973.

- In 1981 Nüsslein-Volhard returned to Tübingen, where she served as director of the Max Planck Institute for Developmental Biology from 1985 to 2015.
- At Heidelberg, Nüsslein-Volhard and Wieschaus spent more than a year crossbreeding 40,000 fruit fly families and systematically examining their genetic makeup at a dual microscope.
- They assigned responsibility for the fruit fly's embryonic development to three genetic categories: gap genes, which lay out the head-to-tail body plan; pair-rule genes, which determine body segmentation; and segment-polarity genes, which establish repeating structures within each segment.
- Christiane Nüsslein-Volhard also published several books, including Zebrafish: A Practical Approach (2002; written with Ralf Dahm) and Coming to Life: How Genes Drive Development (2006).

19.   Peggy Whitson (born 1960)
American biochemistry researcher and a retired NASA astronaut

"I would certainly encourage young people to pursue their dreams. It isn't always an easy path, but it's worth going after."

Peggy Annette Whitson (Mount Ayr, February 9, 1960) is an American astronaut. The 665 days she spent in space in total is an American record.

Whitson was part of NASA Astronaut Group 16. This group of 44 astronauts began their training in 1996 and was nicknamed *The Sardines*.

Her first space flight was STS-111 to the International Space Station ISS on the space shuttle Endeavour and took place on June 5, 2002. She has a total of three spaceflights to her credit. In total she made ten spacewalks.

In 2009, Whitson became the director of NASA's Astronaut Office. She was not only the first woman to hold this position, but also the first mission specialist. The other directors were always former pilots. Whitson resigned in 2012.

On 17 November 2016, it took off from the Kosmodrome Baykonur rocket launch base in Kazakhstan for a six-month mission to the ISS. This was the fiftieth joint mission (Expedition 50/51) of NASA, ESA and Roscosmos. Whitson was scheduled to return to Earth in May 2017, but her stay was extended and she also stayed on board for ISS Expedition 52. She was finally back on Earth in September 2017. On June 15, 2018, Whitson bid farewell to NASA. In early 2021, it became clear that she is working as a commercial astronaut for Axiom Space and is scheduled as a backup captain on Crew Dragon flight SpaceX Axiom Space-1 (Ax-1) and as a Captain for Ax-2.

Highlights

- Peggy Whitson received a B.S. in biology and chemistry from Iowa Wesleyan College in Mount Pleasant, Iowa, in 1981 and a doctorate in biochemistry from Rice University in Houston in 1985.
- From 2009 to 2012, Whitson was chief of the Astronaut Office, which oversees all NASA astronaut activities, including crew selection and training. Whitson was the first woman and the first civilian to hold that position.
- On April 10, 2017, Peggy Whitson became commander of the ISS Expedition 51 mission, which lasted until June 2. She made four space walks on which station components were maintained or replaced.
- Peggy Whitson spent nearly 666 days in space during her three long-duration tours of duty to the ISS, which made her NASA's most-experienced astronaut.

15 Female Artists

1. Beyoncé (born 1981)

American singer-songwriter and actress with multi-platinum Grammy awards

"If everything was perfect, you would never learn, and you would never grow."

Beyoncé Giselle Knowles-Carter (Houston (Texas), September 4, 1981) is an American R&B singer, songwriter, actress and fashion designer. She was born in Houston, grew up there and participated in several singing and dancing competitions as a child. In the late 1990s, she gained fame as the lead singer of the R&B girl group Destiny's Child. With her father Mathew Knowles as manager, the group became one of the world's best-selling girl groups ever. During a hiatus in the group's existence, Beyoncé released her debut album *Dangerously in Love* (2003), which established her name as a solo artist worldwide; it sold 11 million copies and garnered five Grammy Awards, in addition to the two singles *Crazy in Love* and *Baby Boy* reaching number one on the U.S. Billboard chart.

After the breakup of Destiny's Child in June 2005, Beyoncé released her second solo album, *B'Day* (2006), which spawned the hits *Déjà Vu*, *Irreplaceable* and *Beautiful Liar*. She also ventured into acting, with a Golden Globe Award nominated role in 2006's *Dreamgirls*, and roles in 2006's *The Pink Panther* and 2009's *Obsessed*. Both her marriage to rapper Jay-Z and her characterization of Etta James in the 2008 film *Cadillac Records* exerted influence on her third album, *I Am... Sasha Fierce* (2008), which revealed her alter ego Sasha Fierce and won six Grammy Awards in 2010, a record number for a female artist, including Song of the Year for *Single Ladies (Put a Ring on It)*. Beyoncé then took a career break and took management of her career into her own hands. Her fourth album *4* from 2011 was less edgy in tone, showcasing influences from the 70s (funk), the 80s (pop), as well as the 90s (soul). Her fifth studio album, *Beyoncé* (2013), received rave reviews and was distinguished from previous releases by its experimental production and touch on darker themes. Beyoncé is the face of her own clothing line *House of Deréon*.

A "modern-day feminist," Beyoncé writes songs that often address themes of love, relationships and monogamy, as well as female sexuality and independence. On stage, her dynamic performances and cutting-edge choreography have earned her a reputation among audiences and critics as one of the finest entertainers in contemporary pop music. In the first 18 years of her career, she has sold more than 100 million albums as a solo artist and another 60 million with Destiny's Child, making her one of the best-selling artists of all time. She has won 20 Grammy Awards and is the most-nominated woman in the history of the Grammys. The Recording Industry Association of America recognizes her as the Top Certified Artist in America of the first decade of 2000. In 2009, *Billboard named* her the Best Female Artist of the first decade of 2000 and Artist of the Millennium in 2011. *Time* magazine included her in its list of 100 most influential people in the world in both 2013 and 2014.

Lifecycle

Beyoncé Giselle Knowles was born in Houston to Celestine Ann "Tina" Beyoncé, a hairdresser and salon owner, and Mathew Knowles, who was a sales manager at Xerox. The name Beyoncé is an homage to her mother's birth name. Her younger sister Solange is also a singer. Father Mathew is African-American, while mother Tina, who comes from the creole population of Louisiana, has African, Native American, French, and

85

1/16th Irish blood.Beyoncé attended St. Mary's Elementary School in Fredericksburg (Texas), where she took dance classes. Her singing talent was discovered when dance instructor Darlette Johnson began humming a song and she finished it including the top notes. At age seven, Beyoncé won a school talent show with a performance of John Lennon's *Imagine*, beating the fifteen- and sixteen-year-old contestants.

In the fall of 1990, Beyoncé began attending Parker Elementary School, a music school in Houston, where she joined the school choir. She also attended the High School for the Performing and Visual Arts and later Alief Elsik High School. In addition, Beyoncé was a member of the choir at St. John's United Methodist Church, where she was a soloist for two years.

At the age of eight, Beyoncé and her friend Kelly Rowland auditioned for a girl group and met LaTavia Roberson. Along with three other girls, they were put into the group Girl's Tyme to rap and dance on the Houston talent show circuit. After seeing the group, R&B producer Arne Frager took them to his studio in northern California and gave them a spot on *Star Search*, the biggest talent show on American television at the time. However, Girl's Tyme did not win and Beyoncé later felt that their song was no good. In 1995, Beyoncé's father quit his job to become the group's manager. This ran the income of Beyoncé's family by half and the parents were forced to live separately. Mathew reduced the original line-up to four people and the group continued to perform as an opening act for established R&B girl groups. After a few auditions, the group signed a contract with Elektra Records and moved to Atlanta Records for some time to work on their first recording, but the label dropped them. As a result, relations within the family became more strained and Beyoncé's parents split up. On October 5, 1995, Dwayne Wiggins' company Grass Roots Entertainment signed the group. In 1996, the girls began recording their debut album under a deal with Sony Music and the parents reunited. Shortly thereafter, the group signed a contract with Columbia Records.

1997-2001: Destiny's Child

In 1996, the group changed its name to Destiny's Child, after a passage in the biblical book of Isaiah. In 1997, Destiny's Child debuted with a major record label with the song *Killing Time* on the soundtrack for the 1997 film *Men in Black*. The following year, the group released their *Destiny's Child* titled debut album and had their first major hit with *No, No, No*. The group now became established and the reasonably selling album earned them three Soul Train Lady of Soul Awards: for Best R&B/Soul Album of the Year, Best R&B/Soul or Rap New Artist, and Best R&B/Soul Single for *No, No, No*. Their second, multi-platinum-winning album, *The Writing's on the Wall,* was released in 1999, featuring some of the group's best-known songs, including *Bills, Bills, Bills* (their first U.S. No. 1 single), *Jumpin' Jumpin*, and *Say My Name*, the latter of which became their most successful and a recognition song of the group.

Say My Name won the Grammy Award for Best R&B Performance by a singing duo or group and that for Best R&B Song at the 43rd Annual Grammy Awards. The album *The Writing's on the Wall* sold over eight million copies worldwide. During this period, Beyoncé recorded a duet with Marc Nelson, one of the original group members of Boyz II Men, *After All Is Said and Done* for the soundtrack to the 1999 film *The Best Man*.

The way Mathew managed the group led to dissatisfaction with LeToya Luckett and Roberson. They were eventually replaced by Farrah Franklin and Michelle Williams. After the breakup, Beyoncé fell into a depression as she was held responsible in the media, blogs and by critics. Around this time, her boyfriend also broke off the relationship. The depression lasted for several years, during which she would occasionally not leave her bedroom for days and refused to eat. According to her, Beyoncé found it difficult to talk about her depression because Destiny's Child had just won their first Grammy Award and she feared no one would take her seriously. Later, Beyoncé would name her mother as the one who helped her rise above it. Franklin was kicked out of the group and only Beyoncé, Rowland and Williams remained.

Destiny's Child was successful from 1997 to 2005. The songs were mainly of the R&B genre.

Dangerously in Love

In 2003, Knowles released her first solo album *Dangerously in Love*, which sold more than twelve million copies worldwide. For this album she worked with Missy Elliott, Sean Paul, Jay-Z and others. The first single, *Crazy in Love*, was a worldwide success: it reached number 1 in the United States and the top 10 in almost all countries. The following singles were equally successful - *Baby Boy* and *Naughty Girl* reached the top ten, and *Me, Myself and I* peaked at 14. In the United States, all four singles reached the top five. With this album she won five Grammys in one night.

B'Day

Her second album was called *B'Day* and was released on September 4, 2006, her twenty-fifth birthday. The album was recorded within two weeks of the completion of filming for the movie *Dreamgirls*. The album entered the US Billboard 200 at #1 with over 541,000 copies sold in its first week. In April 2007, she re-released *B'Day*, under the name *B'Day Deluxe Edition* - this release has a slightly different track list than the first version of the album. The deluxe edition (*Deluxe Edition*) includes Spanish-language songs and a duet with singer Shakira, *Beautiful Liar*.

I Am... Sasha Fierce

In November 2008, Knowles released her third solo album *I Am... Sasha Fierce*. In an interview, producer Rodney Jerkins said the album was inspired by the movie *Cadillac Records*, for which Knowles was cast to play the role of Etta James. The album is divided into two CDs. The first part of the album, "I Am...", contains mostly quiet songs in which Knowles' vocal performances dominate. The second part of the album, "Sasha Fierce", contains uptempo songs. The album's photo booklet also distinguishes between Knowles and Sasha Fierce; for "I Am..." she poses quietly in sober clothing, while for "Sasha Fierce" she looks into the camera in a biker jacket and heavy makeup. The album's first two singles were released in October 2008: *If I Were a Boy* (from the part "I Am...") and *Single Ladies (Put a Ring on It)* (from "Sasha Fierce"). This made Knowles one of the first artists to release two singles at the same time. The singles both had their video premieres on the Internet. The album also includes the song *Videophone*, which she released with Lady Gaga. The music video for it was released in November 2009.

4

The first single from the album *4* was *Run the World (Girls)* and was released on 21 April 2011. One day after its release, *Run* the World debuted at number 60 in the Single Top 100. The next week it shot up to number eight, its highest position. The accompanying album was released on 28 June in the United States. The second single was *Best Thing I Never Had*.

Beyoncé

On December 12, 2013, just before midnight, Knowles released her fifth studio album *Beyoncé (album), which* contains 14 songs and 17 music videos, exclusively via iTunes. As of December 20, the album was available in stores. The first single from the album was *XO*. On November 24, 2014, *Beyoncé's* Platinum Edition was released. It is a box set consisting of two CDs and two DVDs, which includes two new singles, four remixes, HBO X10 Live and the original *Beyoncé album.*

Lemonade

On April 6, 2016, the single *Formation* was released as a preview of the album *Lemonade, released* on April 23, 2016, which contains 12 tracks. *Lemonade* is the singer's most acclaimed album to date and was nominated for nine Grammy Awards, winning those for Best Urban Contemporary Album and Best Music Video.

Films

Knowles is also active as an actress. She starred in the third part of *Austin Powers* and in *The Pink Panther* in 2006. In 2006, *Dreamgirls* was also released in theaters. In this film, Knowles starred alongside Eddie Murphy, Jamie Foxx and *American Idol finalist* Jennifer Hudson. Knowles also appeared in the film *Cadillac Records*, in which she plays the role of blues singer Etta James. For this role, she was coached by Etta James herself and had to gain at least eight kilos. The film was released in America at the end of December 2008. In 2009, the film *Obsessed* was released, a thriller starring Knowles as Sharon. In the American animated film *Epic* she spoke the voice of Queen Tara. In 2019, she played Nala in the live-action remake of The Lion King.

Private life

Beyoncé's father was her business manager from the beginning of her career until March 2011 and her mother was her stylist. Knowles is a Methodist and married Jay-Z privately on April 4, 2008. On January 7, 2012 at Lenox Hill Hospital in New York, their daughter was born.On June 18, 2017, it was announced that Beyoncé had given birth to twins.

Music and voice

Knowles grew up listening to the music of Anita Baker and Luther Vandross, with whom she later recorded a duet. Beyoncé also uses influences in her music from American artists such as Prince, Aretha Franklin, Mariah Carey, Whitney Houston, Janet Jackson, Michael Jackson, Mary J. Blige, Diana Ross, Donna Summer and Tina Turner, with whom she performed at the 2008 Grammy Awards ceremony.

Beyoncé's music is described as a modern form of R&B but is also influenced by music genres such as dance pop, pop and soul. The singer also recorded several songs in Spanish for her re-released second solo album *B'Day*. She had previously recorded a Spanish song with Destiny's Child. Beyoncé was taught Spanish at school when she was young but nowadays she only speaks a few words of Spanish. To record the Spanish songs she was coached by Rudy Perez over the phone. She sang in French once during the Oscars ceremony.

In 2010, Beyoncé introduced her own fragrance called Beyoncé Heat. She had previously starred in television advertisements for Tommy Hilfiger and Emporio Armani perfumes. A sequel to Beyoncé Heat followed in 2011: Heat Rush. The third fragrance in the series was Midnight Heat, released in 2012. More fragrances were released alongside this series.

Highlights

- Days after a triumphant headlining performance at England's Glastonbury Festival, Beyoncé released 4 (2011), a genre-bending mix of ballads and dance tracks that evoked influences ranging from Motown-era torch songs to the audio collages of rapper M.I.A. In early 2013 Destiny's Child reunited for a halftime appearance at the Super Bowl and released a new song, "Nuclear."
- Shortly thereafter Beyoncé collected a Grammy for her single "Love on Top."
- The single "Drunk in Love," which featured Jay-Z, was awarded several Grammys, including best R&B song.

2. Lady Gaga (born 1986)

American singer, songwriter, actress, and eleven-time Grammy winner

"Fight and push harder for what you believe in, you'd be surprised, you are much stronger than you think."

Stefani Joanne Angelina Germanotta (New York, March 28, 1986), better known as **Lady Gaga**, is an American singer, songwriter, actress and pianist. She broke through worldwide in 2009 with the singles *Just dance* and *Poker face*, which became number 1 hits in many countries. After that, she also scored mega-hits with songs like *Paparazzi* (2009), *Bad Romance* (2009), *Telephone* (2010), *Alejandro* (2010), *Born This Way* (2011), *Applause* (2013) *Shallow* (2018) and *Rain on Me* (2020).

Gaga has won several Grammy Awards, including in 2010 for her debut album *The Fame* (best dance album) and in 2011 for her album *The Fame Monster* (best pop vocal album). Her song *Poker Face*, which was the best-selling single of 2009 worldwide, won a Grammy for best dance record. *Poker Face* (13 million copies sold) and *Bad Romance* (12 million copies sold) are among the best-selling singles of all time.

Lady Gaga took her stage name from the song *Radio Ga Ga Ga* by the British rock group Queen.

Biography

Lady Gaga was born in New York on March 28, 1986. Her mother is of French-Canadian descent. Her father's family is originally from Sicily. She is the eldest of two children. Her sister was born in 1992.They grew up in Manhattan's Upper West Side in an affluent family that had risen from the lower social class with hard work. Lady Gaga was raised Roman Catholic.

Stefani started playing the piano at the age of four. She had her first major performance at thirteen.

In September 2006, Lady Gaga signed a contract with record label Def Jam Recordings to make an album in nine months. However, after only three months, the label dropped her. After Def Jam dropped her, Gaga decided to spend Christmas 2006 with her family. After this, she started experimenting a lot with alcohol and drugs. She performed with performer Lady Starlight in nightclubs. According to Gaga herself, Starlight helped her a lot to gain more stage experience. They were both invited to perform at the Lollapalooza festival in August 2007. Meanwhile, Gaga was recording songs with producer RedOne. RedOne sent the songs to Vincent Herbert, owner of the label Streamline Records. Soon after, Gaga got a contract with Streamline Records, until the label stopped in late 2007.

2008 - 2009: International breakthrough with The Fame

In 2008, Gaga and RedOne began recording three songs that would later become big hits: *Just Dance, Poker Face* and *LoveGame. Just Dance* was released in April 2008. The song was written within 10 minutes. *Poker Face* and *LoveGame were written* in one week. After this, she signed a contract with the Interscope Records record label and officially started making her debut album. In October 2008 she filled in during the tour of New Kids On The Block. She also wrote songs for the Pussycat Dolls and Britney Spears, among others.

On December 1, 2008, Lady Gaga performed on The Ellen DeGeneres Show.

Lady Gaga wrote her debut album *The Fame* in 2008 together with producer Nadir Khayat, a.k.a. RedOne. The album was released on August 12, 2008. The Fame is a synthpop and dance-pop album with influences from 80s pop music. Lyrically, the album visualizes Gaga's love for celebrity in general, but also visualizes dealing with topics such as love, sex, money, drugs and sexual identity.

The first single from the album, *Just Dance*, was released in April 2008. The song reached the number 1 position in seven countries. The song was a collaboration with American singer Colby O'Donis and was nominated for a Grammy Award. The music video was shot on 31 March 2008. The second single *Poker Face* from the same album was released in September 2008. The music video was filmed on 3 October 2008 at Bwin Pokerisland in Ibiza. The song reached number one on the charts in 20 countries and was awarded a Grammy Award. The single was the most listened to song on the US Digital Hot Songs for 83 weeks. The music video was shot on January 9, 2009. In other countries, the song *Eh, Eh (Nothing Else I Can Say) was* released first. Its music video was recorded on January 10, 2009, one day after the shooting of "LoveGame". Because the lyrics of the song *LoveGame* were considered too explicit in some countries, it was replaced by *Paparazzi*.

On January 6, 2009, Lady Gaga's first EP was released, titled *The Cherrytree Sessions*. The EP was recorded in November 2008.

In September 2009 Lady Gaga was nominated nine times for the MTV Video Music Awards with this first album. She won the awards for best new artist and with *Paparazzi* for best *special effects* and best direction. During the ceremony she performed and sang the song *Paparazzi*.

2009 - 2010: The Fame Monster

On September 5, 2009, a photo shoot for the album cover of *The Fame Monster was held* by Gaga herself and Haus of Gaga, her production team.

In November 2009, Lady Gaga launched her second album with *The Fame Monster, an* eight-song EP. The album is about dealing with the dark side of celebrity, which Gaga has experienced in her musical career while touring the world. According to Gaga, the album is "expressed in a monster metaphor". As the first single from the album, *Bad Romance* was

93

released. The song became another chart success and the accompanying music video was the first video to be viewed over two hundred million times.As the second single, *Telephone* was released, a duet with Beyoncé. *Telephone was* originally written for Britney Spears. On 8 June 2010 the third single *Alejandro was released*. The song was quite successful, it reached the fifth place in the United States. The music video for *Alejandro* was considered by some to be very daring and singer Katy Perry was particularly critical. Then *Dance in the Dark* was also released as a promotional single.

At the 2010 Grammy Awards, Lady Gaga was nominated six times. She opened the show with *Poker Face* and then sang a remix of *Speechless* and *Your Song* with Elton John. She won the Grammy for best dance recording with Poker *Face* and for best dance album with *The Fame*.

In February 2010, Lady Gaga dominated the Brit Awards by winning three awards. She performed a rendition of *Telephone* on the piano and then performed a remix of *Dance in the Dark* with which she honored Alexander McQueen, who had ended his life a week earlier.

The album was promoted with the world tour The Monster Ball Tour. The concert of 21 and 22 February 2011 at Madison Square Garden in New York won the Emmy Award for *Outstanding Picture Editing for a Special*. The tour lasted a year and a half and attracted more than two and a half million visitors over a total of 200 days.

2010 - 2012: Born This Way

At the MTV Video Music Awards ceremony in September 2010, Lady Gaga announced the title of her third studio album, *Born this way*. Lady Gaga became the big winner at the 27th edition of the awards show. The singer had a record thirteen nominations and won eight awards at the Nokia Theatre in Los Angeles, including best female video, best pop video and best choreography.The album reached number one on the charts in numerous countries. The first single *Born This Way* caused a commotion when it showed striking similarities with Madonna's *Express Yourself.Judas was released* as the second single, *The Edge of Glory as the* third single and *Hair* followed a week later. *Yoü and I* became the fifth single from the album and was nominated for a Grammy in 2012. *Marry the Night* then became her twelfth No. 1 hit on the *Billboard* Dance Club chart. The Born This Way Ball Tour with four hundred and fifty concerts in two years started in February 2012.

Since the summer of 2011 she has a relationship with actor Taylor Kinney who is best known for his role as Mason Lockwood in the series 'The Vampire Diaries. Lady Gaga met Taylor during the shooting of her music video for *Yoü and I*.

At the MTV Video Music Awards in August 2011 she won prizes for best music video by a female artist and best video with an edifying message with *Born this way*. She opened with *Yoü and I* as her male alter ego *Jo Calderone*. At the MTV Europe Music Awards in November 2011 she won four awards: for the best woman, for the biggest fan base, for the best song and for the best music video, with *Born this way*.

November 2011 saw the release of her fourth EP, called *A Very Gaga Holiday*, taken from the Thanksgiving Day television special *A Very Gaga Thanksgiving*. In the same month, Lady Gaga ended her collaboration with choreographer Laurieann Gibson after four years, and Richard Jackson took over.

Lady Gaga was one of the artists who performed at former President Bill Clinton's 65th birthday in 2011. She also performed at the New Year's Rockin' Eve concert at Times Square in New York at the end of 2011.

At the 53rd edition of the Grammy Awards, *Born this way* was nominated for 3 awards. For *Best Album* and *Best Pop Vocal Album* and for *Best Pop Solo Performance*, but all three awards went to British singer Adele. She was also nominated for *Best International Female Artist* at the Brit Awards, but this award went to Rihanna.

2013-2014: Artpop

On August 3, 2012, Lady Gaga announced her next album. She collaborated with producer Fernando Garibay for this. The album was released in 2013. The first single was *Applause*. The song would initially be released on August 19, 2013, along with the music video. The second single was *Do what u want*, a collaboration with R. Kelly. The third single was titled *G.U.Y.*. The album itself is titled *Artpop*. To promote the album Gaga went on a world tour, with the "ArtRave: The Artpop Ball", she performed 79 times in all continents. The tour included shows that the singer cancelled during her previous tour.

2016-2017: Joanne , Super Bowl and "FiveFootTwo"

In December 2014, Gaga confirmed that she had begun work on her fifth studio album and had reunited with producer RedOne for this purpose. At the 87th Oscar ceremony, she performed in tribute to The Sound of Music by singing a medley of songs from that film. At the opening ceremony of the 2015 European Games in Baku, Azerbaijan, she sang John Lennon's song *Imagine*. On October 2, 2015, she became the first artist to pass 7 million downloads in the United States for the songs *Poker Face* and *Bad Romance*. In 2015, Gaga was named *Billboards woman* of the year. During the press conference at the Golden Globes, Gaga confirmed that the album would be released in 2016.For this album, titled *Joanne*, she has worked with Mark Ronson, Kevin Parker, BloodPop, Florence Welch, Beck, Father John Misty and Hillary Lindsay, among others. The album was released on October 21, 2016. The first single from *Joanne* was *Perfect Illusion*, which had been released September 9, 2016 and the second promo single *Million Reasons* was released on October 6, 2016. The album *Joanne* is a tribute to her aunt who struggled with the disease lupus. The album represents family and life. Gaga promoted her album with a three day tour called: The Dive Bar Tour. Lady Gaga received two nominations for the album at the Grammy Awards for *Million Reasons* and the album.

After *Perfect Illusion* came out, the NFL announced that Gaga got to host the halftime show during Super Bowl LI. The show was watched over 150 million times in the United States, making it the best watched halftime show ever since Katy Perry performed in 2015. Immediately after the performance, it was announced that Gaga was going on another world tour. On September 8, 2017, a documentary of Gaga was released worldwide called: Five Foot Two. This documentary gives an insight during the making of the album Joanne, the promotion of the album, a 'behind the scenes' during the rehearsal of the halftime show of the Super Bowl and how she struggles with her illness. She received an NME Award nomination for best music film for this documentary.

2018-present: A Star is Born

In March 2018, Lady Gaga released a cover of Elton John, namely *Your song*. In October 2018, the singer appeared as the lead in the movie *A Star Is Born*, along with Bradley Cooper, who is her antagonist. The movie became a huge success. Lady Gaga received an Academy Award nomination for this, for best original song and best female lead. The music also earned her a Grammy Award nomination, including for 'Record of the Year' and 'Song of the Year'. Earlier the singer received a Critics' Choice Award for best actress and best original song. The single *Shallow* became the album's lead single, reaching the #1 position in more than ten countries. *Shallow* became the song with the most awards ever in 2019, winning an Oscar, two Grammys, a Golden Globe and a BAFTA Award, among others.

In January 2021, she sang the American national anthem, *the Star-Spangled Banner*, at Joe Biden's inauguration as president.

Work with other artists

Lady Gaga collaborated on Cher's single *The Greatest Thing* and on *3-Way (The Golden Rule)* on Justin Timberlake's album The Lonely Island. Lady Gaga was also featured on New Kids on the Block's album *The Block*, where she contributed on *Full Service* and *Big Girl Now*. In 2011, Gaga sang the song *The Lady is a Tramp* with jazz singer Tony Bennett on his album *Duets II*. It became the second single from the album. Lady Gaga then recorded the jazz album *Cheek To Cheek* with him. On 29 July 2014 *Anything goes* was released as the first single from this album. It reached number one on the Billboard Jazz digital song chart.

Acting

Lady Gaga made her acting debut in Robert Rodriguez's film *Machete Kills*, in which she plays the role of La Chameleón; the film was released in theaters on September 13, 2013. In 2014, the film *Sin City: A Dame to Kill For* by Robert Rodriguez and Frank Miller was released. In it, Lady Gaga plays the character Bertha. In October 2015, Gaga starred in the fifth season of FOX's horror-drama American Horror Story titled *Hotel*. Here, she played the role of *The Countess* , the owner of this titular hotel. For this role, she received a Golden Globe in January 2016. In 2018, she starred as a budding singer Ally in the film A Star Is Born, alongside Bradley Cooper. At the 2019 Academy Awards ceremony, she was nominated both in the category of best actress in a leading role, and for best original song. She won the latter.

Style and appearance

Lady Gaga sees herself as a living work of art. According to her, her artistic clothing style is a tribute to the artist Andy Warhol. Because of her extravagant appearance, she has been compared to new wave acts from the 1980s. In February 2010, she was voted both best dressed and worst dressed artist at the Shockwaves NME Awards.

Tattoos

On the inside of her upper left arm she has an excerpt from a poem by Rainer Maria Rilke tattooed:

prüfen Sie, ob er in der tiefsten Stelle Ihres
Herzens seine Wurzeln ausstreckt, gestehen
Sie sich ein, ob Sie sterben müßten, wenn es Ihnen
versagt würde zu schreiben. muß ich schreiben?

Below the Rilke excerpt is "Little Monsters," the pet name Lady Gaga uses to address her fans. She also has the peace sign tattooed on her left wrist. On her lower back she also has a tattoo, consisting of a kind of music key with roses. On her upper left leg she has the name of her album "Born this Way" tattooed. On her shoulder blade she has three flowers with the text "Tokyo Love". She also has a heart with the word "Dad" in it.

She only puts tattoos on the left half of her body because her father also wants to see "the pretty side" of his daughter.

Highlights

- Lady Gaga, byname of Stefani Joanne Angelina Germanotta, was born into an Italian American family in New York City.
- Her second album, The Fame Monster, was released in November 2009 (it was originally conceived as a bonus disc) and almost instantly produced another hit, "Bad Romance."
- Lady Gaga's third album, Born This Way (2011), found the entertainer reaching back to earlier musical eras for inspiration.

- In addition to recording music, Lady Gaga made occasional film appearances, notably in Machete Kills (2013) and Sin City: A Dame to Kill For (2014). For her performance in the anthology series, Lady Gaga received a Golden Globe Award.
- Lady Gaga garnered critical acclaim and an Oscar nomination for her first lead role, a guileless up-and-coming singer-songwriter in the 2018 remake of the movie A Star Is Born.

3. Celine Dion (born 1968)

Canadian singer and one of the best-selling artists of all time

"It's the moment you think you can't, that you can"

Céline Marie Claudette Dion (Charlemagne (Quebec), March 30, 1968) is a Canadian singer.

The youngest of fourteen children, Dion was born in Charlemagne, Quebec, Canada. At the age of 12, her mother introduced her to manager René Angélil, who believed in her so much that he mortgaged his house to finance her career. In 1981, Dion released her first album (*La Voix du bon Dieu*). It made her a star in Quebec. The following year she won the gold medal at the World Song Festival in Tokyo. In the years that followed Dion released several albums with French chansons, mostly about the emotional life of this young girl. In 1987, Canada released the album *Incognito*, Dion's first real pop album.

In 1988 she competed on behalf of Switzerland in the Eurovision Song Contest, which she won with the song *Ne Partez Pas Sans Moi*. The victory made Dion known in Europe. From 1988, Dion worked on his first English-language album *Unison*, which was released in 1990. Record label Sony Music wanted Dion to break through in the US with the English repertoire. It turned out to work. The single *Where Does My Heart Beat*

Now reached the top 5 of the American Billboard Hot 100 and the album achieved platinum status.

In 1991, Dion was approached by the Walt Disney Studios to collaborate on the soundtrack of the feature film *Beauty And The Beast*. Together with singer Peabo Bryson, Dion recorded the title song of this Disney film and at the end of 1991 the song became a huge success. The duet even earned Dion and Bryson an Academy Award. In early 1992 *Celine Dion* was released, the singer's second album in English. With the released singles *If You Asked Me To, Love Can Move Mountains* and *Nothing Broken But My Heart* she scored high in the charts.

Final breakthrough

At the end of 1993 *The Colour Of My Love* was released, Dion's third album of English-language material. In North America the first single *The Power of Love* (originally recorded by Jennifer Rush) became an unparalleled success. The single was number 1 in the American Billboard Hot 100 for weeks. In Europe, the single *Think Twice* achieved great success. The album gave Dion her definitive breakthrough in almost every country in the world. Despite all the success of her English-language work, she decided to take a temporary step back to basics: she remained a Canadian with French roots. In 1994 Jean-Jacques Goldman wrote 12 French songs for the singer that eventually ended up on the album *D'Eux*. The album was released in early '95 and produced the hit *Pour que tu m'aimes encore*. The album became the best selling French-language album of all time, with 9 million copies sold worldwide.

For her fourth English-language album *Falling into You* from 1996, Dion recorded various covers by different artists. *Falling into You* was officially released in March 1996 and soon sold millions of copies. Dion scored hit after hit with songs like *Because You Loved Me* and *It's All Coming Back To Me Now*. The album sold 32 million copies. It is considered one of the best selling albums by a singer in music history. With this album, Dion went on tour again. Although the previous tour only focused on a few European countries, the 'Falling into You Tour' took her all over the world. More than 100 concerts were given in 17 different countries. Recordings of the tour appeared on the VHS cassette *Live In Memphis*. Irish pop band The Corrs were the support act during the European tour. With 100 sold-out shows and millions in CD sales, Dion appeared to have achieved 'superstardom' status. *Falling into You* earned Dion numerous awards, including two American Grammys.

Good luck

Her participation in the opening ceremony of the 1996 Olympic Games in Atlanta was watched by 3.5 billion people on TV. The next English-language album *Let's Talk About Love* was released at the end of 1997, with recordings taking place in London, Los Angeles and New York. Artists such as Barbra Streisand, Luciano Pavarotti, Bee Gees, Carole King, George Martin and Diana King contributed to various songs. *Tell Him*, a duet by Dion and Streisand, was the album's first hit single. *My Heart Will Go On*, another single and also the title song of feature film Titanic, became an unprecedented success. It is considered Dion's best selling single ever. The song reached number one worldwide in no time and earned Dion numerous awards, including an Academy Award and several Grammy Awards. It sold 31 million copies worldwide and is Celine's second best-selling album of her career.

In September 1998 *S'il Suffisait d'Aimer* was released, a French-language album again with compositions by Jean-Jacques Goldman. Dion's first English-language Christmas album *These Are Special Times*, featuring the hit *I'm Your Angel* (duet with R. Kelly), was released at the end of 1998 and sold 15 million copies worldwide. Again the singer went on a world tour with her latest albums. In June 1999 Dion performed in the Amsterdam ArenA. To this day, that concert is the stadium's event with the most visitors (68,083). A compilation album containing Dion's greatest English-language successes up to that point and some new songs was released at the end of 1999 under the name *All The Way.... A Decade Of Song*. Its first single, *That's The Way It Is*, became a huge success. She sold 20 million copies of this album. By early 2000, Dion appeared to have sold a record 140 million records worldwide. Her status as 'super diva' was further underlined in April 1998 when the singer performed at the benefit concert 'Divas Live' for music channel VH1, together with fellow artists Mariah Carey, Shania Twain, Gloria Estefan and Aretha Franklin.

Break and comeback

After years of performing, Dion thought it was high time to take a break. The singer wanted to focus on family and friends, but she had also been wanting to become a mother for a while. She temporarily ended her period
102

of success with a number of concerts. In 1999 Dion's husband René was diagnosed with cancer. The singer wanted to support her husband during the chemotherapy treatments. Eventually René recovered from the disease. On 25 January 2001, Dion gave birth to a son in Florida: René-Charles Dion-Angélil. Although she had indicated to take a break of more than two years, Dion still gave a number of performances during that period. During a benefit concert to raise money for the families of the victims of September 11, 2001 Dion sang *God Bless America*.

In March 2002 - two years after her previous album - a new English language album was released under the name *A New Day Has Come*. Singles like *I'm Alive*, *A New Day Has Come* and *Goodbye (The Saddest Word)* became chart successes. The album sold 12 million copies, proving that Dion was still hot after two years of silence, and had made a very successful comeback. With the release of the album, it was announced that the singer would have her own show in Las Vegas starting in 2003. This show, called *A New Day... Live in Las Vegas*, started in March 2003 at the Caesars Palace. Especially for this show, and thus for Dion, a brand new venue was built, "The Colosseum", a building in the shape of the Roman Colosseum. Initially, Dion was supposed to perform 600 shows in three years, but due to its great success, the show was extended by a year and a half. At the end of the run, on 15 December 2007, the counter stood at a total of 750 shows. The show - designed by Franco Dragone - contains Dion's greatest hits, mixed with set pieces, dance and visual effects.

Before the show started in 2003, *One Heart*, Dion's 10th English-language album, was released. It sold 8 million copies and spawned hit singles such as *I Drove All Night*, *One Heart* and *Have You Ever Been In Love*. Dion closed 2003 successfully with a new French-language album: *1 Fille & 4 Types* which sold 2.5 million copies. From Dion's show in Las Vegas, the live album *A New Day.... Live in Las Vegas*. In the fall of 2004, Dion launched the *Miracle* project in collaboration with photographer Anne Geddes; an album of songs about motherhood was accompanied by a book containing photos of Dion with various babies. The album sold 3.5 million copies. Dion's first French compilation album, *On Ne Change Pas*, was released in 2005.

The French-language album *D'elles* was released on May 21, 2007. Seven of the thirteen songs were recorded in Montreal in December 2006. The album's first single, *S'il N'en Restait Qu'une (Je Serais Celle-Là)*, made its radio debut on French-language radio on February 14, 2007. The music video for the song was shot in New York in late January/early February 2007. In the same week, Dion also sang her part of the song *Sing*. The song, which was sung by 23 singers, was an initiative of Annie Lennox, who wanted to use it in the fight against AIDS and poverty in Africa. The song can be found on Lennox' album *Songs Of Mass Destruction*.

Dion indicated in late October 2015 that she was working on a French-language album.

Tours

A new English-language album, *Taking Chances*, hit the stores on November 12, 2007. A promotional tour for this album and the album *D'elles*, also released in 2007, took place in October 2007. Her show in Las Vegas had its last performance on December 15, 2007, after almost five years. A DVD of this concert recording, recorded during the week of January 15-21, 2007, was released on December 11, 2007.

On February 14, 2008, Dion embarked on a world tour to perform outside of Las Vegas for the first time since 1999. The tour spread from Canada to Japan to South Africa. The new single from the self-titled album *Taking Chances* did well in America. Other promotional singles released in mid-2008 were *Eyes On Me* and *Alone*. To date, 6.5 million copies of the album have been sold.

Return to Caesar's Palace

Céline returned to the Caesar's Palace in 2011, planning to perform 70 shows a year. The premiere was on March 15, 2011.In August 2014, Dion canceled all her scheduled concerts and announced to stop singing immediately. This was because she wanted to take care of her sick husband.

In the second half of 2015, Dion returned to Caesar's Palace.

Private life

In 1994 she married her twenty-six year older manager René Angélil (1942-2016). On January 25, 2001, the couple had a son; on October 23, 2010, Dion gave birth to twins, also boys. On January 14, 2016, Angélil died of throat cancer. Dion lives in Henderson, Nevada.

Highlights

- Céline Dion, in full Céline Marie Claudette Dion, is the youngest of 14 children raised in a small town near Montreal, Dion began singing with her musically inclined family when she was five years old.
- She recorded numerous hit albums in both French and English and was the recipient of several prestigious awards.
- At the beginning of the 21st century, Dion took a hiatus from her career to focus on her family.
- She returned with the albums A New Day Has Come (2002) and One Heart (2003), which flirted with dance pop in addition to her usual adult contemporary fare.
- Despite the fact that Dion was no longer the dominant cultural force that she had been a decade earlier, it was reported in 2007 that worldwide sales of her albums had surpassed 200 million.

4. Kate Bush (born 1958)

British singer, musician, singer-songwriter, and producer

"Mozart didn't have Pro Tools, but he did a pretty good job."

Catherine (Kate) Bush CBE (Bexleyheath (London), 30 July 1958) is a British singer, musician, singer-songwriter and producer. Her father was English and her mother Irish. When she was only 16, David Gilmour of Pink Floyd got her signed to EMI.

Her experimental style and unusual singing technique have made her appreciated by fellow musicians and by a not overly large, but dedicated fan base. This is proven by the fact that her records always sell, although she often takes years to make an album; for *Aerial* even twelve years.

Biography

Bush debuted in 1978 at nineteen with the hit song *Wuthering Heights*, which was inspired by Emily Brontë's book of the same name. The song topped the charts in the United Kingdom for four weeks.

Her debut album *The Kick Inside* was appreciated both artistically and commercially. The album, produced by David Gilmour, included hits such as *Them heavy people* and *The man with the child in his eyes*. David Gilmour has been called her discoverer and mentor because he supported her both financially and morally while recording her first demos and further promoted her at his own record label, EMI. According to pop critics, Gilmour's influences are evident on every track.

Bush undertook only one tour, *The Tour Of Life*, in 1978-1979. She caused quite a stir with her mime-like way of dancing. After 1979, she did not tour again until the 2014 tour, 35 years later.

Subsequent albums such as *Lionheart* and *Never for Ever* were somewhat less commercially successful than her debut but nevertheless *Babooshka* and *Army dreamers* became hits. Later hits included *Cloudbusting* and *Running up that hill*. For the music video for *Cloudbusting* Bush had her hair cut short and Donald Sutherland played her father. In the same year Bush scored a hit with Peter Gabriel with the song *Don't Give Up*. In 1986 she also recorded a duet with the Scottish band Big Country (*The Seer*).

In 1989 she released her album *The sensual world*, which became her best-selling album in America. After the album *The Red Shoes* (1993), Bush retreated to an island in the Thames for years, where she worked on her album *Aerial* (2005), from which the song *King of the Mountain* became a modest hit. On 18 January 2002, Bush returned to the stage for the first time in years as a special guest of David Gilmour during a concert at the Royal Festival Hall.

In 2007 a documentary about Kate Bush was made entitled *Come Back Kate*, in which devoted fans recount their special bond with the singer. Although her particular style is not easy on everyone's ears, Kate Bush is widely respected among fellow musicians. Tori Amos, Björk and Sinéad O'Connor have indicated in interviews that they have been influenced and inspired by Kate Bush.

A compilation album entitled *Director's Cut* was released on May 16, 2011. In this release, Bush re-edited her previous albums *The Sensual World* and *The Red Shoes*, and provided them with new recordings and remasters. After years of absence, Kate Bush still proved popular.

On 21 November 2011 the album *50 Words For Snow* was released, on which Bush's son Albert (Bertie), Elton John and Stephen Fry collaborated.

In August 2012, rumors circulated that Bush would perform at the closing ceremony of the August 12 Olympics. This would be a special event because Bush hardly ever performs. She feels rather uncomfortable performing her songs in front of an audience. At the ceremony only her recently released remake of R.U.T.H. was played. She herself was nowhere to be seen. Afterwards, Kate did let the organisation of the final performance know that she appreciated the performance of her remake.

In January 2013, Bush was made a Commander of the Order of the British Empire for her achievements in music.

Bush announced on her website in March 2014 that she would perform a series of fifteen concerts at London's Hammersmith Apollo theatre under the name *Before the Dawn for* the first time in 35 years. She added seven more performances a few days later. The 22 performances sold out in less than fifteen minutes. On August 26, 2014, Kate gave her first concert in 35 years. The performances were a huge success. In the week after the first performance, eight of Kate Bush's albums were in the UK Top 40. No other woman had achieved that before.

Highlights

- Kate Bush, byname of Catherine Bush, was the youngest child of an artistic family.
- After directing and starring in The Line, the Cross & the Curve (1993), a short film featuring songs from The Red Shoes, Bush took a 12-year hiatus from music.
- She resurfaced with the atmospheric Aerial (2005), a double record imbued with themes of domesticity and the natural world that earned her some of the most favorable reviews of her career.
- In 2014 Bush returned to the stage for the first time in 35 years. Her 22 concerts were stage spectaculars, featuring puppets, illusionists, and dancers, and they were followed by the three-disc live recording Before the Dawn (2016).

- Bush was made Commander of the Order of the British Empire (CBE) in 2013.

5. Aretha Franklin (1942-2018)

American singer and the first woman inducted into the Rock and Roll Hall of Fame

"Sometimes, what you're looking for is already there."

Aretha Louise Franklin (Memphis (Tennessee), March 25, 1942 - Detroit (Michigan), August 16, 2018) was an American gospel, soul and R&B singer. On the ranking of 100 best singers (m/f) of all time by the American music magazine *Rolling Stone,* she ranks first.

Lifecycle

As a child, Aretha Franklin sang with her sisters, Carolyn and Erma, at the Baptist church where her father was a minister. She made her first recordings when she was 14 years old. She was discovered by John Hammond and signed a contract with Columbia Records. In the early 1960s, she performed a few songs that became popular, including *Rock-a-*

bye Your Baby with a Dixie Melody, originally released by Al Jolson in 1918. In 1968, Aretha Franklin gave a legendary concert at the Concertgebouw in Amsterdam. It was part of her first tour outside the United States. She performed *Satisfaction*, *Dr. Feelgood* and *A Natural Woman*.

After leaving Columbia Records, she signed a contract with Atlantic Records. Her producer became Jerry Wexler, with whom she made some very influential R&B recordings, such as *I Never Loved a Man (The Way I Love You)*. The style of this song had much more "soul" than her earlier work. By the late 1960s, Aretha Franklin was nicknamed "The Queen of Soul" because she had become so famous and was also seen as a role model for the African-American community.

Aretha Franklin had many top 10 hits, including covers of other celebrities such as The Beatles (*Eleanor Rigby*), The Band (*The Weight*), Simon & Garfunkel (*Bridge Over Troubled Water*), Sam Cooke and The Drifters. Other major hits included *Chain of Fools*, *A Natural Woman*, *Think*, *Baby I Love You*, *The House That Jack Built*, *I Say a Little Prayer* and *Respect*. *Spanish Harlem* was number one in the Thirty Thousand.

In the early eighties it seemed her career was over, until she recorded a cover of the Doobie Brothers-hit *What a Fool Believes*. Shortly thereafter, she was featured in the classic John Belushi musical film *The Blues Brothers*. It took another seven years before she hit the charts again, but she did so with the huge hit *I Knew You Were Waiting (for Me)*, a duet with George Michael that spent several weeks at number 1 in the Top 40 and the National Hit Parade. The song was written by Simon Climie of Climie/Fisher. In 1994 she sang *A Deeper Love* for the blockbuster *Sister Act*.

On January 3, 1987, she became the first woman to be inducted into the Rock and Roll Hall of Fame. In 1999, she received America's highest art award, the National Medal of Arts. On January 20, 2009, Franklin sang *My Country, 'Tis of Thee* during the inauguration of Barack Obama as the 44th President of the United States. In 2010, Franklin was named the best singer of all time by American music magazine *Rolling Stone*. In 2012, she was inducted into the Gospel Music Hall of Fame.

On October 17, 2014, her 38th studio album *Aretha Franklin Sings the Great Diva Classics* was released. This album features songs by other famous singers. The first released single from this album was a rendition of Adele's *Rolling in the Deep*. In February 2017, Franklin reported that she would retire after the release of her latest album in September.

Private

Franklin has been married twice. She has four sons, with three different fathers.

Health

In December 2010 it was announced that the singer was ill. She was suffering from pancreatic cancer. In response to media speculation, the singer stated in August 2013 that she had overcome the disease and wanted to focus entirely on her career again. However, the disease returned. On August 13, 2018, it was announced that she was receiving palliative care at home and was dying. On August 16, 2018, Franklin passed away. She was 76 years old.

Highlights

- By the late 1970s disco cramped Aretha Franklin's style and eroded her popularity.
- In 1982, with help from singer-songwriter-producer Luther Vandross, Franklin was back on top with a new label, Arista, and a new dance hit, "Jump to It," followed by "Freeway of Love" (1985).
- In 1987 Aretha Franklin became the first woman inducted into the Rock and Roll Hall of Fame. In addition, she received a Kennedy Center Honor in 1994, a National Medal of Arts in 1999, and the Presidential Medal of Freedom in 2005.
- The documentary Amazing Grace, which chronicles her recording of the 1972 album, premiered in 2018.

6. Margaret Bourke-White (1904-1971)

American photographer and first female allowed to work in combat zones

"The beauty of the past belongs to the past."

Margaret Bourke-White (born **Margaret White**) (New York, June 14, 1904 - Stamford, Connecticut, August 27, 1971) was an American photographer. As a lieutenant colonel, she was the first war reporter for the United States Army and, toward the end of World War II, a photographer for the United States Air Force. One of her photographs, *The Living Dead of Buchenwald*, is one of the most famous of the 20th century.

Life

Margaret Bourke-White was the daughter of Roman Catholic Minnie Bourke and non-practicing Jew Joseph White and grew up in the Bronx, New York. Bourke-White had an older sister, Ruth, and a younger brother

Roger. In her youth, it was not yet common for girls to pursue college education.

Architectural and Industrial Photography

After completing her studies in 1927, Bourke-White opened her first photographic studio in Cleveland, Ohio and began her career as an architectural and industrial photographer. Her shots of industrial plants provided a new and highly valued photographic image of the rapid economic development of the United States.

Photojournalist

Bourke-White received commissions from renowned magazines. In 1930, the bridges and steelworks she photographed formed the cover story of the first edition of *Fortune* magazine, of which Bourke-White was co-editor. In 1931 she opened her photo studio in the Chrysler Building in New York.

In 1930, at the time of industrialisation, Bourke-White travelled to the Soviet Union for the first time. This produced images of gigantic building projects (factories and power stations) but also of simple, exploited workers. During the thirties Bourke-White made photo essays about IG Farben and the shipyards of Hamburg and on the construction site of the Soviet industrial city of Magnitogorsk in Western Siberia.

In the first issue of *Life-Magazine* in November 1936, of which Bourke-White was a founding member, her photographs accompanied the cover story on the Fort Peck Lake dam in the United States. Alongside Walker Evans and W. Eugene Smith, Bourke-White is one of the pioneers of photo essays.

Because of her extravagant lifestyle and energetic performance in the media, Bourke-White was something of a role model for the modern, emancipated woman.

In 1937 Bourke-White published a book with the writer Erskine Caldwell about the living conditions of field workers in the southern US (Dust Bowl), whose livelihoods were threatened during periods of extreme drought. Her photograph *You Have Seen Their Faces* is considered one of her most important works. In 1939 she married Caldwell, from whom she divorced in 1942. In 1938 she began a journey through Europe and worked on a photo reportage about the Sudeten crisis in Czechoslovakia.

Second World War

In 1941, she went to Moscow for *Life-Magazine*. During the German invasion of the Soviet Union, she was the only Western photojournalist in the city, documenting in particular the German air raids on the Soviet capital. She became the U.S. Army's first female war correspondent, including in England, North Africa, and Italy. As an American Air Force photographer, Bourke-White traveled through Germany with General George S. Patton and was present at the liberation of the Buchenwald concentration camp and the Leipzig-Thekla labor camp. Her 1945 photograph *The Living Dead of Buchenwald* is one of the most famous and impressive photographs of the 20th century.

Bourke-White has portrayed many celebrities such as Franklin Roosevelt, Joseph Stalin, Winston Churchill or Marlon Brando.

Post-war years

In the fall of 1945, Bourke-White was commissioned by the Air Force to document the destruction of German cities with aerial photographs. In 1946, she photographed one of her most famous images for Life: Mahatma Gandhi at the spinning wheel. In the following years Margaret Bourke-White documented the partition of the British East Indies and later the Korean War. She also travelled through South Africa during the apartheid era.

In the mid-1950s, Bourke-White contracted Parkinson's disease and had to increasingly cut back on her work. Her autobiography, published in 1963, was on the New York Times bestseller list for weeks. Bourke-White died of Parkinson's disease in 1971.

In 1955 Edward Steichen selected six Bourke-White photographs for the world famous and now world heritage exhibition *The Family of Man.*

Highlights

115

- Margaret Bourke-White, original name Margaret White, began her career in 1927 as an industrial and architectural photographer, she soon gained a reputation for originality, and in 1929 the publisher Henry Luce hired her for his new Fortune magazine.
- After World War II Bourke-White traveled to India to photograph Mohandas Gandhi and record the mass migration caused by the division of the Indian subcontinent into Hindu India and Muslim Pakistan.
- During the Korean War she worked as a war correspondent and traveled with South Korean troops.
- Stricken with Parkinson's disease in 1952, Bourke-White continued to photograph and write and published several books on her work as well as her autobiography, Portrait of Myself (1963).

7. Dorothea Lange (1895-1965)

American documentary photographer

---

*"The camera is an instrument that teaches people how to
see without a camera."*

Dorothea Lange (Hoboken (New Jersey), May 26, 1895 - October 11,
1965) was an American photographer best known for her documentary
work commissioned by the Farm Security Administration on the effects of
the Great Depression.

Biography

Lange was born Dorothea Nutzhorn in Hoboken, New Jersey. At the age
of 7, she contracted polio, a disease for which there was no treatment at
the time. It left her with a deformed right foot. Her father abandoned her
and her mother when she was 12, which led her to take her mother's last
name. After working for several years as an assistant for various
photographers, she opened a portrait studio in San Francisco in 1918,

which became a success. In 1920 she married painter Maynard Dixon, with whom she had two sons. In early 1935, she obtained a position as a photographer for the U.S. government's Resettlement Administration, later renamed the Farm Security Administration. Her assignment was to record the effects of the Depression on the impoverished American countryside. A form of social photography. She worked closely with economist Paul Schuster Taylor, whom she married in 1935, after divorcing Dixon.

The photographs taken by Lange and her colleagues for the FSA were provided free of charge to American newspapers and magazines.

Her most famous photograph is titled *Migrant Mother* from 1936, showing Florence Owens Thompson with three of her children. However, Mrs. Thompson's identity remained unknown until 1978.

During World War II, commissioned by the War Relocation Authority, Lange focused on capturing the conditions under which Japanese Americans were interned after the attack on Pearl Harbor. After World War II, she taught photography at the San Francisco Art Institute. After suffering from various illnesses, she died of esophageal cancer in 1965.

Highlights

- Dorothea Lange studied photography at Columbia University in New York City under Clarence H. White, a member of the Photo-Secession group.
- In 1918, Lange decided to travel around the world, earning money as she went by selling her photographs. Her money ran out by the time she got to San Francisco, so she settled there and obtained a job in a photography studio.
- During the Great Depression, Lange began to photograph the unemployed men who wandered the streets of San Francisco.
- Lange's first exhibition was held in 1934, and thereafter her reputation as a skilled documentary photographer was firmly established.

8. Leni Riefenstahl (1902-2003)

German motion-picture director, actress, producer, and photographer

Berta Helene Amalie (Leni) Riefenstahl (Berlin, 22 August 1902 - Pöcking, 8 September 2003) was a German filmmaker and photographer. She began her career as a dancer and actress, but became best known as a film director.

Leni Riefenstahl was born in Wedding, a district of Berlin known at the time as a 'criminals and workers' colony', the daughter of a plumber. In her youth she was kept short by him. She enjoyed her attraction to men from an early age. Her trademarks in her work were therefore *Körperkultur*, sports, and obsession with nature. The glorification of the human body is especially expressed in her films *Der heilige Berg* and *Die weiße Hölle am Piz Palü*.

119

Film director

Riefenstahl's films are best known for their cinematic (camera-technical) innovations, such as those about the Nuremberg party days (*Der Sieg des Glaubens* from 1933 and *Triumph des Willens* and *Tag der Freiheit - Unsere Wehrmacht* from 1935). They were commissioned by the minister of propaganda Joseph Goebbels and propagated the Nazi ideology.

The report of the 1936 Berlin Olympics (*Olympia*) also features technical innovations such as moving the camera on a tripod on a trolley on rails along the inside of the racecourse. This film was commissioned by the International Olympic Committee.

Another innovative technique: the Olympic divers were filmed without any fixed objects (such as the diving board) in the picture. The viewer, who at the time was not used to such camera work, saw a completely different, free view of the world. Olympia is also striking for its technical perfection: advanced camera work, surprising, suggestive editing, use of slow motion and active underwater photography. The special combination of image and music is striking, and in the second part the aesthetics of sport are emphasized, for instance in the sequence of the men's clean jump.

Triumph of the Will

The 1935 film *Triumph des Willens*, about an NSDAP party day in the previous year, is not a pure documentary because the filmmaker edited retrospective scenes between real footage of the party day in order to convey this focused message: that as early as 1934, all of Germany was ready to follow Hitler in his adventure with the chanted words, "Hier stehen wir, wir sind bereit, wir tragen Deutschland in die neue Zeit. Deutschland!" Closing with, "Ein Volk!, ein Reich!, ein Führer!" where successively an eagle, the swastika and Hitler come into view. This is not an academic question, because initially a large part of the population had many doubts about the new rulers. The popularity of the NSDAP and the SA reached a low point shortly before the Night of the Long Knives in 1934 (see Willem Melching and Marcel Stuivenga in *Ooggetuigen van het Derde Rijk*).

The opening sequence, in which the shadow of the plane used to land Hitler is shown for minutes on end, is a real find. The message: the "Saviour of the Fatherland" is sent from heaven. The ingenious decoupage of the various shots in Speers' stadium that follow one another shortly
120

after each other, in which the "German Youth" eagerly await the Führer's arrival, is also significant.

This film was compulsorily shown in all German schools in the 1930s. In other words, Hitler and Goebbels were keenly aware of the "Power of Images".

Olympia

The 1938 film *Olympia*, about the 1936 Berlin Olympics, consists of two parts:

1. Fest of the Völker
2. Festival of Beauty

The artistic qualities of these films are not controversial; however, some parts were *later* discussed negatively because they could have been used as Nazi propaganda. There are the constantly recurring images of flags waving swastikas and the recurring images of the Führer. She herself has always maintained that she was unaware of the true nature of the regime when she made the documentaries and that she was only aiming for aesthetic purposes. With regard to *Olympia* she has noted that she even came into conflict with the regime to some extent because she explicitly showed images of the victory of black athletes.

It has been noted that Riefenstahl's sports world is of a hushed, icy beauty. With her, athletes know no emotions, no happiness or disappointment, no fatigue. It is their bodies that the filmmaker falls in love with. The mighty hands of a basketball player; the muscular thigh of a pristinely naked javelin thrower, the curved arms of a gymnast who splits on the beam without a single strand of her hair being ruffled. This is the addition to the cinematography.

Subsequent criticism

Riefenstahl's films acquired a stigma after the Second World War: controversial because the documentaries were commissioned by the Nazis and because, like the architect Albert Speer, she put her talent at the service of the glorification of Hitler and his regime (1933-1945). After a series of trials she was acquitted of complicity with Nazi policy and was merely labelled *a Mitläuferin*. She continued to deny all responsibility until

121

the end of her days and showed no remorse. However, it came to light that during the war she had requisitioned gypsies from a concentration camp to act in her film *Tiefland*. She had even personally sampled the extras on their appearance. Even after it turned out that most of these "actors" had died in the Dachau concentration camp, she kept denying it.

After the war, she could no longer obtain financing for film projects and for years earned a meagre living as a photographer.

Later, prompted by images by British photographer George Rodger, she discovered the Nuba's in Sudan, which she photographed extensively (first published in 1974). Magazines like *Life* and *National Geographic* showed interest in her camera work. This elicited a merciless critique from Susan Sontag in her essay discussing the *fascinating fascism* of Riefenstahl's new work. Sontag saw connections between Riefenstahl's portrayal of Africans and the Nazi ideal of beauty prevalent at the time; she compared the glorification of the Nubian *Körperkultur* to that of Hitler's *Aryan race*. According to Sontag, Riefenstahl's vision had not changed since then.

Renewed interest

In the 1970s there was renewed interest in Riefenstahl among pop stars and American feminists in the United States. Mick Jagger, for example, liked to have himself photographed by her.

Highlights

- Leni Riefenstahl studied painting and ballet in Berlin, and from 1923 to 1926 she appeared in dance programs throughout Europe.
- Riefenstahl began her motion-picture career as an actress in "mountain films"-a type of German film in which nature, especially the mountain landscape, plays an important role-and she eventually became a director in the genre.
- In 1931 she formed a company, Leni Riefenstahl-Produktion, and the following year wrote, directed, produced, and starred in Das blaue Licht (1932; The Blue Light).
- Riefenstahl's films were acclaimed for their rich musical scores, for the cinematic beauty of the scenes of dawn, mountains, and rural German life, and for brilliant editing.

- Much of Riefenstahl's later life was devoted to photography, and Korallengärten (1978; Coral Gardens) and Wunder unter Wasser (1990; Wonders Under Water) are collections of her underwater photographs; a documentary on marine life, Impressionen unter Wasser (Impressions Under Water), was released in 2002.

9. Käthe Kollwitz (1867-1945)

German artist known for her drawings and prints

---

*"If everyone recognizes and fulfills his cycle of obligations,
genuineness emerges."*

Käthe Kollwitz (Koningsbergen, July 8, 1867 - Moritzburg, April 22,
1945), born Käthe Schmidt, was a German graphic artist and sculptress.

Lifecycle

Käthe was a sculptor and illustrator for the weekly *Simplicissimus* and was
married to the social democratic doctor Karl Kollwitz who died on 19 July
1940. She was the mother of two sons, Hans Kollwitz and Peter Kollwitz.

Käthe's talent for drawing became apparent at an early age and she
received her first instruction in this subject at the age of fourteen in her
home town from the copper engraver Rudolf Mauer.

After her training with Mauer, she went to Berlin for a year (1884-1885) to attend classes at Karl Stauffer-Bern's school.Back in Koningsbergen, Käthe continued her studies under Emil Neide.

During her student years Kollwitz developed a keen interest in social democracy, the women's movement and the new naturalism in literature. This interest was to leave its mark on the rest of her career, which began in 1889 when she turned to etching.

After her marriage in 1891 she settled with her husband, the fund specialist Karl Kollwitz, in a working-class neighbourhood in Berlin, where Karl had his medical practice to care for the poor. Captivated by social needs and the bond between mother and child, she made them the subject of her prints. She devoted herself entirely to graphic techniques, which lent themselves best to the evocative nature of her work.

In 1899 she joined the Berliner Sezession, a separatist movement in which artists wanted to distance themselves from the aims of an existing association and pursue new ideals or reach new audiences. Five years later she moved to Paris where she trained in sculpture.

Twice she was in Paris, where (in 1904) she received her first training in sculpture.

In 1907 she was awarded the Villa Romana prize, which was accompanied by a year's stay in the villa of the same name in Florence.

During the war years 1914-1918 she began to sculpt. On 23 October 1914 her 17-year-old son Peter Kollwitz, who was a musketeer in the German army, died in an attack on Diksmuide in Flanders. In April 1915 Käthe started working on the first plans for a memorial stone for the grave of her son Peter, and after 1919 she mainly depicted the suffering of war, for example in posters and in the woodcut series "Der Krieg". She then sought her undiminished power of expression in a greater simplification of form and a striving for abstract, stylized monumentality.

In 1929, the Knights of the Order 'Pour le Mérite für Wissenschaften und Künste' elected Käthe Kollwitz, as the first woman, as a member of their exclusive order.Kollwitz was part of the scientific research into giftedness and psychiatric problems conducted by Adele Juda

125

On 23 July 1931 the stone statues of 'The grieving parents' were placed on *Het Roggeveld* between Zarren and Esen, near Diksmuide.

In 1956 Peter was transferred, together with 1538 comrades, to the "Deutscher Soldatenfriedhof Vladslo", near the Praetbos in Vladslo. On this German military cemetery more than 25,000 fallen soldiers from World War I received their final resting place. At the same time the sculpture moved to be placed near his grave, as before in Esen, Kollwitz gives shape to the boundless sorrow that the war caused her. It is a double image of a grieving parental couple. The father, Peter's own father, looks down on the thousands of graves, including that of his son. The mother, Käthe Kollwitz herself, is kneeling down. In this work the artist wanted to be the mother not only of Peter, but of all those who died with him on the Iron Front.

The cemetery is sung by Willem Vermandere in his song "Vladslo".

On 22 April 1945 Käthe Kollwitz died in Moritzburg at the age of 77.

Style

Kollwitz made numerous drawings, etchings, lithographs and woodcuts and, early in her career, some genre pieces in oil. It was only around the age of forty-five that she began to sculpt.

After early family and self-portraits, which were under a realist influence, she formulated her first testimonials. These consisted of detailed etchings, in historical cycles (e.g. 'The Revolt of the Weavers' and 'The Boer War'). Impressed by the work of the Norwegian painter Edvard Munch, she shaped her accusations into silent, expressionless figures. Later, however, she transformed realism into her own expressionism.

Work

In 1933, her work was declared 'entartet' (degenerate) and she was expelled by the National Socialists from the Berlin Academy, where she had been professor of the graphics department since 1928. She was also expelled from the Pour le Mérite order. In 1936 she was banned from exhibiting and after that she only drew and sculpted. The depiction of mother and child took a central place in her late work.

Highlights

- Käthe Kollwitz, original name Käthe Schmidt, grew up in a liberal middle-class family and studied painting in Berlin (1884-1885) and Munich (1888-1889).
- Impressed by the prints of fellow artist Max Klinger, Käthe devoted herself primarily to graphic art after 1890, producing etchings, lithographs, woodcuts, and drawings.
- The death of her youngest son in battle in 1914 profoundly affected her, and she expressed her grief in another cycle of prints that treat the themes of a mother protecting her children and of a mother with a dead child.
- From 1924 to 1932 Kollwitz also worked on a granite monument for her son, which depicted her husband and herself as grieving parents. In 1932 it was erected as a memorial in a cemetery near Ypres, Belgium.
- Kollwitz's last great series of lithographs, Death (1934-1936), treats that tragic theme with stark and monumental forms that convey a sense of drama.

10. Doris Lessing (1919 - 2013)

British writer and Nobel Prize winner

"What I had that others didn't was a capacity for sticking to it."

Doris Lessing, maiden name: **Doris May Tayler** (Kermanshah (Persia), 22 October 1919 - London, 17 November 2013), was a British writer, awarded the Nobel Prize in Literature in 2007. Her work reflects deep engagement with political and human issues, but is also autobiographical, describing then her African childhood experiences.

Biography

Doris Lessing was born the daughter of a British officer and a nurse. The family moved to Rhodesia (now Zimbabwe) in 1924, where Doris Lessing lived until 1949. She attended primary school and left the family home when she was fifteen years old.

In 1937 Lessing moved to Salisbury, where she became a telephone operator; there she married her first husband, Frank Wisdom. She had two children with him before divorcing him in 1943.

In the "communist book club" she met her second husband, Gottfried Lessing, whom she soon married and had a child with. In 1949 this marriage also ended in divorce.

Lessing moved to London with her youngest son in 1949, where her first novel, *The Singing Grass*, was published. She made her breakthrough in 1962 with *The Golden Book*.

Lessing's fiction literature is usually divided into three phases. Communist involvement (1944-1956 and later in *The Good Terrorist*), when she wrote radical texts on social problems, psychological themes (1956-1969) and then Sufi themes (Canopus series).

In choosing Doris Lessing, the jury of the 2007 Nobel Prize for Literature paid tribute to "that hero poet of the female experience, who with scepticism, fire and visionary power has put a divided civilization under the microscope". Due to back problems, the author was unable to receive the award herself in Stockholm on 10 December 2007. The award was presented to her in London.

Feminism

Doris Lessing was regarded as a prominent feminist - especially on account of her seminal work *The Golden Book*. In this respect, however, she was rather cautious:

What the feminists want from me is something they have not researched, because it is religious. They want me to bear witness. What they would most like to hear me say is, "Ha, my sisters, I stand side by side with you in your struggle toward the golden days council where all those beastly guys will be no more. Do they really want people to make oversimplified statements about men and women? Yes, they do. I deeply regret that I had to come to this conclusion.

Highlights

- In her early adult years, Doris Lessing was an active communist.

129

- In 1994 Lessing published the first volume of an autobiography, Under My Skin; a second volume, Walking in the Shade, appeared in 1997.
- Her first published book, The Grass Is Singing (1950), is about a white farmer and his wife and their African servant in Rhodesia.
- Among her most substantial works is the series Children of Violence (1952-1969), a five-novel sequence that centres on Martha Quest, who grows up in southern Africa and settles in England.
- Doris Lessing was awarded the Nobel Prize for Literature in 2007.

11. J. K. Rowling (born 1965)

British author who created The Harry Potter series

"You sort of start thinking anything's possible if you've got enough nerve."

Joanne (Jo) Rowling (Yate near Bristol, 31 July 1965) is a British author. She is best known as the creator of the *Harry Potter fantasy series*. The *Harry Potter books* received worldwide attention and won multiple awards, selling over 500 million copies. The books formed the basis for the *Harry Potter film series*, with Rowling acting as producer in two of the eight parts. Rowling's parents are named Peter Rowling and Anne Volant Rowling.

Rowling wrote mainly under the name **J.K. Rowling**, in which the 'K' stands for her grandmother Kathleen's name. In reality, Rowling does not have a middle name. She added the 'K' when the publisher of the *Harry Potter books* stated that boys would not read books written by a woman. By using only her initial this would be hidden. Only the 'J' was not enough, so she added an initial.

Some of her later books were published under the pseudonym **Robert Galbraith**.

Biography

In 1986 Rowling graduated from the University of Exeter in French and Classical Culture, after which she took various office jobs. In 1991 she moved to Portugal to teach English. There she met TV journalist Jorge Arantes, whom she married. In 1993 her first daughter Jessica was born. The marriage failed and Rowling went to live in Edinburgh with her daughter. There she wrote two books for adults, but neither of them was good enough to be sent to a publisher.

Rowling and her second husband, Neil Murray, had a baby son in 2003. Two years later, in 2005, the couple had a daughter.

In 2003, it was calculated that Rowling would be richer than the British monarch, and for a while she was the richest woman in the country, having sold 500 million copies of the seven books translated into 69 languages (in whole or in part), which together brought in over $8 billion.

Rowling was named the 'Most Influential Woman in Britain' by editors of leading magazines in 2010. She became a notable philanthropist and helped found the Children's High Level Group, among other things. She also put a lot of money into organisations such as Comic Relief, One Parent Families and the Multiple Sclerosis Society of Great Britain. Rowling's wealth was estimated at $1 billion by *Forbes* in 2011; however, a year later the magazine estimated her wealth at $160 million, the difference is said to be due to the tax levied on high incomes in Britain and her donations. In 2016, her wealth was estimated at £584 million.

In 2011, a film was released about Rowling's life entitled *Magic Beyond Words: The J.K. Rowling Story*.

On 12 December 2017, Rowling was appointed a member of the Order of the Companions of Honour. She received the accompanying decorations from the hands of Prince William.

Harry Potter

In 1990, during a four-hour delayed train journey from Manchester to London, Rowling conceived the story of Harry Potter. Over the next five years, she developed the storylines into a seven-part series. The first volume was returned by twelve publishers, so it was not published until 1997 by Bloomsbury Publishing. Her literary agent, Christopher Little, later sold the book to American publisher Scholastic, earning Rowling a sloppy $105,000 (about 77,000 euros).

After a hesitant start, the books, of which three had already been published by then, reached the first three places of the book top ten in both the United States and the United Kingdom in 1999. The last four books in the series became the fastest selling books in history. More than 500 million copies have been sold worldwide.

After the publication of the seventh *Potter book*, *Harry Potter and the Deathly Hallows*, Rowling decided that enough was enough and that she would take a long rest. Nevertheless, in 2008 the *Harry Potter fairy tale book The Tales of Baker the Bard* was published. Rowling also promised fans a *Harry Potter encyclopedia*, with never-before-published background information. In 2012, she said she was working on the encyclopedia.

In 2010 she indicated in an interview with Oprah Winfrey that she still had plenty of ideas in her head for an eighth Harry Potter book. This eventually became the script for the play *Harry Potter and the Cursed Child*. For another project called Pottermore a website was created. Through this website people were directed to a YouTube channel where they counted down to 13:00 on 23 June 2011. At this time the author announced the new project. Her agent made it clear that it will not be a new *Harry Potter book*, but an online computer game, which became accessible to everyone in 2012.

On September 12, 2013, Rowling announced that she will create a spin-off film series based on the world of Harry Potter. The main character will be Newt Scamander, the author of *Fantastic Beasts and Where to Find Them*. The film will be called *Fantastic Beasts and Where to Find Them*. There is also already a second film In April 2015, it was announced that actor Eddie Redmayne would star in the film.

On 30 July 2016, the Palace Theatre on the West End premiered the play *Harry Potter and the Cursed Child*. The script of the play was based on a

brand new *Harry Potter story* by J.K. Rowling and is set nineteen years
after the seventh book.

Robert Galbraith

After Rowling published her first book for adults, *The Casual Vacancy*,
under her own name in 2012, she decided (under the pseudonym Robert
Galbraith) to devise a detective in the tradition, as she herself points out,
of Agatha Christie, Ruth Rendell, Margery Allingham and P.D. James,
starring Cormoran Strike. The stories are therefore characterised as
puzzle detectives, in which the reader only finds out who the culprit is after
incremental clues and via detours. In 2013 the detective, *The Cuckoo's
Calling* was published. This book turned out to be the beginning of a new
series. Rowling had started writing this series under a pseudonym to re-
experience what it was like to be a beginning writer. After it was
discovered that Rowling was hiding behind the name Galbraith, sales rose
explosively. The pseudonym is a combination of the first name of her hero
Robert F. Kennedy and the last name she had coined for herself as a little
girl (Ella Galbraith).

The main character of the series, Cormoran Strike, is a former military
man who returned from Afghanistan with an amputated leg and started a
detective agency. Strike is the son of a famous pop star, but has only met
his father twice. Rowling indicates that this fact allows her to write about
dealing with celebrity in a more objective way.

His detective agency is not too successful until he solves a complicated
murder in *Cuckoo's Boy, set in* the upper-class world of London. He does
so in collaboration with Robin Ellacott, whom he has hired as his
secretary, but who turns out to be a skilled assistant sleuth.

In *Silkworm* another mysterious disappearance and murder is solved, this
time in the publishing world. Furthermore, the relationship between Strike
and Robin deepens, which in turn leads to problems between Robin and
her fiancé.

The third volume in the series, *Career of Evil*, was released in 2015. Robin
Ellacott takes delivery of a package from a courier at the office of her
employer, Cormoran Strike. When it turns out that the package contains
the lower leg of a woman, Strike is able to name four people who qualify
as the sender.

Highlights

- After graduating from the University of Exeter in 1986, Rowling began working for Amnesty International in London, where she started to write the Harry Potter adventures.
- The first book in the Harry Potter series, Harry Potter and the Philosopher's Stone (1997; also published as Harry Potter and the Sorcerer's Stone), was released under the name J.K. Rowling.
- A book version of the script, which was advertised as the eighth story in the Harry Potter series, was published in 2016.
- In May 2020, during the COVID-19 pandemic, Rowling began serializing a new children's book, The Ickabog, for free online; it was then published in November.

12. Margaret Atwood (born 1939)
Canadian writer

---

*"A voice is a human gift; it should be cherished and used,
to utter fully human speech as possible. Powerlessness
and silence go together."*

Margaret Eleanor Atwood OC (Ottawa, November 18, 1939) is one of
Canada's leading contemporary writers. She is a poet, novelist, literary
critic, feminist, and political activist. She receives both national and
international recognition.

Life

Margaret Atwood was born in Ottawa, Ontario, and is the second of three
children of Carl Atwood, an entomologist, and Margaret Killiam, a dietician.
Because her father did much research in the vast forests of Canada, she
spent many of her younger years in remote areas of northern Ontario,
commuting back and forth between Ottawa, Sault St. Marie, and Toronto,
attending many different schools. She became an avid reader, and began
writing at 16.

From 1957 she studied at Victoria University in Toronto, receiving her Bachelor of Arts degree in English, with Philosophy and French as minor subjects. She studied at Radcliffe College in Harvard from 1961, on a Woodrow Wilson Scholarship after winning the E.J. Pratt Prize for her collection of poetry entitled *Double Persephone*. She received her master's degree in 1962 and continued her studies at Harvard. She went on to teach at various universities.

After divorcing her first husband, Jim Polk, she married Graeme Gibson, with whom she moved to Alliston and with whom she had a daughter in 1976. Today, Margaret Atwood lives in Toronto and on Pelee Island in Ontario.

Work

Margaret Atwood has written books with many different themes and in different genres and traditions. She is often described as a feminist writer, and gender issues figure prominently in her work. Her work also focuses, among other things, on the identity of Canada, relations between Canada and the United States and Europe, human rights, environmental issues, the representation of the female body in art, and the relationship of women to each other and to men.

Her best-known critical work is *Survival: A Thematic Guide to Canadian Literature* (1972), which is said to have sparked a renewed interest in Canadian literature.

Atwood was vice president of the Writers' Union of Canada and from 1984 to 1986 president of PEN International, an international lobby group that seeks to free writers held as political prisoners. In April 2006, she attended the annual PEN World Voices festival in New York, organized by Salman Rushdie, then president of PEN America. Among the guests, besides Atwood, were David Grossman, Toni Morrison, Jeanette Winterson, Anne Provoost and Orhan Pamuk.

She was elected as a Senior Fellow of Massey College at the University of Toronto, and she holds many honorary doctorates (including from Oxford University, Cambridge University and the Sorbonne). She was added to Canada's Walk of Fame in 2001.

In 2017, she was awarded the Peace Prize of the German Book Trade and the Czech Frans Kafka Prize.

Politics

Atwood has spoken out for feminism and environmental politics on several occasions. Although an opponent of the Canadian Conservatives, she considers herself a *Red Tory*. She rejects cultural boycotts against Israel.

In 2018, Atwood claimed that those responsible for the September 11, 2001 attacks were inspired by Star Wars.

Highlights

- In Margaret Atwood's early poetry collections, Double Persephone (1961), The Circle Game (1964, revised in 1966), and The Animals in That Country (1968), Atwood ponders human behaviour, celebrates the natural world, and condemns materialism.
- In 2019 The Testaments, a sequel to The Handmaid's Tale, was published to critical acclaim and was a cowinner (with Bernardine Evaristo's Girl, Woman, Other) of the Booker Prize.
- Her nonfiction includes Negotiating with the Dead: A Writer on Writing (2002), which grew out of a series of lectures she gave at the University of Cambridge; Payback (2008; film 2012), an impassioned essay that treats debt-both personal and governmental-as a cultural issue rather than as a political or economic one; and In Other Worlds: SF and the Human Imagination (2011), in which she illuminated her relationship to science fiction.
- She won the PEN Pinter Prize in 2016 for the spirit of political activism threading her life and works.

13. Agatha Christie (1890-1976)
English detective novelist and playwright

"The impossible could not have happened, therefore the impossible must be possible in spite of appearances."

Dame Agatha Mary Clarissa Miller (Torquay, 15 September 1890 - Wallingford, 12 January 1976) was a British writer who became one of the most successful authors of all time. Her works have been translated into at least 108 languages, with over 3 billion sold worldwide.

Agatha Christie's oeuvre includes 66 detective novels, 20 plays, 4 non-fiction works, 6 novels under the pseudonym Mary Westmacott, and approximately 150 short stories. Nearly 200 film adaptations of and about Christie's work and about the author's life have appeared on the big screen and television.

She is spiritual mother of Hercule Poirot, Miss Marple, Tommy and Tuppence and Mr. Harley Quin, among others.

Lifecycle

Agatha Mary Clarissa Miller was born on 15 September 1890 in Torquay, a stately coastal town in Devon (south-west England). She is the second daughter and third child of American Frederick Alvah Miller and British Clarissa Boehmer. Ten and eleven years earlier, sister Margaret (Madge) and brother Louis (Monty) were born into the family. Agatha's father inherited his fortune from his father (a merchant of clothing and perishable foods). He is often in the United States where he works as a stockbroker. The "upper-middle-class" Miller family occupy the villa bought in 1881 called Ashfield, on the outskirts of Torquay. There is a large garden in which Agatha plays a lot and there are maids. Agatha enjoys a carefree childhood. She is a quiet and somewhat dreamy girl. Her sister and brother are much older and there are few children in the neighborhood. Therefore she plays a lot alone and is often with her mother, to whom she gets very attached.

Agatha doesn't go to school. Her mother doesn't think it's necessary. She and Madge home-schooled Agatha and taught her to play the piano and the mandolin. Her mother thinks Agatha should only learn to read and write from the age of eight, but she teaches herself to do this out of curiosity about books when she is four or five years old. Because of Frederick's health problems the family leaves for the South of France in 1896. This region is known for its warm climate and pure air. The Millers stayed there for six months. Here Agatha learns a few French words. In 1901 her father dies of an acute lung disease.

After the death of father Frederick, the family is in increasing financial difficulty. Sister Madge has married and moved away and brother Monty serves in the army in the US. At the age of 12 Agatha writes her first poems and short stories. Some of these are published in regional magazines. In the winter of 1905, her mother rents Ashfield to generate income and leaves with Agatha for Paris. Agatha is taught at a boarding school there. Her mother returned to Torquay after a few months while Agatha remained in Paris for another two years. During this time she tries to break through as a professional pianist and singer, but fails. Her sister Madge, who also writes, bets that Agatha will not succeed in writing a full-fledged crime novel. Agatha would eventually win the bet years later.

140

Agatha's mother suffers from health problems. In late 1907 she rents Ashfield and she and Agatha travel for the winter to the then popular (and cheap) holiday destination of Cairo. The warm and sunny climate does Agatha's mother good. After returning to Torquay Agatha enjoys her social life: going out with friends to dance parties, strolling along the promenade along the beach, roller skating, amateur theatre, making music. During these years she also writes several short stories. She offers them to publishers but they are all rejected.

First marriage and debut

In 1912 Agatha has incorporated the experiences of her trip to Cairo into her first novel - *Snow Upon the Desert* - and submits it to the well-known author Eden Phillpotts, who lives near the Millers. Phillpotts thinks Agatha has a 'talent for dialogue', but advises her to put the work aside and to continue writing. In 1914 she meets army officer Archibald Christie ('Archie') at a dance party and both fall quickly in love. After only three months Archie proposes marriage, which she accepts. The First World War breaks out shortly afterwards and Archie is stationed in France for the RAF. During the Christmas period Archie is on leave in England and the couple take the opportunity to marry quickly on Christmas Eve. Shortly after Christmas Archie leaves for France again. Agatha works first as a nurse and later as a pharmacist's assistant in an emergency military hospital in Torquay. Here she is introduced to various kinds of poison.

After the war Agatha and Archie move to London. Archie went to work in the financial world. In 1919 Rosalind, Agatha's first and only child, is born. Three poems - *World Hymn*, *Dark Sheila* and *A Passing* - are Agatha's first works to be published professionally. The poems find their way into *The Poetry Review* and *Poetry of Today*.

Agatha enjoys reading detective novels, especially Sherlock Holmes by Sir Arthur Conan Doyle, who solves crimes together with his friend Watson. Agatha draws much inspiration from this. In 1916 she had already written her first crime novel, encouraged by her mother: *The Mysterious Affair at Styles*. Herewith she wins the old bet with her sister. Her detective Hercule Poirot is introduced in this story. The wounded Belgian soldiers she nursed and the many Belgian refugees sheltered in Torquay gave her inspiration to make her detective a Belgian. By analogy with Watson in the Sherlock Holmes stories, the figure of Hastings appears in her novel. The manuscript is rejected several times and it is not until 1920 that a publisher

(The Bodley Head) is willing to publish the work after some modification of the ending of the story. The novel is well received. Agatha signs a contract for five more books.

Archie is asked in 1922 by an army acquaintance of his (Ernest Belcher) to make a trip around the world for the British Empire Exhibition, visiting the British colonies. The trip will take just under a year and will serve to promote the great exhibition to be held in London in 1924 and 1925. Agatha accompanies her husband and enjoys this trip around the world. After her return, *The Road of Dreams* - a collection of poetry - is published by Geoffrey Bles. It is the only work of Christie's to be published by this London publisher.

The Christies move to London because Archie starts working in finance there. They live in a few flats and then move to Sunningdale, famous for its large golf course. They name their home *Styles*, after the mansion at the centre of Christie's debut novel. The earth-shattering *The Murder of Roger Ackroyd* is published in 1926. Christie is said to have fooled the reader and tensions in the writing world run so high that the author is almost expelled from the prestigious *Detection Club*, a bastion of the cream of crime authors.

Disappearance

In April 1926 Agatha's mother dies. Four months later Archie announces that he wants a divorce because he is in love with Nancy Neele - a friend of Major Belcher. Her mother's death and poor marriage to Archie led to a mental setback for Christie. On December 8, 1926, she disappeared without a trace. Her car (with only some clothes and a driving licence in it) was found the next morning on the edge of a quarry near Guildford. Christie was found eleven days later in a hotel in Harrogate, where she had checked in under the surname of her husband's mistress. Police and thousands of volunteers had been searching across the country for the missing author. Christie is lodged in her sister's home, where she will have no contact with the outside world for the time being. The background of this disappearance has always remained unknown and still gives rise to conspiracy theories and conjecture. A publicity stunt and amnesia are some of the explanations put forward. Christie herself has never commented on this disappearance. Her family has always held to the theory of temporary amnesia. Author Jared Cade wrote a documented book about this period. According to Agatha's daughter, that book was far

142

from the truth. She wanted the work banned from bookstores. Some people close to Agatha Christie, however, have stated that they agree with the findings of Cade's book.

Second marriage

Agatha and Archie divorce in 1928. At the express request of her publisher, Agatha keeps the surname Christie as her author. *Alibi* is the first play to be staged. Agatha realizes that she must now write in order to earn a living - during her marriage she only wrote because she enjoyed it. Writing is hard and Agatha still suffers emotionally from the after-effects of the difficult year 1926. She wants to travel and is suggested by a fellow guest at a dinner party to go to Baghdad to visit excavations and experience the culture of the Middle East. She does so and travels on the Orient Express via Istanbul to Iraq. There she meets the archaeologist Leonard Woolley in Ur. He invites her to return in early 1930 to stay at the excavation site. She accepts this invitation and in February 1930 meets Max Mallowan, a fourteen year younger archaeologist who works as Woolley's assistant. He guides Agatha and other guests around the sites. A friendship develops. Later in England, Max proposes marriage, which Agatha accepts. They married on September 11, 1930.

In 1931 Agatha bought *Winterbrook House* in Wallingford. This is conveniently close to Oxford - where Max often works - and not too far from London. She accompanies Max on excavation work at Tell Arpachiyah near Mosul. *Death in the Clouds* sold over 10,000 copies in 1936, making it Christie's first bestselling novel. The following year she wrote the play *Akhnaton*. The play is never performed. The work does not appear in book form until 1973.In the years between 1930 and 1945, Agatha has an enormously productive writing period and her most successful and famous detective novels are written during this time. She draws on her experiences in the Middle East in many of her detective novels, as in Murder on the Nile.

Her native Torquay continues to attract her but the feeling she used to have there is no longer there. Torquay is expanding and the atmosphere has changed. Agatha sells her birthplace Ashfield. Then in 1938 she buys Greenway House as a country house and holiday home. This house in the green, overlooking the Dart, she had often seen from a distance as a child. Daughter Rosalind marries Hubert Pritchard in World War II 1941. Max

143

moves to Cairo as an Arabia expert in the *British War Department*. Agatha herself goes back to work as a volunteer in the hospital.

Presumably during this period Agatha wrote *Curtain: Poirot's Last Case* and *Sleeping Murder* (Miss Marple's last). Both books are kept in a vault and may not be published until after the author's death. In 1943 her grandson Mathew is born. Under the pseudonym Mary Westmacott, Agatha writes *Absent in the Spring*; this in only three days and without any rest. Agatha's son-in-law - and thus father of grandson Mathew - was killed in the war. In May Max returned to England. The couple again took up residence in *Greenway House*. On the occasion of her birthday, Queen Mary asked Agatha Christie to write a radio play for *BBC Radio*. *The Mousetrap* is the result.

Agatha accompanies Max to Nimrud (Iraq). She calls her makeshift accommodation *Beit Agatha* (Agatha's house). Daughter Rosalind marries Anthony Hicks. A *London Sunday Times* columnist reveals the true person behind the pseudonym Mary Westmacott. Agatha joins the *Royal Society of Literature*. In 1950 she meets theatre impresario Peter Saunders and records the first lines of her autobiography on paper. *The Mousetrap* was first performed in London in 1952.

Recognition

Agatha wins the *Grand Master Prize* from the *Mystery Writers of America* in 1954. The following year Agatha Christie Limited is formed, and in 1956 she is pinned on the decorations of a "Commander of the British Empire". She may place the letters "CBE" after her name.The author is also appointed president of *The Detection Club* (the body she was previously nearly expelled from after the intended foul play in *The Murder of Roger Ackroyd*). Max finishes his excavations in Nimrud. Max is also decorated and may henceforth call himself Max Mallowan CBE.The University of Exeter awards Agatha Christie an honorary Doctor of Letters degree in 1961.

In 1962 ex-husband Archibald Christie dies.Agatha Christie completes her autobiography in 1965 and Max publishes his standard work *Nimrud and Its Remains*. Max is also knighted. As his wife, Agatha is now "Lady Mallowan". Agatha in turn is then promoted to "Dame Commander of the British Empire". She may have herself called Dame Agatha Mallowan, or

144

Dame Agatha Christie, and put the letters "DBE" after her name.Madame Tussaud unveiled a wax figure of Agatha Christie in 1972.

She made her last public appearance in 1974. She dies on January 12, 1976 in Wallingford, Oxfordshire.

After her death

Agatha's autobiography appears in bookstores. *Mallowan's Memories* also ends up on many a bookshelf.Max Mallowan died in 1978. *Partners in Crime* (a ten-part television series) appears on the tube. The first Joan Hickson portrayals as Miss Marple find their way to a wide audience.David Suchet makes his first appearance as Hercule Poirot in the 1989 Poirot television series. Agatha's 100th birthday, the *Agatha Christie Centennial*, is celebrated en masse. The *Agatha Christie Society* is founded. *Black Coffee* (1997 adaptation by Charles Osborne) and *Unexpected Guest* (Charles Osborne, 1999) are published posthumously.

Style and storytelling techniques

Almost all of Agatha Christie's books are whodunits, set in the British middle and upper classes. Usually the detective stumbles upon the murder by chance, or is called in by an acquaintance who is involved. Gradually the detective interviews all the suspects, and investigates the crime scene, pointing out all the clues so that the reader can analyze the case and try to solve the mystery himself. Usually one of the suspects dies halfway through or during the denouement, often because he has discovered the identity of the murderer and must be silenced. In some novels, including *En het einde is de dood* and *Tien kleine negertjes*, there are several victims. Eventually the detective arranges a meeting with all the suspects and the culprit is revealed, revealing all the secrets, sometimes over thirty pages or more. The murders are always ingeniously constructed, and some form of deception is usually used. The stories are known for their taut atmosphere and strong psychological suspense. Twice the murderer is surprisingly the unreliable narrator of the story.

In five stories, Christie lets the killer escape justice (and in the last three, she almost implicitly approves of the crime): *Witness for the Prosecution, The Man in the Brown Suit, Murder on the Orient Express, Curtain,* and *The Unexpected Guest.* In many cases the killer is not brought to justice but dies (with death proving a more "sympathetic" outcome), for example
145

in *Death Comes as the End*, *And Then There Were None*, *Death on the Nile*, *Dumb Witness*, *The Murder of Roger Ackroyd*, *Crooked House*, *Appointment with Death*, *The Hollow*, *Nemesis*, and *The Secret Adversary*. In some cases, the detective plays a role in this.

Highlights

- Agatha Christie, in full Dame Agatha Mary Clarissa Christie, née Miller, was educated at home by her mother.
- Christie began writing detective fiction while working as a nurse during World War I. Her first novel, The Mysterious Affair at Styles (1920), introduced Hercule Poirot, her eccentric and egotistic Belgian detective; Poirot reappeared in about 25 novels and many short stories before returning to Styles, where, in Curtain (1975), he died.
- Christie's first major recognition came with The Murder of Roger Ackroyd (1926), which was followed by some 75 novels that usually made best-seller lists and were serialized in popular magazines in England and the United States.
- Other notable film adaptations included And Then There Were None (1939; film 1945), Murder on the Orient Express (1933; film 1974 and 2017), Death on the Nile (1937; film 1978), and The Mirror Crack'd From Side to Side (1952; film [The Mirror Crack'd] 1980).

14.   Alexandra Danilova (1903-1997)

Russian ballerina known for her vivacity and theatrical flair

Aleksandra Dionisievna Danilova (Russian: Александра Дионисиевна Данилова) (Peterhof, November 20, 1903 - New York City, July 13, 1997) was a Russian ballerina and dance pedagogue who later assumed American citizenship.

Life

Danilova received her dance training at the Mariinsky Theatre in Saint Petersburg. In 1921 she also joined the 'corps de ballet' of the Mariinsky ballet. Together with dancer-choreographer George Balanchine (with whom she had a long-standing relationship), she left Russia in 1924 to become a soloist in Sergei Diaghilev's Ballets Russes. After Diaghilev's death she danced for a long time in the Ballet Russe de Monte Carlo.

During her career, Danilova has danced just about every major classical ballet role and worked with great choreographers such as Marius Petipa and Michel Fokine. She was much praised for her interpretation of *Swanhilda* in Coppélia and *Odile* in Swan Lake. Her last performance was in 1951.

After her career as a ballet dancer, she emigrated to the United States and worked as a choreographer at the Metropolitan Opera and as a dance teacher at the School of American Ballet. She also performed occasionally in musicals and films, including "The Turning Point" by Herbert Ross.

Danilova died in 1997 in New York, at the age of 93.

Highlights

- Alexandra Danilova attended the Russian Imperial and Soviet State Ballet schools in Leningrad, where she studied under Agrippina Vaganova and became soloist at the Mariinsky (formerly Kirov) Theatre.
- Danilova appeared as guest artist with several ballet companies, including Sadler's Wells Ballet, and with her own company (Great Moments of Ballet, 1954-56) toured Japan, the Philippines, and South Africa.
- Alexandra Danilova won note both for her extensive repertoire, ranging from romantic to abstract Balanchine roles, and for the individuality of her characterizations, particularly the street dancer in Le Beau Danube, the glove seller in Gaîté Parisienne, Odette in Swan Lake, and Swanilda in Coppélia.
- She also appeared in musical comedy (Oh Captain!, 1958), taught, and made lecture tours.
- Alexandra Danilova played a small but significant role in the motion picture The Turning Point (1977).

15.   Josephine Baker (1906 - 1975)

American-born French dancer famous for her theatrical performances

"You must get an education. You must go to school, and you must learn to protect yourself. And you must learn to protect yourself with the pen, and not the gun."

Josephine Baker or **Joséphine Baker**, stage name of *Freda Josephine McDonald* (Saint Louis (Missouri), June 3, 1906 - Paris, April 12, 1975) was an American-French dancer, singer and actress.

Life

Josephine Baker grew up in poverty. As a child, she was a servant to several families before living as a homeless person from the age of twelve. She begged by dancing in the streets for passers-by. At fifteen she performed in the Vaudeville in Saint Louis. After this she moved to New York and debuted on Broadway in her early twenties. After this she performed in Europe and South America, in Paris for the first time in 1925, among others at the Folies Bergère. During this time she also appeared

149

almost naked on stage and became famous for her banana skirt and her erotic dances. She often had a cheetah with her.

In 1937, she assumed French citizenship by marrying Frenchman Jean Lion and went to live permanently in France. During World War II, she did resistance work for the Résistance by using her position to obtain intelligence. For this she was later awarded the War Cross, the Medal of Remembrance for the Volunteers of Free France and the Resistance Medal. She was also awarded the Knight's Cross of the Legion of Honour in December 1957.

After the war, Baker campaigned for the rights of African-Americans. She refused to perform in segregated venues. In 1951 she was refused entry to a club in New York. Grace Kelly, who was admitted, immediately decided to leave the premises with all her friends and never come back. After this Baker and Kelly became good friends. In 1963 she walked with Martin Luther King in the March on Washington where she was the only female speaker. After the assassination of Martin Luther King, she was asked to take his place. She declined the honor because she felt her children were too young to lose their mother.

On April 12, 1975, four days after opening a successful premiere of a new revue, Baker was found dead in bed. She had suffered a brain hemorrhage. She is buried in the Cimetière de Monaco in Monte Carlo. In Château des Milandes there is an exhibition of wax figures, clothing and objects about her life.

Private life

In 1941 she had a miscarriage, after which her uterus had to be removed. Later she adopted twelve children from all over the world; her children were therefore called the rainbow children (la tribu arc-en-ciel). For a while she lived with her children in the Castle des Milandes in Castelnaud-la-Chapelle in the Dordogne.

Joséphine Baker was bisexual. Married to several men, she also maintained relationships with women throughout her adult life. However, no public attention was ever paid to this part of her personality. Her famous lovers included the French writer Colette and Frida Kahlo. One of her children, Jean-Claude Baker, in the biography about his mother, mentions four more of her lovers: Clara Smith, Evelyn Sheppard, Bessie

Allison and Mildred Smallwood, all of whom she met on the circuit during her early years on the stage in the United States.

Despite her own bisexuality and her commitment against racism (notably through her participation in certain actions of the African-American civil rights movement), she was found to have homophobic traits herself; for example, she sent one of her sons, Jarry Bouillon Baker, to his father because he was gay. According to the latter, she feared he would "infect" his brothers.

Highlights

- Between the ages of 8 and 10 Josephine Baker was out of school, helping to support her family. As a child Baker developed a taste for the flamboyant that was later to make her famous.
- In 1923 Baker joined the chorus in a road company performing the musical comedy Shuffle Along and then moved to New York City, where she advanced steadily through the show Chocolate Dandies on Broadway and the floor show of the Plantation Club.
- In 1925 Baker went to Paris to dance at the Théâtre des Champs-Élysées in La Revue Nègre and introduced her danse sauvage to France.
- Josephine Baker sang professionally for the first time in 1930, made her screen debut as a singer four years later in Zouzou, and made several more films before World War II curtailed her career.
- Her life was dramatized in the television movie The Josephine Baker Story (1991) and was showcased in the documentary Joséphine Baker.

18 Female Freedom Fighters

1. Malala Yousafzai (born 1997)

Pakistani education advocate

*"One child, one teacher, one book, one pen can change
the world."*

Malala Yousafzai (born Mingora, July 12, 1997) is a Pakistani child rights
activist. In 2014, she was awarded the Nobel Peace Prize along with
Kailash Satyarthi.

Lifecycle

Malala Yousafzai, daughter of a teacher, has become known for her fight
for girls to be allowed to go to school. In 2009 she gained fame at the age
of eleven when she kept a weblog on the BBC website under the
pseudonym *Gul Makai* (Cornflower). In the form of a diary, she wrote
about the violence of the Taliban in the Swat Valley, where, since the
Taliban seized power in 2007, girls have been excluded from school and
many other human rights violations have been committed.

While on a bus returning from school on October 9, 2012, a Taliban fighter
carried out a targeted attack on her, seriously injuring her with a bullet to
her head and neck. Doctors removed the bullet from her head at a hospital
in Rawalpindi. The Taliban threatened to kill her anyway.

153

On 15 October she was flown to England, where she received further specialist treatment at the Queen Elizabeth Hospital in Birmingham. Here she was also better protected from Taliban attacks. Her father got a job there so the family could accompany her in the UK.

She was discharged from hospital in January 2013, but went back to Birmingham in early February. Part of her skull was repaired with a titanium prosthesis made to the shape of her head using a 3D technique. She received a cochlear implant on her left ear. She left the hospital on February 8.

Malala studied at Oxford University.

International recognition

In 2011, Malala was nominated for the *International Children's Peace Prize*. The same year, she was awarded the *National Youth Peace Prize* by the Government of Pakistan. This prize was later renamed the *National Malala Peace Prize* in her honour.

10 November 2012 was declared *Malala's Day* by the United Nations, with which the UN wants to draw attention to the 32 million girls and 29 million boys in the world who receive no primary education. A petition on the internet from October 2012 calling for her to be awarded the Nobel Peace Prize in 2013 was signed by more than 250,000 people.

The April 29, 2013 issue of *Time named* Malala as one of the 100 most influential people in the world. Her photo was featured on the cover of the magazine. On July 12, 2013, on her sixteenth birthday, Malala addressed 500 young people at the UN. On this occasion, this day was declared as "Malala Day". On 6 September 2013, Malala was awarded the International Children's Peace Prize 2013 in the Ridderzaal in The Hague. She came to the Netherlands at the invitation of the Dutch children's rights organization KidsRights. The winner of the Nobel Peace Prize 2011, Tawakkul Karman, presented the award on behalf of KidsRights. On 20 November 2013 Malala received the *Sakharov Prize for Freedom of Expression* from the European Parliament in Strasbourg. She is the youngest winner of this prize to date.

On May 24, 2014, she received the Four Freedom Award for Freedom from Fear in Middelburg, presented by Blof in the presence of the
154

Roosevelt family and the royal family. On October 10, 2014, it was announced that she was awarded the 2014 Nobel Peace Prize. At 17, she was the youngest ever winner of a Nobel Prize. In July 2014, she traveled to Nigeria, where she visited the parents of some 200 schoolgirls kidnapped by Boko Haram in April.

In April 2015, space agency NASA named an asteroid between Mars and Jupiter after Malala with the official name '316201 Malala'. The celestial body has a diameter of four kilometers and orbits the sun every five and a half years.

Highlights

- Malala Yousafzai gained global attention when she survived an assassination attempt at age 15.
- In October 2011 she was nominated by human rights activist Desmond Tutu for the International Children's Peace Prize.
- In 2014 Yousafzai and Kailash Satyarthi were jointly awarded the Nobel Prize for Peace in recognition of their efforts on behalf of children's rights.
- In July 2015, with support from the Malala Fund, she opened a girls' school in Lebanon for refugees from the Syrian Civil War.
- She discussed her work with refugees as well as her own displacement in We Are Displaced (2019).

2. Angela Davis (born 1944)
African American political activist and author

Angela Yvonne Davis (Birmingham (Alabama), January 26, 1944) is an American feminist philosopher, writer,activist, and professor. She has taught for several decades at universities throughout the United States, Europe, Africa, the Caribbean, and the former Soviet Union. She has also written and edited a large number of articles, essays and books.

Personal

Angela Davis was born on January 26, 1944, in Birmingham, Alabama. Her mother, Sallye Bell Davis, played an important role within the Southern Negro Youth Congress, which had ties to the Communist Party of the USA. Around the time of Davis' birth and her childhood, her parents were in communist circles; they were good friends with black members of the Communist Party. Her surroundings strongly influenced Davis: she herself cannot remember a time when she did not have some kind of relationship with the party.

156

Davis attended a segregated black elementary school and went to a
middle school in Birmingham. She eventually attended the progressive
Elisabeth Irwin High School in New York , where Davis says she began to
take an interest in Marxism.

Growing up in a southern state, Davis soon had to deal with segregation
and racism. Birmingham in the late 1940s was one of the most segregated
cities in America. Davis lived with her parents and brothers in a middle-
class neighborhood also known as Dynamite Hill. The homes of African-
American families were terrorized with dynamite and explosions by the Ku
Klux Klan, so frequently that the area was given that nickname, and
Birmingham itself nicknamed "Bombingham. Davis experienced
discrimination himself, and knew the girls who were victims of the 1963
church bombing in Birmingham by the Ku Klux Klan.

Angela Davis was married to Hilton Braithwaite from 1980 to 1983. She
came out of the closet as a lesbian in *Out* magazine in 1997.

Career

Davis worked as a philosophy lecturer at the University of California - Los
Angeles in 1969 and 1970, but she was fired there due to her association
with the Communist Party of the United States and her "inflammatory
language."

Because of her ties to the Soledad Brothers, Davis was eventually
charged with complicity in the 1970 kidnapping and murder of Judge
Harold Haley. Davis provided weapons that allowed three African-
American prisoners (George Jackson, Fleeta Drumgo, and John
Clutchette) to free themselves. During their escape, Haley was murdered.
Davis spent some time in prison for this, but was eventually acquitted.
Possible motivation for Davis' complicity was her connections to one of the
three prisoners, George Jackson. He was the leader of the Black Panther
Party, of which Davis was a spokeswoman for a time.

In the early 1980s, Davis taught at San Francisco State University. From
1991 to 2008, she was a professor at the University of California - Santa
Cruz and Rutgers University. At Santa Cruz, she served for a time as
director of the Department of *Feminist Studies*. One of her specialties is
penitentiary reform. She received an honorary doctorate from the
California Institute of Integral Studies in 2016.

In 1980 and 1984, she ran for Vice President of the United States on behalf of the Communist Party of the United States, as a *running mate* of Gus Hall. The pair obtained 0.05% (1980) and 0.04% (1984) of the vote. In addition to the Communist Party, Davis was involved in the fight for equal civil rights for blacks, the Black Panther Party, and protests against the Vietnam War. Davis was one of the recipients of the 1979 International Lenin Peace Prize, awarded by the Soviet Union. In 1991, Davis left the Communist Party and founded the Committees of Correspondence for Democracy and Socialism. Davis is still active in communist and feminist activism.

In September 2018, she was awarded the Fred L. Shuttlesworth Human Rights Award by the Birmingham Civil Rights Institute. However, in January 2019, it was announced that the award ceremony could not take place, as well as the gala evening, because Davis did not meet all the criteria. Mayor Randall Woodfin of Birmingham (Alabama) was appalled by this decision. According to him this was caused by "the protest voices that had been heard from the Jewish community and its allies". Angela Davis has long defended the rights of Palestinians and the BDS movement. Protests were held at the Institute. As recently as November, the president of the BCRI, Andrea Taylor, had said she was "thrilled to be able to present the award to such a world-renowned champion of human rights."

Feminist activism

Angela Davis dedicated much of her work to researching and writing about women and feminism, especially the oppression of black women. She recognized that the black liberation movement was not standing up for the rights of black women, but also that the feminist movement was not standing up for black women. For this reason, she joined the Communist Party. In an interview she said the following: *there were also very strong sexist tendencies in the black movement. In the Student Non-Violent Coordinating Committee (SNCC), for example, we women ran the office, but when it came time to represent the organization publicly at press conferences and meetings, the men came out and took credit for our work. We knew something was very wrong here*

Along with Kimberly Crenshaw, who coined the term intersectionality in 1989 , Davis became one of the figureheads of black feminism.

Davis wrote *Women, Race and Class* in 1981, in which she discusses the intersection between the women's movement, the black liberation movement, and the class struggle. The book is a collection of thirteen essays, describing the origins and progression of the American women's liberation movement. Slavery in America is also covered. It is Davis' third book and contains an intersectional analysis from Marxist feminism on gender, race, and class. Within Marxist feminism, intersectionality is typically applied to study the interaction between different aspects of identity as a result of structured, systematic oppression, in Davis' case how the aspects of gender, race, and class interact as a result of systematic oppression.

The convergence of the factors of gender, race, and class in the lives of black women is a major focus of Davis' work. Davis can be considered one of the founding fathers of black feminism. Black feminism, according to Davis, is said to have emerged as a theoretical and practical attempt to demonstrate that race, gender, and class are inseparable in the social worlds in which we live. During the early years of black feminism, black women were still often asked to choose between the black movement and the women's movement and this, according to Davis, was wrong.

Angela Davis has many criticisms of (white) feminism. She states that when feminism is discussed in the United States, people almost always tend to assume that it is something created by white women. "Women like Ida B. Wells, women like Mary Church Terrell, women like Anna Julia Cooper, are responsible for the feminist approach that we tend to call intersectionality today." During a lecture at the Copley Library in 2019, Davis already stated that the white suffragettes, despite drawing inspiration from the activism of the anti-slavery movement, did not allow black suffragettes to protest alongside them, and when white women gained the right to vote, they voted no differently than white men.

Davis foresaw that the problems of racism, sexism, and classism would remain if these factors were not all combined in fighting them: black women were excluded from the black liberation and feminist movements, and within the movement for black women there was discrimination based on economic class.

"Any feminism that will help us transform today's world must be able to incorporate perspectives that challenge white supremacy" (Davis, 2019).

159

Highlights

- Angela Davis, in full Angela Yvonne Davis, (born Jan. 26, 1944, Birmingham, Ala., U.S.), militant American black activist who gained an international reputation during her imprisonment and trial on conspiracy charges in 1970-1972.
- Because of her political opinions and despite an excellent record as an instructor at the university's Los Angeles campus, the California Board of Regents in 1970 refused to renew her appointment as lecturer in philosophy.
- In 1991, however, Davis became a professor in the field of the history of consciousness at the University of California, Santa Cruz.
- In 1974 she published Angela Davis: An Autobiography (reprinted 1988).

3. Mae Jemison (born 1956)
American physician and NASA astronaut

"Never limit yourself because of others' limited imagination; never limit others because of your own limited imagination."

Mae Carol Jemison (Decatur, October 17, 1956) is an American former astronaut. She was the first African-American woman in space. In 1993, she left NASA and retired as an astronaut.

Jemison was part of *NASA Astronaut Group 12*. This group of 15 astronauts began their training in June 1987 and became astronauts in August 1988. Jemison's first and only space flight was STS-47 with the space shuttle Endeavour and took place on September 12, 1992. During the mission, several experiments were conducted in the Spacelab module.

After her NASA career, Jemison became professor of environmental studies at Dartmouth College, where she conducted research on the possibilities and limitations of interstellar spaceflight and also headed the

Jemison Institute for Advancing Technology in Developing Countries. There she also founded *The Jemison Group*, whose mission is to use technology to improve health care in developing countries. Jemison also actively promotes the rights of women and minorities. In 1994 Mae Jemison founded the *Earth We Share programme* for young people, in which she links a socio-educational objective to her scientific mission.

Personal info

Mae was born on October 17, in Decatur, Alabama, but she considers Chicago, Illinois her hometown. Her hobbies include traveling, graphic arts, photography, sewing, skiing, collecting African art, and she has an extensive dance and sports background. Charlie and Dorothy Jemison live in Chicago.

Training

She graduated from *Morgan Park High School* in Chicago in 1973. In 1977, she graduated from Stanford University with a *bachelor's degree* in science and as a chemical engineer and a doctorate in medicine from Cornell University in 1981.

Highlights

- Mae Jemison, in full Mae Carol Jemison, (born October 17, 1956, Decatur, Alabama, U.S.), American physician and the first African American woman to become an astronaut.
- In 1977 Jemison entered medical school at Cornell University in Ithaca, New York, where she pursued an interest in international medicine.
- She graduated from medical school in 1981, and, after a short time as a general practitioner with a Los Angeles medical group, she became a medical officer with the Peace Corps in West Africa.
- In 1992 she spent more than a week orbiting Earth in the space shuttle Endeavour. At the time she was the only African American woman astronaut.

4. Rosa L. Parks (1913-2005)

African-American civil rights activist

*"You must never be fearful about what you are doing
when it is right."*

Rosa Louise Parks-McCauley (Tuskegee (Alabama), February 4, 1913 -
Detroit (Michigan), October 24, 2005) was an American civil rights activist.
She is best known for her act of resistance in 1955 when she refused to
give up her seat in the rear section reserved for blacks to white
passengers. This happened when the front section of the bus reserved for
whites became full.

Biography

Parks was born in Tuskegee, Alabama. She worked most of her life as a
seamstress. In the early 1950s, she became active in the African-
American civil rights movement. She also worked as a secretary for the
NAACP in Montgomery. On December 1, 1955, she refused to give up her
seat in the "black section" of a bus to white passengers when the "white
section" became full, as required by Alabama law at the time. The police
were called and Parks was fined $10 (plus $4 court costs). When she
refused to pay, she was arrested and tried for disorderly conduct in
February 1956.

Martin Luther King got wind of the issue, and started the non-violent "Montgomery bus boycott," which nearly bankrupted the bus company and eventually forced it to abolish the segregation of whites and blacks on its buses. This led to more protests against racial segregation. Meanwhile, Rosa Parks' lawsuit had reached the U.S. Supreme Court, which ruled in her favor and declared the separation of whites and blacks unconstitutional.

Her action got her fired and also threatened with death, so she moved to Detroit in the early 1960s, where she lived until her death. Between 1965 and 1968, she worked as a staffer for John Conyers, a member of the House of Representatives. In 2004, a medical report revealed that Parks was suffering from dementia. She eventually died in her sleep a year later, at the age of over 92.

Highlights

- When she was two years old, shortly after the birth of her younger brother, Sylvester, her parents chose to separate. Estranged from their father from then on, the children moved with their mother to live on their maternal grandparents' farm in Pine Level, Alabama, outside Montgomery.
- In 1932, at age 19, Rosa married Raymond Parks, a barber, and a civil rights activist, who encouraged her to return to high school and earn a diploma.
- In 1987 she cofounded the Rosa and Raymond Parks Institute for Self-Development to provide career training for young people and offer teenagers the opportunity to learn about the history of the civil rights movement.

5. Nellie Bly (1867-1922)
American journalist, industrialist, inventor, and charity worker

"Energy rightly applied and directed will accomplish anything."

Nellie Bly (Cochran's Mills, Pennsylvania, May 5, 1864 - New York, January 27, 1922) was the pseudonym of American journalist **Elizabeth Jane Cochrane**. She was an innovative reporter, known for her Around the World in 72 days (faster than Jules Verne's fictional adventurer Phileas Fogg's Around the World in 80 days) and for a report for which she feigned insanity in order to study the interior of a mental hospital. She was a pioneer in her field and the originator of a new kind of investigative journalism. In addition to her writing, she was also an industrialist and did charity work.

Early years

She was born **Elizabeth Jane Cochran** in Cochran's Mills, present part of the Pittsburgh suburb of Burrell Township in Armstrong County,

Pennsylvania. Her father Michael Cochran was a modest laborer and millwright who married Mary Jane. Cochran taught his young children an urgent lesson about the virtues of hard work and determination by purchasing the nearby mill and most of the land surrounding his family farm. As a young girl, she was often called "Pinky" because she usually wore pink clothing. In her teens she wanted to make herself more worldly, dropped her nickname and changed her surname to **Cochrane**. She went to boarding school, but had to drop out after just one term due to lack of money.

In 1880 Elizabeth and her family moved to Pittsburgh. A highly misogynistic column entitled *What Girls Are Good For* in the *Pittsburgh Dispatch* prompted her to write a fiery retort to the editor-in-chief under the pseudonym Lonely Orphan Girl. Chief editor George Madden was impressed by her sincerity and enthusiasm and placed an advertisement, calling for the author to come forward. When Elizabeth introduced herself to the editor-in-chief, he offered her to write a story for the paper, again under the pseudonym 'Lonely Orphan Girl'. After her first article for the *Dispatch*, entitled 'The Girl Puzzle', Madden offered her a full-time job. He chose the pseudonym 'Nellie Bly' for her, derived from the title role of the famous song 'Nelly Bly' by Stephen Foster. She originally wanted her pseudonym to also be written as 'Nelly Bly', but her editor-in-chief accidentally spelled it as 'Nellie' and that mistake stuck.

As a writer, Bly focused her early work at the *Dispatch* on the plight of working women and wrote a series of investigative journalism articles on female factory workers, but editorial pressure pushed her to the so-called women's pages to cover fashion, society, and gardening, typical topics that women journalists were expected to cover at the time. Dissatisfied with these duties, she took matters into her own hands and traveled to Mexico to work as a foreign correspondent. Although she was only 21, she spent nearly six months reporting on the daily life and customs of Mexicans. Her reports were published in book form in 1888 under the title *Six Months in Mexico*. In one report she protested the imprisonment of a local journalist who criticized the Mexican government, then a dictatorship under Porfirio Díaz. When Mexican authorities heard of Bly's reportage, they forced her to leave the country. Once safely home, she denounced Díaz as a tyrannical czar who oppressed the Mexican people and controlled the press.

Report on an insane asylum

After being reassigned to cover theater and art, Bly left the *Pittsburgh Dispatch* in 1887 and moved to New York. When her money ran out after four months, she asked for work at Joseph Pulitzer's newspaper the *New York World*. There she accepted an undercover assignment where she would feign insanity in order to investigate rumors of atrocities and neglect at the *Women's Lunatic Asylum* on Blackwell's Island.

Bly spent an evening in front of the mirror practising imitating the facial expressions of psychiatric patients. The next day she found lodging in a boarding house for workers. She refused to go to bed and told the boarders that she was afraid of them because they looked disturbed. They alerted the police the next morning. She was taken away and brought to court. There she pretended to suffer from amnesia. The judge ruled that she must have been drugged.

She was examined by several doctors, all of whom stated that she was mentally disturbed. "Definitely demented," said one, "I consider this a hopeless case. She should be placed somewhere where someone will take care of her." The head of psychiatric facility Bellevue Hospital described her as "undoubtedly deranged." The case of the "pretty crazy girl" caught the attention of the press: "Who is this crazy girl?" wondered *The Sun*. *The New York Times* wrote of the "mysterious waif" with a "wild, haunted look in her eyes" and her desperate complaining, "I don't know, I don't remember."

After her admission to the asylum as a patient, Bly was introduced to the daily living conditions there. The meals consisted of watery porridge, rotten beef, bread that was little more than dried dough, and filthy, undrinkable water. Patients who might pose a danger were tied up with ropes. The sick were forced to sit for much of the day on hard benches in a poorly heated room. There was rubbish everywhere around the dining tables and rats in the building. One bath consisted of buckets of cold water being poured over the patient. The attendants were unpleasant and abusive, telling patients to shut up and beating them if they did not. Bly became convinced through contact with other patients that some were as mentally healthy as she was. She wrote about her experiences in the asylum:

Is there anything except torture that would produce derangement faster than this treatment? Here a class of women are sent to be cured. I wish that expert doctors who condemn me for my actions, which their skill has

167

proved, would take a perfectly mentally and physically healthy woman under their care, shut her up, force her to sit on straight-backed couches from six in the morning until eight at night, forbid her to speak or move during these hours, give her nothing to read and let her know nothing about the world or what goes on in it, give her bad food and cruel treatment, and then see how long it takes for her to go mad. Two months would make her a mental and psychological wreck.

...My teeth chattered and my limbs were ...numb from the cold. Suddenly I got three buckets of ice cold water ...one of which went into my eyes, nose and mouth.

After ten days, Bly was released after intervention by *The World*. Her account, published in book form under the title *Ten Days in a Mad-House*, caused a sensation and brought her lasting fame. Embarrassed doctors and other asylum staff tried to explain in detail how so many experts had been fooled. A grand jury conducted an investigation into conditions at the asylum, seeking Bly's advice. The grand jury report recommended that the changes suggested by the journalist be made. The Department of Charities and Penitentiaries increased its budget for insane care by $850,000. It also assured that future inspections would be more thorough and that only seriously ill people would be admitted to the asylum.

World trip

In 1888, Bly suggested to her managing editor at the *New York World* that she take a trip around the world to try to make the fictional *Around the World in Eighty Days* a reality for the first time. A year later, as she had announced two days earlier, she boarded the *Augusta Victoria*, a steamship of the Hamburg-America Line, at 9:40 a.m. on November 14, 1889, and began her 40,071-mile journey.

Her luggage was the dress she wore, a sturdy overcoat, a pile of clean underwear and a small travel bag containing her toiletries. She carried most of her money (a total of £200 in English banknotes and gold, plus some American currency) in a bag she had tied around her neck.

The New York newspaper *Cosmopolitan* sponsored its own reporter, Elizabeth Bisland, to cover both Phileas Fogg and Bly's time. Bisland would travel around the world in opposite directions. To maintain interest in the story, *The World* organized a "Nellie Bly Gambling Contest," asking readers to estimate Bly's arrival time down to the second. The grand prize was initially a free trip to Europe, but this was changed to money to spend during that trip.

During her world travels, Bly passed through England, France (where she met Jules Verne at Amiens), Brindisi, the Suez Canal, Colombo (Ceylon), the Straits Settlements of Penang and Singapore, Hong Kong, and Japan. The development of efficient submarine cable networks and the electric telegraph enabled Bly to send short progress reports, although longer messages had to be carried by regular mail and were often delayed by several weeks as a result.

Bly travelled by steamships and the existing rail network, which occasionally caused delays, especially in the Asian leg of her journey. During these delays she visited a leper colony in China and bought a monkey in Singapore.

Because of severe weather during her Pacific crossing, she did not arrive in San Francisco until January 21 on the White Star Line ship *Oceanic*, two days behind schedule. But *The World owner* Pulitzer chartered a private train, renamed the *Miss Nellie Bly Special*, to bring her home and she arrived back in New Jersey on January 25, 1890 at 3:51 pm.

"Seventy-two days, six hours, eleven minutes, and fourteen seconds after her departure from Hoboken" Bly was back in New York. She had traveled the earth almost unaccompanied. Bisland was still crossing the Atlantic at that time, arriving in New York four and a half days later. Like Bly, she had missed a connection and had to board a slow, old ship (the *Bothnia*) instead of a fast ship (*Etruria*). Bly's trip was a world record, although it was bettered a few months later by George Francis Train, who completed the journey in 67 days. By 1913 Andre Jaeger-Schmidt, Henry Frederick and John Henry Mears had surpassed the record, with the latter completing the voyage in 36 days.

Later years

In 1895, Nellie Bly married millionaire manufacturer Robert Seaman, who was 40 years older. She retired from journalism and became the president of the *Iron Clad Manufacturing Co.* , which made steel containers such as milk cans and central heating boilers. Her husband died in 1904. In the same year, *Iron Clad* began producing the steel drum that served as the model for the 55-gallon oil drum, still widely used in the United States. Although it is sometimes claimed that Nellie Bly invented the barrel, it is assumed that the actual inventor was Henry Wehrhahn, who probably attributed his invention to her (US Patents 808.327 and 808.413). However, Nellie Bly was equally an inventor herself, acquiring US Patent 697,553 for a new milk can and US Patent 703,711 for a waste storage can, both under her married name Elizabeth Cochrane Seaman. For a time she was one of the leading women manufacturers in the United States, but embezzlement of goods by her employees led to her bankruptcy.

She returned as a reporter and wrote stories about Europe's Eastern Front during World War I did notable coverage of Women's Suffrage Parade of 1913. Her headline for the parade story was "Suffragists Are Men's Superiors" ("Suffragettes Are Above Men") but she also predicted in her story "with uncanny foreknowledge" that it would be until 1920 before women gained the right to vote.

In 1916, a mother entrusted a baby to Nelly to care for him and have him adopted by someone. The child was unreal and difficult to place because he was half-Japanese. He spent the next six years in an orphanage run by the *Church For All Nations* in Manhattan.

When Bly fell ill near the end of her life, she asked her niece Beatrice Brown to care for the little boy - and several other babies that had caught her interest. Her interest in orphanages may have been part of her ongoing efforts to improve the social organizations of her day.

Bly died of pneumonia at St. Mark's Hospital in New York in 1922 at the age of 57. She was given a modest grave in the Woodlawn Cemetery in the Bronx.

Highlights

- Nellie Bly, pseudonym of Elizabeth Cochrane, began her career in 1885 in her native Pennsylvania as a reporter for the Pittsburgh Dispatch, to which she had sent an angry letter to the editor in response to an article the newspaper had printed entitled "What Girls Are Good For" (not much, according to the article).

- Her first articles, on conditions among working girls in Pittsburgh, slum life, and other similar topics, marked her as a reporter of ingenuity and concern.
- Nellie Bly's Book: Around the World in Seventy-two Days (1890) was a great popular success, and the name Nellie Bly became a synonym for a female star reporter.

6. Marie Curie (1867-1934)

First woman to win a Nobel Prize

"Nothing in life is to be feared, it is only to be understood.
Now is the time to understand more, so that we may fear
less."

Maria Salomea (Marie) Skłodowska-Curie (Warsaw, 7 November 1867 -
Passy, 4 July 1934) was a Polish-French chemist and physicist. She was
a pioneer in the field of radioactivity, receiving two Nobel prizes and
discovering the elements polonium and radium. In her second homeland
France she is known as Marie Curie and she is often referred to as
Madame Curie, which is also the title of her biography written by her
daughter Ève.

Lifecycle

Maria Skłodowska was born on 7 November 1867 in Russian-occupied
Poland. She was the youngest of five children of Władysław Skłodowski
(1832-1902) and Bronisława Boguska (1836-1878). Both parents came

172

from impoverished families belonging to the lower landed gentry. Her childhood was marked by the death of her sister Zofia from typhoid fever in 1876 and the death of her mother from tuberculosis two years later.

As a 15-year-old she passed her high school exams cum laude, but shortly afterwards she suffered from depression and was sent by her father to relatives in the countryside where she stayed for a year. Because of Russian measures after the failed January Uprising in 1863 education in Poland was "Russified". The language of instruction at universities became Russian, Polish was banned, and women were denied access. As a result, Maria Skłodowska was not admitted to the (then Royal) University of Warsaw in 1883. To contribute to the family's living expenses (after their father lost his job), she worked as a teacher. In the evenings she attended classes at the clandestine Flying University of Warsaw, a secret 'mobile' university where Polish women could attend classes in Russia-occupied Poland.

Paris

Maria made an agreement with her older sister Bronisława (Bronia): Bronia would go to Paris to study medicine, while Maria would look for work as a teacher. With her earnings she would contribute to her sister's livelihood in France. Once Bronia would be a doctor, Maria in turn would come to Paris and her sister would help her to pay for her studies. From 1886 to 1889 Maria worked as a governess with the Żorawski family where she fell in love with the eldest son Kazimierz Żorawski. The rich family did not feel anything for an engagement of their son with a girl without money. She lost her job as a governess until she found another job with the Fuchs family in Sopot on the Baltic coast.

In 1891 she was able to move to Paris to study chemistry, physics and mathematics at the Sorbonne with Gabriel Lippmann and the mathematician Paul Appell. In the summer of 1893 Maria Skłodowska passed her physics degree as the best of her year, and the following year she obtained the degree in mathematics. At the instigation of physics lecturer Lippmann she was allowed in early 1894 to carry out research for the *Society for the Promotion of National Industry* on the magnetic properties of hardened steel. For her research she needed a good instrumental approach and through professor Józef Kowalski she met the physicist Pierre Curie who was doing research on magnetism at the École

173

de Physique et Chimie. They married on 26 July 1895 (after Pierre Curie's promotion).

Radioactivity

In 1897 Marie Curie completed her research on the magnetization of hardened steel. For her doctorate, she began researching the phenomenon of uranium rays discovered by Becquerel. Marie later discovered that these rays are a property of the atomic nucleus and gave it the name radioactivity.

On 25 June 1903 she defended at the Sorbonne her dissertation *Recherches sur les Substances Radioactives*, the first dissertation in physics written by a woman. She obtained her doctoral degree with the qualification *très honorable*. In the same year Marie and Pierre Curie received part of the Nobel Prize in Physics "for their research on the radiative phenomena discovered by Henri Becquerel". Becquerel received the other part of that prize. After being awarded the Nobel Prize, Pierre Curie was appointed head of the physics laboratory at the Sorbonne.

Although Marie Curie was now recognised and appreciated by most academics as a leading scientist, not everyone was yet convinced of the value of her discoveries. Especially the eminent physicist Lord Kelvin, long a friend of Pierre Curie, publicly doubted her theory of radioactivity. In an open letter of 9 August 1906 to *The London Times,* he wrote, wrongly, as it would later turn out, that radium was not an element but rather a compound of lead and helium. Stimulated by this criticism, Curie, with the help of her befriended colleague André-Louis Debierne and after years of diligent research, succeeded in 1910 to place radium as a (separate) element in the Table of Mendeleev.

Following the death of her husband Pierre Curie, the Sorbonne faculty council unanimously awarded a chair to Marie Curie on 11 May 1906. She was also appointed lecturer. This made her the first female professor at the Sorbonne. In 1910 Curie wrote the two-volume *Traité de Radioactivité (Treatise on* Radioactivity) in which she recorded all the knowledge she had acquired about radioactivity. In the same year she succeeded in isolating radium. She also defined the unit of radioactivity, the curie, which was named after her and her husband Pierre.

Langevin affair
174

Despite her fame, she was not elected to the French Académie des sciences in 1911. In a fierce pre-election campaign, conservatives and Catholics had portrayed the liberal Curie as a licentious atheist who could not be a true Frenchwoman because of her Polish ancestry. They even speculated that Curie was Jewish. In her place was chosen Édouard Branly, physicist and a pioneer of wireless telegraphy. Only 50 years later, a student of Curie, Marguerite Perey, was elected the first female member of the Académie.

In 1911, the year of her second Nobel Prize, Curie visited the cold laboratory of Leiden physicist Heike Kamerlingh Onnes. The purpose of her visit was to study the effect of low temperatures on radioactivity. The radium preparation she took with her is still in the possession of Rijksmuseum Boerhaave. In that same year she took part, together with the French physicist Paul Langevin, in the First Solvay Conference in Brussels. Her relationship with the de facto divorced but legally still married Langevin caused a major scandal in the public opinion stirred up by the press. When she returned home to Paris, an angry crowd was waiting for her. In order to escape verbal and physical aggression she and her daughters sought protection with a writer friend, Camille Marbo, and her husband, the mathematician Émile Borel, who immediately offered her shelter. Once again she fell into depression and renamed herself Skłodowska. In the same year Albert Einstein wrote her a letter expressing his indignation at the way she was treated in France after losing the elections to the Académie and her relationship with Paul Langevin.

War years

After the outbreak of the First World War, Curie went to the war front in the Westhoek in the autumn of 1914 at the request of the Flemish battalion doctor Frans Daels and under the protection of her former lawyer, the French Minister of War Alexandre Millerand. With the help of "ambulances radiologiques" (vans equipped with an alternator and an X-ray machine; later called "les petites Curies"), which she designed herself, Curie, together with her eldest daughter Irène and with the support of the French Red Cross, examined the wounded soldiers in the field hospitals along the front line.

Although around 1930 the daily management of the Radium Institute was taken over by her daughter Irène, Curie remained its director until her death. She died in 1934 in the French sanatorium Sancellemoz at the age of 66 from leukemia, almost certainly caused by exposure to enormous doses of radiation through her work. She was buried next to her husband in Sceaux. In 1995, the remains of Pierre and Marie Curie were transferred to the Panthéon.

Work

Initially Maria Skłodowska studied steel for a metal company, her only research that did not involve radioactivity. In December 1895 her attention shifted when Wilhelm Röntgen discovered X-rays. Shortly thereafter, Frenchman Henri Becquerel discovered that minerals containing uranium also gave off an unknown radiation. To investigate whether other materials possessed the same property, Marie tested all kinds of possible substances she could obtain. She found that thorium, the second heaviest element after uranium, was also radioactive.

She studied radioactive materials, in particular uranium ore, also known as uraninite or pitchblende. pitchblende was found to be more radioactive than the uranium and thorium extracted from it, even though no other radioactive elements were known to exist. The logical explanation was that pitchblende must contain traces of another, unknown, radioactive substance, which produced much more radiation than uranium. However, the radioactive substance in pitchblende was so small that it eluded any chemical analysis and could only be detected thanks to Pierre Curie's sensitive electrometer.

Marie obtained permission from the college to set up a primitive laboratory behind the school in an old, unheated barn. Pierre and Marie Curie applied various chemical separation techniques to the pitchblende, proceeding only with the residue that showed the strongest radiation activity. Through several years of tireless work, they finally isolated two new chemical elements from several tons of ore.

The first element was named polonium after Marie's homeland and the second radium, because of its intense radioactivity. Marie regretted afterwards that polonium was much less applied than radium. The couple received the Davy Medal in 1903 and the Matteucci Medal in 1904. Especially for her work the Institut du Radium in Paris was completed in 1914.

Nobel Prizes

176

Together with Becquerel, the Curie couple received the Nobel Prize for Physics in 1903. Marie's poor health prevented Marie and Pierre Curie from receiving the prize in person.

Eight years later Marie Curie again received the Nobel Prize in Chemistry, this time undivided, "in recognition of her services to the advancement of chemistry by the discovery of the elements radium and polonium, by the isolation of radium and the study of the nature and composition of this remarkable element".

Marie Curie was the first woman to receive a Nobel Prize and one of four people to ever win two Nobel Prizes (the others were Linus Pauling, John Bardeen and Frederick Sanger) and one of two people to win Nobel Prizes in two disciplines (Linus Pauling was the other).

Posthumous recognition

In 1995 Curie was the first woman to be interred in the Panthéon in Paris on her own merits. During a period of hyperinflation, her image appeared on the Polish banknotes of 20,000 zloty. Together with her husband she was depicted on the 500 French franc note; also in 1997 a gold coin of 500 francs was minted with a depiction of the Curie couple on the obverse and a pestle and mortar on the reverse with the text *Ra 226,0*, a reference to the isotope 22688Ra. A unit for radioactivity, the curie, is based on this isotope. Nowadays physicists hardly ever use the unit *curie,* but the becquerel is used instead. The element curium (Cm) is also named after the couple.

Around 1995, the archives containing all the notes and writings of Marie and Pierre Curie were donated by their descendants to the *Bibliothèque nationale* in Paris. Since these documents were in almost constant contact with the radioactive materials in Curie's laboratory, they first had to be thoroughly cleaned. However, this did not rule out the possibility that radioactivity still posed a problem; visitors wishing to consult them had to sign a paper declaring that they would bear the health risks for themselves.

Highlights

- Marie Curie was a Polish-born French physicist, famous for her work on radioactivity and twice a winner of the Nobel Prize.

177

- With Henri Becquerel and her husband, Pierre Curie, she was awarded the 1903 Nobel Prize for Physics.
- She was the sole winner of the 1911 Nobel Prize for Chemistry.
- Marie Curie was the first woman to win a Nobel Prize, and she is the only woman to win the award in two different fields.

7. Sacagawea (1788?-1812?)

Native American interpreter and guide

*"Amazing the things you find when you bother to search
for them."*

Sacagawea (Lemhi County, circa 1788 - Fort Lisa (Nebraska), December 1812), also called *Sacajawea* and *Sakakawea*, was a Native American woman of the Shoshone tribe. Her husband and she were recruited from Fort Mandan for Lewis and Clark's expedition. They accompanied this expedition as interpreters and guides while exploring the western part of the United States. She became a symbol of women's emancipation in the United States and her image has been on the obverse of one of the current one US dollar coins since 2000.

Biography

Sacagawea was born as Shoshone. When she was about twelve, she was kidnapped by members of the neighboring Hidatsa tribe. A year later she married French explorer Toussaint Charbonneau. Her husband was hired in 1804 as an interpreter by Meriwether Lewis and William Clark for their expedition, with which Sacagawea also accompanied. By the end of 1805

179

they reached the Pacific Ocean. In September 1806, the expedition came to an end in Saint Louis.

After the expedition was over, Sacagawea and her husband lived with the Hidatsa for three years. After this they settled with the settlers. She probably died of diphtheria at Fort Lisa (Nebraska) on the Missouri River in 1812 when she was about 25 years old. However, there is also evidence that she returned to the Shoshone on the Wind River reservation, where she is believed to have died in 1884.

Highlights

- Sacagawea, also spelled Sacajawea, translates into "Bird Woman."
- Enslaved and taken to their Knife River earth-lodge villages near present-day Bismarck, North Dakota, she was purchased by French Canadian fur trader Toussaint Charbonneau and became one of his plural wives about 1804.
- Sacagawea was not the guide for the expedition, as some have erroneously portrayed her; nonetheless, she recognized landmarks in southwestern Montana and informed Clark that Bozeman Pass was the best route between the Missouri and Yellowstone rivers on their return journey.

8. Ruby Bridges (born 1954)

American civil rights activist

"Racism is a grown-up disease, and we should stop using our kids to spread it."

Ruby Nell Bridges (b. September 8, 1954) was the first black student admitted to the William Frantz Public School in New Orleans, an elementary school with only white students.

Biography

Ruby Nell Bridges was born in Tylertown, Mississippi, the first daughter of Aborn and Lucille Bridges. When Ruby was four years old the family moved to New Orleans, Louisiana. Her father went to work as a clerk in a gas station and her mother worked nights to support the family.

End of segregation in the South

By court order, New Orleans schools were required to admit black students in 1960. This was intended to promote the integration of black children into white schools. A test determined whether or not black children would be admitted. Ruby passed this test, along with five other children.Of the six children, two stayed at their old school, three went to

Mc Donaugh, Ruby was the only one to go to William Frantz Public School.Ruby's father hesitated to send his daughter to the school, her mother saw it as a big step forward for all black children and was able to convince her husband.

First day of school

Attempts were made to stop the court order in any way possible. As a result, Ruby missed the start of the school year in her new school. It wasn't until November 14, 1960 that she traded in her old school for William Frantz Public School.On that day Ruby and her mother, under escort of US marshals, stepped into William Frantz for the first time. At the school gate they were met by an angry mob, people shouting racist slogans. Ruby later said that the crowd and noise reminded her of Mardi Gras.Because of all the commotion caused by her arrival, Ruby did not make it to her classroom. She and her mother stayed in the principal's office all day.

From the moment Ruby became a student at William Frantz Elementary School, white parents pulled their children out of school en masse. All teachers refused to teach a black student, except Barbara Henry (from Boston, Massachusetts). From the second day on, she taught Ruby, who would be her only student during that year.

Protest and its consequences

The huge protest did not stop at the school gate. A woman threatened to poison Ruby, preventing her from entering the school cafeteria and allowing her to eat only things she brought from home. She remained under escort of US marshals.

The consequences for the family were not long in coming. Ruby's father was fired. The grocery store where the family did their shopping no longer wanted them to do their shopping with them. Her grandparents, who had been sharecroppers on a farm in Mississippi for 25 years, were asked to move.

People from all over the country sent the family messages of support and gifts. One neighbor gave Ruby's father a job as a house painter. Child psychiatrist Robert Coles counseled Ruby during her first year at William

Frantz. Every week he visited Ruby at home and they talked about how things were going at school. By the end of the school year, the protest had largely died down and by September of the new school year, it had completely disappeared. Ruby then sat with other children in class, among them even some black children. It seemed that the difficult period of school integration of black children was over.

Family

Ruby married Malcolm Hall in 1984 and they had four sons. Ruby worked as a travel agent for fifteen years but after the birth of her children she became a full-time stay-at-home mom.In 2005, Ruby Bridges lost her home in the passage of Hurricane Katrina.

William Frantz

When Ruby briefly cared for her late brother's daughters and took them to school in 1993, the memories returned to her. She decided to become a volunteer in the school. Through the publisher of Dr. Coles' book, Barbara Henry found Ruby again. After many years they got in touch again. The William Frantz Public School was largely destroyed by Hurricane Katrina in 2005. The Ruby Bridges School of Community Services & Social Justice is rebuilding the school and will focus on equitable education where cultural differences are seen as an enrichment.

The Ruby Bridges Foundation

This foundation was founded by Ruby in 1999. The mission of the foundation is to draw permanent attention to tolerance and respect for all who are different. She herself says the following: "racism is a disease of adults and we must stop using our children to spread it".

Highlights

- Ruby Bridges, in full Ruby Nell Bridges, was the eldest of eight children, born into poverty in the state of Mississippi.
- Of the six African American students designated to integrate the school, Bridges was the only one to enroll.
- On November 14, 1960, her first day, she was escorted to school by four federal marshals.

- Bridges spent the entire day in the principal's office as irate parents marched into the school to remove their children.

9. Greta Thunberg (born 2003)
Swedish climate activist

Greta Thunberg (Stockholm, 3 January 2003) is a Swedish climate activist.

She became famous when she decided to strike every school day after the summer holidays until the Swedish parliamentary elections on September 9, 2018, and take up post outside the Swedish parliament with a protest sign to draw attention to the threat of climate change. After the election, she went on strike every Friday. In November 2018, she declared in an opinion piece in *The Guardian* that she would continue to do so until politicians would comply with the Paris Agreement.

Inspiration

In an interview with Amy Goodman of *Democracy Now!* and later on her Facebook page, Thunberg said the idea of a school strike first came to her after the Shooting at Stoneman Douglas High School on February 14, 2018, when a number of young people refused to go to school anymore. Shortly after she won a writing contest from *Svenska Dagbladet* in May

2018, Bo Thorén from the environmental group *Fossil Free Dalsland* raised the possibility of a school strike as a means of action. Greta liked the idea, but received little support from other members of the environmental group, nor from her parents. So she decided to go on strike on her own.

Greta Thunberg was discovered as early as August 20, 2018, the first day of her protest, by *We Don't Have Time*, a Swedish tech start-up led by CEO Ingmar Rentzhog, an acquaintance of her mother Malena Ernman. The foundation/company is committed to providing support for sweeping climate investments (Green New Deal) via social media. Greta Thunberg briefly joined the foundation's board as a special youth advisor. In February 2019, the organization *We Don't Have Time* admitted that they had used her name without the knowledge of Greta Thunberg and her family.

Activism

Greta Thunberg was regularly in the press for her sharp statements at climate rallies. During an action of civil disobedience in front of the UK Parliament on 31 October 2018, organised by *Extinction Rebellion*, Thunberg spoke of "an extraordinary and urgent crisis that has never been recognised as such, and our leaders are all acting like little children". At the November 24, 2018 TED conference in Stockholm, Thunberg stated "we've heard pep-talk and positive talk for thirty years. And sorry, but it's useless. Had it helped, emissions would have dropped by now - and they haven't".

At the Katowice 2018 Climate Conference, Thunberg repeatedly addressed attendees, accusing current world leaders of "stealing the future [of their children] where they stand" and "you are not mature enough to tell the truth. Even that burden you leave to us children".

On 23 December 2018, she was interviewed by Fareed Zakaria on the CNN program *GPS*, which normally features politicians, government authorities and diplomats. On January 23, 2019, she arrived in Davos, where she was invited to speak at the World Economic Forum. While Thunberg opted for a 32-hour train journey, 1,500 participants came here by private plane.

Greta Thunberg also served as a role model for the climate actions of schoolchildren (Truancy for Climate) in Belgium, Germany and Switzerland, in January 2019.

On February 21, 2019, Greta Thunberg came to Brussels to walk with Anuna De Wever, Kyra Gantois and Adélaïde Charlier, the Belgian figureheads of *Youth for Climate,* at the front of the seventh climate march on Thursday. Because of the massive press interest, the police had to intervene to protect the young people. In the morning, Thunberg addressed the European Commission in Brussels with President Jean-Claude Juncker. On Friday 22 February 2019, Thunberg attended the climate march in Paris together with Anuna De Wever, Kyra Gantois and Adélaïde Charlier, among others, and was afterwards received by French President Emmanuel Macron together with the Belgian and German delegations. Thunberg participated in the climate marches in Antwerp on 28 February 2019 and Hamburg on 1 March 2019 during a week of school holidays in Sweden. As Thunberg was invited to Berlin for the *Goldene Kamera gala*, she also attended the *Fridays for Future protest* on Friday 29 March, where she addressed the approximately 20,000 participants under the Brandenburg Gate.

On Tuesday, April 16, 2019, Thunberg addressed the Environment Committee of the European Parliament in Strasbourg. A mural of Thunberg by artist Encq, also known as Henk De Ruddere, was painted in the Vlier neighbourhood in the centre of Brussels. On Wednesday, April 17, 2019, Thunberg had a brief meeting in St. Peter's Square in Rome with Pope Francis who encouraged her to continue. On Thursday, Thunberg was invited along with other organizers of the climate strikes (including Anuna De Wever) to speak before the Italian Parliament and on Friday she walked with the school strike for climate in Rome, where she addressed the 25,000 participants in Piazza del Popolo. Thunberg then traveled on by train to London, where on Sunday, April 21, she addressed the activists of the Extinction Rebellion movement who had been campaigning in London for eight days. On April 23, 2019, Thunberg gave a speech at the British Parliament.

In the summer of 2019, Thunberg announced that she would be taking a year off from school (in Sweden, school is compulsory until sixteen) and in August 2019 Thunberg sailed across the Atlantic from the English port city of Plymouth to New York in the Malizia II, an eighteen-metre sailing yacht, type IMOCA 60-single-hull vessel equipped with solar panels and underwater turbines. The voyage was announced as a CO_2-neutral transatlantic crossing as a demonstration of Thunberg's beliefs about the importance of reducing emissions. However, the voyage was criticised because it ended up emitting CO_2: crew members were flown over from Europe to return to the ship, but they were CO_2 compensated. The trip lasted 15 days, from 14 to 28 August 2019. Thunberg attended the UN climate summit in New York on 23 September 2019 and will also speak at the COP 25 climate conference in Santiago, Chile (2-13 December 2019). Upon her arrival in New York, she was met by hundreds of fans and climate activists including fourteen-year-old Alexandria Villaseñor (co-founder of *US Youth Climate Strike* and founder of *Earth Uprising*) and seventeen-year-old Xiye Bastida (one of the organizers of *Fridays for Future New York City*). For several weeks, the trip and the discussion surrounding it was in the news daily. On Friday, August 30 and Friday, September 6, she was on hand at the school strikes in New York for climate. On Friday, September 13, Thunberg joined several hundred activists at the school strike for climate in Washington in front of the White House, and on September 14 she was interviewed by Trevor Noah on The Daily Show.

On September 23, 2019, at the climate summit in New York, Thunberg, immediately after Secretary-General António Guterres addressed the United Nations General Assembly, called the world's ruling leaders and popular representatives to account in a sharp tone for their failure to act decisively against the climate crisis. It was also violently attacked by a series of think tanks and politicians who oppose a radical climate policy.

In an open letter, together with Adélaïde Charlier and Anuna De Wever on 1 December 2019, they announce that further actions will be taken to convince politicians to respond to the clear questions from the scientific community.

After the gap year, Thunberg plans to return to school in the 2020-2021 school year.

Recognition and awards

Thunberg was named "woman of the year" in Sweden in early March 2019, following a poll commissioned by Swedish newspaper *Aftonbladet*. *Expressen*, another Swedish newspaper, also previously named Thunberg woman of the year. On March 13, 2019, Greta Thunberg was nominated for the Nobel Peace Prize by three Norwegian MPs, Freddy André Øvstegård and two other members of the Socialist Left Party after she was also nominated by German politician Lisa Badum in early February. On 30 March 2019, Thunberg was awarded the *Sonderpreis Klimaschutz* in Berlin at the *Goldene Kamera gala* and on the same day she was honoured as Swedish Woman of the Year by the *Swedish Women's Educational Association* (or SWEA International, Inc.).

On April 2, 2019, it was announced that Thunberg was the winner of the *Prix Liberté* of the French region of Normandy, an award presented to young people working for freedom and peace. On April 12, Thunberg won the Norwegian Fritt Ords Pris together with the Norwegian environmental association *Natur og Ungdom*.

Wednesday, April 17, 2019, she met Pope Francis in St. Peter's Square. She invited him "to join the Climate Strike" written on a sign from the Laudato Si generation. He encouraged her to continue her action. She also spoke at the Senate in Rome and participated in a climate march there.

In August 2019, Thunberg received the *Game Changer Of The Year award* from British magazine GQ. On September 16, Thunberg (along with *Fridays for Future*) received Amnesty International's *Ambassador* of Conscience Award in Washington from the hands of Kumi Naidoo, secretary general of the human rights organization.She was also awarded the Right Livelihood Award in 2019.

In 2019, a beetle was named after her, the *Nelloptodes gretae*. In 2020, a snail also received a reference to Thunberg in its name: *Craspedotropis gretathunbergae*.

She also received the annual environmental prize in 2019 from the Nordic Council, which promotes cooperation between the Danish, Finnish and Swedish parliaments. She turned down the cash prize of 350,000 Danish kroner (about 46,800 euros), immediately stating that, despite good efforts for climate and environment, the Nordic region is energy hungry.

On November 20, 2019, Thunberg received the International Children's Peace Prize along with Divina Maloum. She was unable to receive the award herself because she was in the process of crossing from the United

States to Europe by sailboat on her way to the Madrid 2019 Climate Conference.

On December 11, 2019, Thunberg was named *2019 Person of the Year* by Time magazine.

In 2020, Thunberg received a million euro award from the Calouste Gulbenkian Foundation in Lisbon and promised to donate it to charities as soon as possible, starting with 100,000 each to the *Stop Ecocide movement* and the SOS Amazonia campaign of the Brazilian branch of *Fridays for Future*.

In 2021, the Swedish Post Office released a stamp with Thunberg on it, within a series on the environment.

Movie

In 2020, *I am Greta* arrived in cinemas, a documentary film. She is followed from her first day on strike at school to the moment she crosses the Atlantic by racing yacht with her father as a world-renowned environmental activist. In New York City she addresses the United Nations Assembly. The film won the science prize at the Zurich Film Festival 2020.

Family and private life

Thunberg's mother is Malena Ernman, a Swedish opera singer and participant in the 2009 Eurovision Song Contest. Her father is Svante Thunberg, an actor named after Svante Arrhenius, a cousin of his great-grandmother. Arrhenius won the 1903 Nobel Prize in Chemistry for his theory of electrolytic dissociation.

Greta Thunberg had a strong interest in the environment and science from an early age. To reduce her carbon footprint, she convinced her family members to eat vegan, consume and stop traveling by plane.

At the TEDx Conference in Stockholm in November 2018, she stated that she has been diagnosed with obsessive-compulsive disorder, selective mutism and Asperger's syndrome. She explains the doggedness of her commitment in part from her autism.

Highlights

- Greta Thunberg, in full Greta Tintin Eleonora Ernman Thunberg, was diagnosed with Asperger syndrome, which is now considered an autism spectrum disorder (ASD).
- In addition to her environmental work, Thunberg was credited with raising awareness about Asperger's and inspiring those who had the disorder.
- While acknowledging that Asperger's had hampered her in some ways, she also noted its advantages, at one point tweeting, "I have Aspergers and that means I'm sometimes a bit different from the norm. And-given the right circumstances-being different is a superpower."
- No One Is Too Small to Make a Difference (2019) is a collection of her speeches.
- The documentary I Am Greta appeared in 2020.

10.   Jane Goodall (born 1934)
British primatologist, ethologist, and anthropologist

"The least I can do is speak out for those who cannot speak for themselves."

Valerie Jane Morris-Goodall (London, 3 April 1934) is an English anthropologist and biologist specializing in ethology and primatology. She is best known for her 60-year study of the social and family life of the chimpanzee, which she studied in the Gombe Stream National Park in Tanzania. She is the founder of the Jane Goodall Institute and the youth program Roots & Shoots.

Lifecycle

Goodall was the first child of Mortimer Herbert Morris-Goodall and Margaret Myfanwe 'Vanne' Joseph. Her sister Judy was born in 1938. After her parents' divorce, both sisters lived with their mother in Bournemouth, England.

Goodall had been interested in animals since childhood. After a secretarial training, she worked as a secretary for the anthropologist Louis Leakey in Kenya in 1957 and 1958. Because of her fondness for animals, Leakey asked her to contribute to his research on human evolution. This led Goodall to start studying the chimpanzees of Gombe Stream National

Park from July 1960. This study continued for sixty years and is now the longest running study of wild chimpanzees in the world.

Leakey also arranged for Goodall to return to the United Kingdom, where she earned her doctorate in ethology from Newnham College of the University of Cambridge in 1965. She accomplished this without ever having studied before.

Goodall married twice: the first time in 1964 to wildlife photographer Hugo van Lawick. They divorced in 1974. Their son Grub was born in 1967. Then Goodall married Derek Bryceson, a member of Tanzania's parliament. Bryceson was director of Tanzania's national parks from the mid-1970s until his death in 1980.

Scientific contribution

One of Goodall's greatest contributions was the discovery that chimpanzees make and use tools. Some chimpanzees use twigs and branches to catch termites. The twigs are inserted into holes where termites are. The twig is then covered with termites, and withdrawn and eaten by the chimpanzee. Until this discovery, it was thought that only humans used tools.

She also discovered that chimpanzees sometimes eat meat, hunt together and wage war with other ape species and groups of chimpanzees.

In contrast to the then common practice of assigning numbers, Goodall gave names to animals. This humanisation represented a break with the scientific tradition of the time, which was very suspicious of descriptions of chimpanzee behaviour in terms of human drives and emotions. However, her approach proved very fruitful and is now widely used by ethologists.

Jane Goodall is committed to the great apes and the preservation of the great apes (the so-called Great Ape Project). She has been ambassador for the United Nations since 2002. She was appointed lady commander of the Order of the British Empire (DBE) at a ceremony at Buckingham Palace in 2004. In January 2006, Goodall received UNESCO's 60th Anniversary Medal for her efforts.

Films and many documentaries have been made about her and her work. There is also an orchid named after her: *Dendrobium goodallianum.*

Jane Goodall Institute

In 1977 Goodall founded the Jane Goodall Institute. The institute now exists in more than 30 countries and is dedicated to the sustainable protection of chimpanzees and their habitats. The Jane Goodall Institute always works together with local communities in Africa.

Public performance

Jane Goodall gave a presentation at the March 2007 TED meeting about the great similarities and small differences between humans and great apes. TED is one of the meetings that Goodall values highly. She also gives her public lectures at many other places and times, such as at the Commonwealth Club, at various (international) universities, nature reserves and of course her own Jane Goodall Institute.

Goodall also regularly speaks out about the negative impact of humans on nature and the climate. Her own institute is dedicated to the sustainable coexistence of man and nature.

Highlights

- Jane Goodall, in full Dame Jane Goodall, was interested in animal behavior from an early age, left school at age 18.
- She worked as a secretary and as a film production assistant until she gained passage to Africa. Once there, Goodall began assisting palaeontologist and anthropologist Louis Leakey.
- The University of Cambridge in 1965 awarded Goodall a Ph.D. in ethology; she was one of very few candidates to receive a Ph.D. without having first possessed an A.B. degree.
- Goodall wrote a number of books and articles about various aspects of her work, notably In the Shadow of Man (1971).
- Goodall continued to write and lecture about environmental and conservation issues into the early 21st century.

11.   Mary Seacole (1805-1881)

Nurse and a heroine of the Crimean War

"Unless I am allowed to tell the story of my life in my own way, I cannot tell it at all."

Mary Jane Seacole (Kingston, 1805 - London, 14 May 1881) was a Jamaican writer and nurse during the Crimean War.

Life in the Caribbean

Mary Jane Seacole was born in Kingston the daughter of Scottish soldier James Grant and a free Jamaican woman. Her mother was a healer who was familiar with Caribbean and African healing methods. From her mother she learned the profession of nursing. In 1821, she made her first visit to the city of London, only to return to Jamaica after four years where she started working alongside her mother again. In 1836 she married Edwin Horatio Hamilton Seacole, according to the biographer of Mary Seacole, Jane Robinson, he was an illegitimate child of the British naval hero Horatio Nelson.

In 1851 Mary Seacole traveled to Panama, then part of New Granada, where her half-brother lived. Shortly after her arrival, an epidemic of cholera struck the place where her brother lived. She successfully nursed the sick there and after a year returned to Jamaica and then after two years returned to Panama to settle her affairs there. Before leaving, she heard the news about the Crimean War that had broken out and decided to volunteer to work as a nurse there.

Crimean War

Using her own funds, she traveled to the Crimea. In London she formed a partnership with Thomas Day, bought supplies there, and traveled to Constantinople. During a stopover on the island of Malta, Seacole met a doctor who had just returned from the front and he wrote her a letter of recommendation for Florence Nightingale. She then travelled on to the British bridgehead at Balaklava.

Using driftwood and iron plates, she built her British Hotel at Kadikoi, five kilometers from Sebastopol. From this place, Seacole treated her patients. She also often went to the front as a marketeer to sell goods to the soldiers. She continued her work after the fall of Sebastopol. When the Treaty of Paris was signed in 1856 and the troops left the peninsula, Mary Seacole was the last to leave the region. She had consumed much of her financial resources during her time in the Crimea.

Later life

After the war she returned to London where she was declared bankrupt in August 1856. A fund was set up for her on which many donated and a large festival was held at the Royal Surrey Gardens to raise money. In 1860 Mary Seacole converted to Catholicism and returned to Jamaica. When she returned to the capital of the British Empire ten years later, there were rumours that she wanted to take up medical aid on the front lines of the Franco-German War. In 1872 she became the personal masseuse of the Princess of Wales, Alexandra of Denmark, who suffered from rheumatism, among other ailments. Seacole died of apoplexy at her home in 1881 and was buried in St Mary's Catholic Cemetery in Kensal Green.

Highlights

- In 1836 Mary Grant married Edwin Horatio Seacole, and during their trips to the Bahamas, Haiti, and Cuba she augmented her knowledge of local medicines and treatments.
- After her husband's death in 1844, she gained further nursing experience during a cholera epidemic in Panama, and, after returning to Jamaica, she cared for yellow fever victims, many of whom were British soldiers.
- Despite her experience, her offers to serve as an army nurse were refused, and she attributed her rejection to racial prejudice.
- In 1855, with the help of a relative of her husband, she went to Crimea as a sutler, setting up the British Hotel to sell food, supplies, and medicines to the troops.

12.   Jane Austen (1775-1817)

English novelist

"I must learn to be content with being happier than I deserve."

Jane Austen (Steventon, 16 December 1775 - Winchester, 18 July 1817) was a prominent English novelist whose work is now part of the Western literary canon. The form and dramatic content of her fiction forms a stark contrast to the reclusive life she led in reality.

Her realism, biting social commentary, and her use of free indirect speech, a hitherto little-used figure of speech, made her one of the most widely read and best-loved writers in English literature.

Lifecycle

Austen grew up in a close-knit family in the lower echelons of English nobility. She was taught mainly by her father and older brothers. She also learned a great deal through much reading. The unwavering support of her family was crucial to Austen's development as a professional writer. Austen continued to develop artistically as a writer until she was about thirty-five years old. All the while she was experimenting with various literary forms, including the epistolary novel, although she discarded that form again rather quickly. The only epistolary novel she wrote was *Lady Susan*. She wrote (and rewrote) three great novels and began a fourth. From 1811 to 1816 she achieved success as a writer with the novels *Sense and Sensibility* (1811), *Pride and Prejudice* (1813), *Mansfield Park* (1814), and *Emma* (1816). She wrote two more novels, *Northanger Abbey* and *Persuasion*; these were published posthumously in 1818. One novel remained unfinished because she died before she could complete it; the latter was eventually titled *Sanditon*.

Austen's works are a critical reaction to *sentimental novels*, a literary genre that was very popular in the second half of the eighteenth century. Her books are part of the transition to nineteenth-century realism. Austen's (essentially comic) plotlines point to the strong dependence of women at the time on marriage to ensure social status and economic security. Her books deal extensively with then-current moral issues, as did those of Samuel Johnson, one of the strongest influences on her work.

Because Austen had chosen to publish anonymously, her work brought her little personal fame and only a few positive reviews during her lifetime. Only after the publication of her cousin James Edward Austen-Leigh's book *Memoir of Jane Austen* in 1869 did this change. She became known to a much wider audience but it was not until the mid-twentieth century that Austen became widely accepted in academia as a "great English writer". In the second half of the twentieth century, knowledge of Austen's life grew and a bevy of fans calling themselves "Janeites" emerged. Her life was described and filmed, including the film *Becoming Jane* starring Anne Hathaway. The film *Miss Austen regrets*, starring Olivia Williams, focuses on her own love life (or what was known about it). Her books were translated into many languages, but television adaptations and film adaptations were the main cause of her popularity. In 2015's *Love Finds You in Charm (Ohio),* Amish girl Emma Miller reads Austen books.

Letters

Little information about Jane Austen's life has survived. Only a few personal letters and letters from her family have survived (only an estimated 160 out of 3000 letters). Her sister Cassandra, to whom most of the letters were originally addressed, burned most of Jane's letters and censored the small number that did survive.Other letters were destroyed by the heirs of Admiral Francis Austen, Jane's brother. Most of the biographical material written in the first fifty years after her death came from her relatives and reflects the subjective view of the family in favor of "the kind and quiet Aunt Jane." However, researchers have been able to find little other information.

Family

Jane Austen's parents, William George Austen (1731-1805) and his wife Cassandra (1739-1827), came from noble families of distinction. George had come from a family of wolf farmers who had risen through their profession to the lower ranks of the landed gentry. Cassandra was a member of the prominent Leigh family, a baronet from Stoneleigh. They married at Bath on 26 April 1764. From 1765 to 1801, so for much of Jane's life, Father George served as minister in the Anglican parishes of Steventon, Hampshire, and a nearby village. From 1773 to 1796 he supplemented his income by farming and by always teaching and boarding three or four boys at a time.

Austen's immediate family was quite large: six brothers (James (1765-1819), George (1766-1838), Edward (1767-1852), Henry Thomas (1771-1850), Francis William (Frank) (1774-1865), Charles John (1779-1852)) and one sister, Cassandra Elizabeth (1773-1845), who, like Jane, remained unmarried. Cassandra was Jane's best friend and confidante throughout her life. Of her six brothers, Jane had the best relationship with Henry, who later became a banker and, after his bank failed, an Anglican minister. Henry was also his sister's literary agent. Within his large circle of London friends and acquaintances were bankers, merchants, publishers, painters and actors, and he thus allowed Jane a glimpse into a social environment that would normally have remained invisible to her from rural Hampshire. Jane's brother George left home at an early age and lived with a local family because, as biographer Le Faye describes, George was "mentally abnormal" and "subject to seizures". He was also possibly deaf. Charles and Frank served in the navy and both reached the rank of admiral. Edward was adopted by his cousin Thomas Knight; he inherited his estate and also took his name in 1812.

Highlights

200

- The earliest of her novels published during her lifetime, Sense and Sensibility, was begun about 1795 as a novel-in-letters called "Elinor and Marianne," after its heroines. Meanwhile, in 1811 Austen had begun Mansfield Park, which was finished in 1813 and published in 1814.
- Of all Austen's novels, Emma is the most consistently comic in tone.
- The enduring popularity of Austen's books can be seen in the numerous film and television adaptations of her work.
- Pride and Prejudice was notably adapted into a 1940 movie starring Greer Garson and Laurence Olivier, a miniseries (1995) with Jennifer Ehle and Colin Firth, and a film (2005) featuring Keira Knightley and Matthew Macfadyen.

13.　Coco Chanel (1883-1971)
French fashion designer

*"The most courageous act is still to think for yourself.
Aloud."*

Coco Chanel (real name **Gabrielle Chasnel**) (Saumur, 19 August 1883 -
Paris, 10 January 1971) was a French designer of women's fashion and
the founder of the Chanel brand. After World War I, Chanel, along with
several contemporaries such as Paul Poiret, ensured that the highly
corseted figure of the fashion of the time was exchanged for more casual,
sporty women's clothing. Chanel is considered the most important fashion
designer ever. She not only made a name for herself with her clothing
designs but also designed jewellery, handbags and perfumes. Her
successful perfume Chanel Nº5 became an iconic product. Chanel was
the only fashion designer on *Time*'s list of most influential people of the
20th century.

Lifetime

During the tumultuous 1920s, Chanel was known as the "Queen of
Fashion. "Being elegant is not a matter of putting on a new dress. You are
elegant because you are elegant." In 1918, she acquired a building at *31*

rue Cambon in Paris. She opened her first "fashion boutique" in 1921, selling clothes, hats and accessories. Between 1921 and 1926, Chanel had a relationship with the poet Pierre Reverdy. In 1927, she owned five buildings on Rue Cambon, namely numbers 23 to 31. She was the one who invented the *Garçonne style*: she dressed women in sweaters and pleated skirts with a lowered waist and decorated their hair with cloche hats and hair bands.

Her great rival Paul Poiret, who before her created a furore with brightly colored creations, called Chanel's style *misérable de luxe*. She in turn punished his exotic collections by presenting a minimalist black evening dress, one of Chanel's most distinctive designs.

Chanel released her perfume Chanel N°5 in May 1921, one of the best-selling perfumes and, at the time, the first artificial perfume that did not make women smell like flowers. Chanel said of it, "A woman should smell like a woman and not like a rose."

In the 1950s she introduced the deux-pièce, known as the Chanel suit, and the shoulder bag 2.55 (after its introduction in February 1955). She was over seventy by then.

Her style was always different from the other big names in fashion, such as her contemporary Elsa Schiaparelli, with whom she was constantly at odds.

Chanel died at the age of 87 in a suite at the Hôtel Ritz in Paris. Chanel's view on fashion was passed on after her death through her fashion empire Chanel, thanks to couturier Karl Lagerfeld (1933-2019).

Collaboration

Chanel allegedly had a relationship with Walter Schellenberg, Major General of the Reichssicherheitshauptamt, during the German occupation of France. Hal Vaughan, in his biography *Sleeping with the Enemy: Coco Chanel's Secret War* (2011), wrote that Chanel collaborated with the German occupiers and that she had an affair with Baron Hans Günther von Dincklage, a German officer who was "held in high esteem by Adolf Hitler and Joseph Goebbels". According to the writer Franck Ferrand, who collaborated on the French documentary series *L'ombre d'un doute*, a document of the French Ministry of Defense would prove that Chanel, under code name *Westminster*, was spying for the Abwehr, the German Military Intelligence. Initially, according to Vaughan, Chanel would have done so to get her cousin André Palasse out of captivity. Later, she would have used her Nazi connections to recover ownership of her perfume Chanel n°5, which she had sold in 1924, from the Jewish Wertheimer family.

Chanel was arrested in September 1944, but was released after only a few hours. According to her through the intervention of "her friend Winston Churchill". She fled with von Dincklage to Switzerland, from where she only returned to Paris in 1953 or 1954.

In film

The film *Coco avant Chanel* (2009) tells the life of Chanel before she became famous as a fashion designer. She is played by Audrey Tautou. In the same year, the film *Coco Chanel & Igor Stravinsky* was released, based on the book *Coco & Igor* by Chris Greenhalgh. Part of the story overlaps with *Coco avant Chanel* and continues where it left off. Chanel is played by Anna Mouglalis.

Highlights

- Coco Chanel was born into poverty in the French countryside; her mother died, and her father abandoned her to an orphanage.
- Coco Chanel's elegantly casual designs inspired women of fashion to abandon the complicated, uncomfortable clothes-such as petticoats and corsets-that were prevalent in 19th-century dress.
- After her death in 1971, Chanel's couture house was led by a series of designers, with Karl Lagerfeld's tenure (1983-2019) being the longest and most influential.
- Chanel's shrewd understanding of women's fashion needs, her enterprising ambition, and the romantic aspects of her life-her rise from rags to riches and her sensational love affairs-continued to inspire numerous biographical books, films, and plays, including the 1970 Broadway musical Coco starring Katharine Hepburn.

 # Frida Kahlo (1907-1954)

Mexican painter

"I don't paint dreams or nightmares, I paint my own reality."

Magdalena Carmen Frida Kahlo y Calderón (Coyoacán, July 6, 1907 - there, July 13, 1954) was a Mexican surrealist painter.

Biography

Kahlo was born in Coyoacán, now a district of Mexico City. Her mother was the Catholic Matilde Calderón. Her father Guillermo (Wilhelm) Kahlo was a German Protestant. According to Kahlo himself, he was a German-speaking Jew of Hungarian descent, but that turned out to be a fabrication. He had six daughters, two of whom were from his previous marriage to María Cardena. He worked as a photographer, especially of architectural works and for the government of Porfirio Díaz, making a good living. After the Mexican Revolution, he struggled to make ends meet.

In 1913, at the age of six, Frida was stricken with infantile paralysis of her right leg. This was the source of a number of complexes that she would carry with her throughout her life. The only nude of her dates from 1930 and shows her sitting on a chair, her skinny leg under the other so that her disability is not noticeable. It was painted by her husband Diego Rivera.

When her father enrolled her in the prestigious National Preparatory School in 1922, she hoped to study medicine later. The students wanted to build a new Mexico that replaced the pervasive European cultural norms with indigenous culture and a more authentic "Mexicanism." Her later husband was in charge of one of the school's murals at the time.

On 17 September 1925 the bus in which the then eighteen-year-old Kahlo was riding with her lover Alejandro Gómes through Mexico City was hit by a tram. A piece of the steel handrail entered her body through her left side and exited through her vagina. Her ribs and hip were broken, her bad leg was broken in eleven places, her spine was broken in several places, and her foot was shattered. For months she had to stay in bed, encased in Band-Aids and bandages, fighting the pain. She decided to take up painting. Kahlo's mother had mirrors attached to her sickbed so Kahlo could paint herself. Despite the inconvenience of corsets and crutches, once she recovered she got back outside and sought out friends. The accident that broke her pelvis prevented her from bearing full-term children. One pregnancy resulted in a painful miscarriage.

In 1928, Kahlo joined the Mexican Communist Party (PCM).

On 21 August 1929, she married Diego Rivera, 21 years her senior, also a communist and already a famous muralist. His ex-wife, Lupe Marin, tried to disrupt the wedding party. Kahlo's sister Cristina confessed in the summer of 1934 that she was having an affair with Diego Rivera. Kahlo subsequently left Diego, but the couple remarried after a fierce struggle on 8 December 1940. However, the marriage contract stipulated that Kahlo no longer had to have sexual relations with her husband.

In 1951 she was quoted in the newspaper Novedades de México: "I have endured two serious accidents in my life; one in which a tram hit me.... the other accident being Diego."

In 1930, she lost her unborn child in Detroit, where Diego painted a fresco for the Detroit Institute of Arts. Her mother died in September. In the summer of 1932 she would have a second miscarriage.

Kahlo and Rivera had frequent extramarital affairs; Kahlo with both men and women. Among her lovers were the Japanese-American landscape artist Isamu Noguchi, the Russian revolutionary Leon Trotsky, who had fled from the Soviet Union to Mexico in 1937, and the Hungarian-New York photographer Nickolas Muray (1892-1965), who made a series of impressive photographs of her.

The couple was very active in the Communist Party. However, after they welcomed Trotsky into their home, both were expelled from the party. Kahlo remained politically active; just a few weeks before her death she took part in a demonstration against American interference in Guatemala.

Kahlo died in 1954, a week after her 47th birthday. She left a note saying 'I hope the end is happy and hope never to return'.

Work

Frida Kahlo's work is characterised by cheerful colours, which contrast with an alienating atmosphere. She did not shy away from controversy. In a painting in memory of the actress Dorothy Hale, for example, she depicted the moment of her suicide very realistically and in great detail. The furrowed eyebrows in her self-portraits are particularly striking. She paints from her fear and loneliness to overcome her pain. Kahlo left behind 143 paintings, 55 of which are self-portraits.

She was initially misunderstood or recognized only as the wife of Diego Rivera; in November 1938 she had her first solo exhibition, in the gallery of art dealer Julien Levy in New York. In 1953 she had her first exhibition in Mexico thanks to Cola Alvarez Bravo.

The classification as surrealist comes from André Breton, founder of the surrealist movement in art. Kahlo herself rejected this label, saying that she never painted her dreams, but her own reality. In January 1939 she travelled to Paris at Breton's invitation to exhibit her work. She did not like the surrealist milieu in that city, which she found bloated and unreal. When, with the help of Marcel Duchamp, she opened her exhibition on March 10, she won the praise of Wassily Kandinsky and Pablo Picasso. The Louvre bought her self-portrait *Autorretrato - El marco* ("the frame") and Vogue magazine placed her hand (with jewels) on the cover.

The following list includes Frida Kahlo's major painting works. It does not include drawings, studies and watercolors.

Memory and influence

The large house in Mexico City where Kahlo was born and died, known as the 'blue house', has housed the Frida Kahlo Museum since 1959. It was established on the initiative of Diego Rivera, who died in 1957.

In the 1960s, interest in the Blue House was limited due to foreign tourists. Her international fame grew rapidly from the 1980s, the major breakthrough being a 1982 exhibition at the Whitechapel Gallery in London dedicated to Kahlo and the photographer Tina Modotti. The Mexican government organized retrospectives in 1974, 1983 and 2004 in parallel with events in the United States, Japan, the United Kingdom and Spain; but the largest and most popular exhibition was that to mark her centenary in 2007.

About the life of Frida Kahlo in 2002 the movie *Frida was* made with Salma Hayek in the lead.

Frida Kahlo is still seen today as a symbol of feminism. Her free spirit was a model for women worldwide. For example, Kahlo categorically refused to shave her body and facial hair.

During her lifetime, Frida was largely in her husband's shadow. As recently as February 1933, the Detroit News called her the "wife of the master muralist [who] amuses herself with works of art." The highest price she ever received for a painting in her lifetime was equivalent to 400 American dollars. Today, Diego Rivera is best known as Frida Kahlo's husband. Her works are coveted and traded for millions of dollars.

Highlights

- Frida Kahlo, in full Frida Kahlo de Rivera, was born to a German father of Hungarian descent and a Mexican mother of Spanish and Native American descent.
- After suffering a miscarriage in Detroit and later the death of her mother, Kahlo painted some of her most-harrowing works.

- In 1943 she was appointed a professor of painting at La Esmeralda, the Education Ministry's School of Fine Arts.
- The Frida Kahlo Museum opened to the public in 1958, a year after Rivera's death.

15.   Mary Anning (1799-1847)
British fossil collector, dealer, and palaeontologist

"It is large and heavy but... it is the first and only one discovered in Europe."

Mary Anning (Lyme Regis (Dorset), 21 May 1799 - 9 March 1847) was an English fossil collector and palaeontologist, known for her discoveries of *Ichthyosaurs* and *Plesiosaurs*. She spent her life searching for fossils in the limestone cliffs of Lyme Regis, now known as the Jurassic Coast.

Finding fossils for work

Anning was born into a poor family. Her father Richard was a carpenter who collected fossils to sell to tourists. When he died of tuberculosis in 1811 Mary and her brother Joseph started collecting fossils fulltime to earn money. In the early 19th century fossil collecting came into vogue as it became increasingly clear that fossils could make important contributions to biology and geology. Although Anning was primarily trying to make money, she came into contact with famous scientists of the time, who bought the fossils from her.

Annings finds

Anning first drew attention to herself in 1811, with her discovery of an almost complete *Ichthyosaur*, a few months after the death of her father. The previous year the skull of the fossil had been discovered by her brother, and a storm had exposed the rest of the fossil as well. This was in fact not the first ichthyosaur ever discovered, there are descriptions of a find in Wales in 1699. Nevertheless, it was an important find, described in the *Philosophical Transactions* of the Royal Society. Anning would later find two other species of ichthyosaurs.

In 1823 Anning was the discoverer of a fossil of a *Plesiosaurus*, which was named by William Conybeare as *Plesiosaurus dolichodeirus*, but is not the holotype of the taxon *Plesiosaurus*. She also found a intact fossil of *Diapedium politum*, a ray-finned fish, described in 1828. In the same year she found the first pterosaurian outside Germany (*Pterodactylus macronyx*, later renamed *Dimorphodon macronyx* by Richard Owen), this fossil was probably the first fairly complete pterosaurian ever found in England. These are the three most important finds of Anning, who also made many minor fossil discoveries.

Significance for science and recognition

Although Anning sought her fossils to sell, she knew a great deal about them and was well aware of the scientific value of her fossils. She was an autodidact who was able to describe, draw and record the exact location of her finds without being trained. It was thanks in part to Annings fossils that biologists gained a much clearer sense of how species went extinct over the geologic time scale while new species emerged. This realization would lead to lamarckism and eventually to the theory of evolution.

Anning was recognized during her lifetime as an authority on paleontology. She was made an honorary member of the Geological Society in recognition of her work and received an annual annuity from the British Association for the Advancement of Science to continue her work. True membership of a society was not common for women at that time.

211

Mary Anning died of breast cancer at the age of 47.

Highlights

- News of Anning's fossil excavations made her a celebrity and prompted palaeontologists, collectors, and tourists to descend on Lyme Regis to buy from her.
- Mary Anning uncovered a pterosaur in 1828, which became known as Pterodactylus (or Dimorphodon) macronyx. It was the first pterosaur specimen found outside Germany.
- In 1829 she excavated the skeleton of Squaloraja, a fossil fish thought to be a member of a transition group between sharks and rays.
- Her excavations aided the careers of many British scientists by providing them with specimens to study and framed a significant part of Earth's geologic history.

16.   Amelia Earhart (1897-1937)
American aviator

> *"Women must try to do things as men have tried. When*
> *they fail, their failure must be but a challenge to others."*

Amelia Earhart (Atchison, July 24, 1897 - Pacific?, missing since July 2, 1937, declared dead on January 5, 1939) was a famous American aviator.

In January 1935 she became the first person to fly solo across the Pacific Ocean, but she is best known for being the first woman to cross the Atlantic Ocean as a pilot in 1932. She also made that trip solo. In 1928 she had already crossed the ocean as a passenger. Here too she was the first woman. Early July 1937 she and navigator Fred Noonan began what was to become the longest flight in the world. However, the final destination of the 47,000 kilometre flight was never reached. What exactly happened is still unknown.

In Sint-Denijs-Westrem a street is named after her.

Biography

Earhart was born the daughter of lawyer Edwart Earhart and Amelia Otis. As a child, Amelia was a *tomboy*; she climbed trees and hunted rats with a rifle. She also collected newspaper articles about women in men's professions. She completed high school in 1915 and from 1917 worked as a military nurse and as a social worker in Boston. In 1919 she began studying medicine at Columbia University in New York, which she dropped out of after a year, returning to her parents in Los Angeles.

Start of her career

In 1920 she was allowed to fly in an aeroplane for the first time. From then on she wanted only one thing: to fly herself. Her flying career began in 1921 in Los Angeles, when she took flying lessons from Neta Snook. Six months later, with savings and borrowed money, she bought her first plane, a Kinner Airster, with which she set an altitude record for women. In 1924 her parents divorced. She moved with her mother to the east coast and to please her mother she sold her plane and bought a sports car instead. Four years later, she bought an Avro Avian airplane and became the first woman to make a solo intercontinental tour flight. At the opening dinner of the Stevens Hotel in Chicago on May 2, 1927, she was one of the guests of honor and her accomplishments were highlighted. From then on she continued to improve her own speed and distance records, in competitions and in personal stunts promoted by publisher and publicist George Palmer Putnam whom she married in 1931.

First transatlantic crossing

After Charles Lindbergh made a solo flight across the Atlantic in 1927, Amy Phipps Guest (1873-1959) expressed interest in becoming the first woman to fly or be flown across the Atlantic. After coming to the conclusion that the crossing would be too difficult for her, she offered to sponsor the flight if it were to be undertaken by another woman. It was Captain Hilton H. Railey who called Earhart at work in April 1928 and asked if she would be the one.

The project coordinators, including George Palmer Putnam, asked her to accompany pilot Wilmer Stultz and co-pilot/mechanic Louis Gordon as a passenger. She was given the task of keeping the logbook on board. The trio took off on June 17, 1928 from Trepassey Harbour (on the south coast of Newfoundland) in a Fokker F.VIIb/3m and landed exactly 20 hours and 40 minutes later at Burry Port, near Llanelli in Wales. About the flight she said: "Stulz did all the flying, he had to. I was just luggage, like a sack of potatoes.", and added: "... maybe one day I'll try to fly it on my own."

In New York, Earhart, Stulz and Gordon were presented with a ticker-tape parade and hosted by President Calvin Coolidge at the White House.

Solo flight Atlantic Ocean

Her name became more famous in 1932, when she became the first woman and the second person to cross the Atlantic solo, exactly five years after Lindbergh. She flew a Lockheed Vega from Harbor Grace in Newfoundland to Londonderry in Northern Ireland.

On January 11, 1935, she became the first person to fly solo across the Pacific Ocean, from Honolulu (Hawaii) to Oakland (California). Later the same year, she flew solo from Los Angeles to Mexico City and back to Newark. In July 1936 she received a Lockheed 10E 'Electra', funded by Purdue University, and began her flight around the world to prepare.

> *"Please understand that I am very aware of the risks. I want to do it because I want to do it. Women should try things just as men have tried things. If they fail, their failure is only a challenge to others."* (Amelia Earhart, 1937)

Earhart's flight would not be the first flight around the world, but it would be the longest: 47,000 km, on a route around the equator. On March 17, 1937, she flew the first part of her flight, from Oakland to Honolulu. When she wanted to continue her flight three days later, she got a flat tire during take-off, causing her to do a ground swing. The plane was badly damaged and had to be taken by ship to California to be repaired, so the flight was cancelled. Earhart made a second attempt from Miami; this time she would fly west to east. Fred Noonan, an ex-Pan Amp pilot, would be her navigator and only company. They departed on June 1 and after several stops in South America, Africa, the Middle East and Southeast Asia, arrived in New Guinea on June 29. They had covered about 35,000 km. The remaining 12,000 was entirely across the Pacific Ocean.

Last flight

On July 2, 1937 Earhart took off with navigator Fred Noonan. Their destination was Howland, a small island with a length of several kilometers, 6 meters above sea level. Especially for the record flight a runway was constructed on this island. The island was 4110 km away. Their last position report and visual contact was after 1300 km, when they flew over the Nikumaroro Islands. A US Coast Guard ship, the cutter *Itasca*, was close to Howland to guide Earhart's plane to the island.

It soon became clear that Earhart and Noonan had little practical experience in using radio navigation. The frequencies that Earhart used were not very suitable for determining the correct direction and the reception of the messages she sent was very poor. The low-frequency transmitting and receiving equipment that the *Itasca* had used to locate the aircraft had been left behind by Earhart in New Guinea. After six hours of fruitless attempts to establish a two-way radio link, the *Itasca* lost all radio contact. A joint Navy and Coast Guard search yielded no trace of the airmen or their aircraft. Earhart's and Noonan's fate has been the subject of much rumor and speculation ever since.

Recent investigations indicate that Earhart deviated from her course after passing the Nukumanu Islands and flew unknowingly to a point 160 km north-northwest of Howland. Researchers generally surmise that the aircraft crashed into the sea due to lack of fuel. However, a research group from *The International Group for Historic Aircraft Recovery* (TIGHAR) claims that the plane made an emergency landing on the island of Nikumaroro (in present-day Kiribati) and that Earhart and Noonan eventually perished there. Research on the uninhabited island has yielded indications that support this theory.

Another theory states that Earhart and Noonan were captured by the Japanese when they made an emergency landing on the island of Saipan, part of the Mariana Islands. They were then allegedly executed on suspicion of espionage.

Hidden time error

A new quantitative theory using the theory and practice of navigational science in the 1930s leads to the conclusion that navigator Noonan, on the route from Gagan on Buka to the Nukumanu Islands, determined his position on the setting sun, using the bubble sextant in conjunction with preliminary calculations from *H.O. Pub. no. 208, Navigation Tables for*

Mariners and Aviators, which he took with him on all his voyages from the publication of the first edition in 1928. When, on the morning of 2 July 1937, he again determined his position at dawn in west longitude before starting the approach flight for Howland, he probably introduced by the use of the seaman's sextant a hidden time error, not of chronometers and watch, but of local hour angle of the sun. The cause was the difference in reference line: for a bubble sextant it is the artificial horizon at the centre of the true sun; for a seaman's sextant it is the horizon at the upper edge [at sunrise] of the visible sun. The deviation of the geographical longitude calculated from the observation was 16 km from the true longitude.

The course deviation for the approach flight was therefore three minutes and fifty seconds too early and when it was thought that Howland should be in sight straight ahead, the true position of the island was 26 km to port. As a result the aircraft did not come within the visibility circle and mainly due to inadequate radio communication and the failure of radio direction finding due to incompatible equipment on board the aircraft and on and near the island the target was missed. At approximately 20.17 GMT Earhart reported she was flying (at an altitude of 1000 feet) over "the" position line of Howland - 26 km to the west. The announced continuation of the radio message was not received, so it must be assumed that due to lack of fuel it was necessary to land at sea. A corresponding time follows from an investigation into the fuel supply on board and the fuel management. The navigation model used for the theory, in combination with the recorded radio transmission, yields a calculated landing site 203 km north of the equator and 300 km east of the Greenwich antimeridian, at 177 degrees 19 minutes west longitude and 1 degree 49 minutes north latitude, 137 km north-northwest of Howland's true position.

An article in the *European Journal of Navigation* in December 2011 showed that the flight range was 4410 km at most. It is therefore impossible that islands other than Howland and Baker could be reached. The last recalculated landing zone is at 117-10-W / 01-31-N, 100 km NW of Howland, compass 323 grad.

Searching for Amelia Earhart

In 2018, the American anthropologist and emeritus professor in the US, Richard Jantz, claimed that the bones already found and examined earlier in 1940 that were found on Nikumaroro, based on the data he entered into the computer from the notes of the doctor who had measured the bones at the time and the resultant result, had to be 99% certain to be those of Amelia Earhart.

 In July 2019, it was announced that Robert Ballard would lead an expedition to recover the plane. In August of the same year, the search actually began.

Highlights

- Determined to justify the renown that her 1928 crossing had brought her, Earhart crossed the Atlantic alone on May 20-21, 1932.
- Her flight in her Lockheed Vega from Harbour Grace, Newfoundland, to Londonderry, Northern Ireland, was completed in a record time of 14 hours 56 minutes despite a number of problems.
- Amelia Earhart's disappearance during a flight around the world in 1937 became an enduring mystery, fueling much speculation. Notably, some believed that she and Noonan had crashed on a different island after failing to locate Howland, and others posited that they were captured by the Japanese.
- Most experts believe that Earhart's plane crashed in the Pacific near Howland after running out of fuel.

17.   Emmeline Pankhurst (1858-1928)
British political activist

"I would rather be a rebel than a slave."

Emmeline Pankhurst (born Emmeline Goulden), (Moss Side (Manchester), 14 July 1858 - London, 14 June 1928) was one of the founders of the British suffragette movement. Her name is associated more than any other with the struggle for women's suffrage in Britain, particularly as she founded a number of organisations whose aim was to advocate women's suffrage. Pankhurst was married to barrister Richard Marsden Pankhurst (1834-1898), who fully supported her work.

Mrs. Pankhurst was appointed in 1894 as Poor Law Guardian, a kind of unpaid social worker. Her dealings with the poor strengthened her conviction that women's suffrage was indispensable in the struggle for social improvement. In 1903, she founded the *Woman's Social and Political Union*. The movement, which included her daughters Christabel and Sylvia, became known for its militant actions. Pankhurst's tactics to attract public attention often landed her in prison, but she received better treatment than most other prisoners because of her high status. On a few occasions, however, she was forcibly fed to end a hunger strike.

When World War I broke out in 1914, activities for women's suffrage were suspended because Pankhurst believed that nothing should stop her country's victory. She began campaigning for women to replace men in factories so that they could go to fight at the front. Throughout the country she made speeches. Supporters of the movement distributed white feathers - a symbol of cowardice - to all men who passed by in civilian clothes. In 1914 she also founded the international peace movement for women.

In March 1918, the British government began granting women the right to vote (the right to vote) in the United Kingdom of Great Britain and Ireland. Although the *Representation of the People Act* of 1918 only gave voting rights to women over 30, and then only with a property requirement , while all men over 21 were included, the suffragettes nevertheless saw this as a great victory. In November 1918, women over 21 were given the right to become members of parliament (passive suffrage), which meant that women could sit in the House of Commons without being allowed to vote themselves. In 1928, women in the United Kingdom finally gained the same voting rights as men.

Emmeline Pankhurst died on 14 June 1928 at the age of 69, a few weeks before her fervently fought for goal was reached on 2 July 1928. She is buried in Brompton Cemetery, London.

Highlights

- In 1879 Emmeline Goulden married Richard Marsden Pankhurst, lawyer, friend of John Stuart Mill, and author of the first woman suffrage bill in Great Britain (late 1860s) and of the Married Women's Property acts (1870, 1882).
- She founded the Women's Franchise League, which secured (1894) for married women the right to vote in elections to local offices (not to the House of Commons).
- From 1895 she held a succession of municipal offices in Manchester, but her energies were increasingly in demand by the Women's Social and Political Union (WSPU), which she founded in 1903 in Manchester.
- In 1926, upon returning to England, she was chosen Conservative candidate for an east London constituency, but her health failed before she could be elected.
- Pankhurst's autobiography, My Own Story, appeared in 1914.

18.   Anne Frank (1929-1945)
German-Dutch diarist

---

*"How wonderful it is that nobody need wait a single
moment before starting to improve the world."*

Annelies Marie (Anne) Frank (Frankfurt am Main, June 12, 1929 -
Bergen-Belsen, February 1945) was a German and later stateless Jewish
girl who became world famous for the diary she wrote during World War II,
while in hiding in the secret annex on the Prinsengracht in Amsterdam.
She probably died of typhus in Bergen-Belsen concentration camp in
February 1945. However, her official date of death has been established
as 31 March 1945. Her diary was published posthumously, and is one of
the most widely read books in the world. Because of her diary, Anne Frank
has become an international symbol of the Holocaust, the murder of six
million Jews during World War II.

First years of life

Anne Frank was born on 12 June 1929 in Frankfurt am Main (Germany),
the second daughter of Otto Frank and Edith Frank-Holländer. Her sister
Margot was just over three years old at the time. The Frank family were
221

liberal Jews and lived in a spacious rented house at 307 Marbachweg, on the outskirts of the city. While Otto worked for the family business, the Michael Frank Bank, Margot and Anne played with the children in the neighborhood. Some were Catholic, others Protestant or Jewish. They were curious about each other's celebrations. Margot was invited to the Communion party of one of her friends, and when the Frank family celebrated Hanukkah, the neighborhood children were sometimes allowed to join in.

Anne's parents were alarmed when in the summer of 1932 groups of the Sturmabteilung, adorned with swastikas, marched through the streets of Frankfurt am Main. Adolf Hitler's National Socialist German Workers Party (NSDAP) was the largest party in Germany, winning over 37% of the vote in the July 1932 elections. Six months later Adolf Hitler came to power in Germany. The Frank couple decided to emigrate.

From Germany to Amsterdam

In July 1933 Anne's father Otto moved from Frankfurt am Main in Germany to Amsterdam to escape increasing anti-Jewish measures by the Nazis. The fact that the Frank family's bank was in trouble due to the economic crisis was an additional motive. In the centre of Amsterdam Otto set up his own company, Opekta, a branch of the parent company Opekta GmbH, founded in Cologne in 1928. Anne's mother Edith Frank and her older sister Margot arrived in Amsterdam at the end of 1933, and Anne herself followed in February 1934 after spending time with her grandmother Rosa Holländer-Stern in Aachen. The family went to live at Merwedeplein 37-2, in a new housing estate in Amsterdam, where many rented houses were vacant due to the economic crisis and where many other German Jewish refugees settled. (Housing corporation Ymere bought the house in 2004 and restored it in collaboration with the Anne Frank House. In 2016 the apartment belongs to the Anne Frank House).

A carefree childhood

Margot went to the Jeker school (Jekerstraat 84), Anne to the Montessori school (Niersstraat 41), where she started kindergarten. The sisters learned Dutch and quickly adapted to their new life. Like her sister, Anne soon had a circle of friends, including Hanneli Goslar and Sanne Ledermann, who, like Anne Frank, had fled with their families from Germany to the Netherlands. Anne Frank grew up in a liberal Jewish family. The Frank family valued Jewish traditions and holidays, but did not follow all religious rules. On Friday evenings the Frank family was often invited to the Goslars' home for dinner. Anne's parents were very worried about developments in Nazi Germany, but did not let their daughters know. Anne's years were carefree. She played with her friends, regularly went to the beach with her family in the summer or visited relatives in Switzerland, and enjoyed skating in the winter.

Yet Anne noted that her mother was very somber in November 1938. On the night of November 9, 1938 Kristallnacht took place in Germany, a pogrom organized by the Nazis. Throughout Germany Jews were attacked, synagogues set on fire, some 7000 Jewish shops looted and many Jewish properties defaced. Two uncles on her mother's side eventually managed to escape to the United States, while Anne's grandmother Rosa Holländer joined the Frank family at Merwedeplein in March 1939. She died in Amsterdam in early 1942.

Netherlands occupied

After the German army occupied the Netherlands in May 1940, one anti-Jewish measure after another followed. From January 1941, for example, people designated by the Nazis as Jews were no longer allowed to visit cinemas. After the summer holidays of 1941 Anne went from elementary school to the first year of the Jewish Lyceum. From then on it was forbidden for Jews to attend non-Jewish schools. Her sister also went to the Jewish Lyceum.

German Jewish refugees, including Anne Frank and her family, were stripped of their remaining German nationality when the new *Reich citizenship law* came into effect on 25 November 1941. The family then became stateless. The Dutch nationality was never granted to her, as it is only granted to living persons. Her father refused the German nationality after the war and became a naturalised Dutch citizen in 1949.

Jews were increasingly banned from public life. Like other Jews in the Netherlands, Anne Frank had to wear a yellow star from 1 May 1942.

On 12 June 1942 Anne Frank turned thirteen. Her best birthday present was a red checked diary, in which she wrote her first sentences that same day: "I hope I will be able to confide everything to you, as I have never been able to confide in anyone before, and I hope you will be a great
223

support to me." Three weeks later, on July 6, 1942, Anne and her family went into hiding in The Secret Annex, after her sister had received a call the day before to "go to work" in Germany. The Secret Annexe was part of her father Otto Frank's business premises *Opekta* on Prinsengracht 263. The door between the front and back part of the house was hidden behind a bookcase. Staff worked in the front part of the house and in the stockroom, but only a few of them knew about the people in hiding: the four helpers, Miep Gies, Bep Voskuijl, Johannes Kleiman, Victor Kugler and Bep Voskuijl's father, who had made the bookcase.

Hiding in the Secret Annexe

The hiding place at the back of the canal house in the heart of Amsterdam was named "The Secret Annexe" after its location, which would later also become the title of her posthumously published diary. Anne Frank hid there with her parents and sister from 6 July 1942 to 4 August 1944. A total of eight people were hiding there: the Frank family, Hermann van Pels, Auguste van Pels and their son Peter van Pels (who served as the model for the Van Daan family in the diary), and later also Fritz Pfeffer, a Jewish dentist (who served as the model for the Dussel character in the diary). The Van Pels family and Fritz Pfeffer were acquaintances of the Frank family and, like them, had fled their fatherland as German Jews.

In the secret annexe Anne Frank and the other people in hiding had to be as quiet as a mouse during the day. Anne missed her friends and the fact that she could never go outside. During these years in hiding, her diary became increasingly important. In it Anne wrote about daily life in the Secret Annex, the fear of being discovered while in hiding, her budding feelings for Peter, the arguments with her parents and other hiders, and her ambitions to become a writer. "The nicest thing of all is that I can at least write down what I think and feel, otherwise I would completely suffocate," Anne wrote in her diary on March 16, 1944. The only piece of nature Anne could see from the secret annexe was a horse-chestnut tree in the courtyard garden. Decades later this tree would be known as the Anne Frank Tree. Anne filled up several notebooks. Following an appeal by Minister Bolkestein on Radio Orange in London on March 28, 1944, to collect diaries that could be published after the war, Anne decided to rewrite her diary on loose sheets of carbon copy paper while still keeping her regular diary. Anne wrote: "Of course they all rushed straight at my diary. Imagine how interesting it would be if I published a novel of the Secret Annex." In ten weeks she wrote 324 sheets, but because of her arrest she was unable to complete the book. Anne's last diary entry was from August 1, 1944.

Discovery

Three days later the people in hiding were discovered after more than two years (25 months). They were arrested on 4 August 1944 by the *Sicherheitsdienst* and Dutch policemen. SS-Hauptscharführer Karl Silberbauer was in charge. For a long time it was thought that the people in hiding had been betrayed, although it was not known by whom. In 2016, the Anne Frank House published the results of a new investigation, suggesting that the people in hiding may have been discovered by accident.

The diary papers (the notebooks and loose sheets) were found after the arrest on the floor of the secret annexe by two members of staff who were among the helpers of the hiders: Miep Gies and Bep Voskuijl (who was the model for Elly Vossen in the diary). Miep Gies hid them in her desk drawer, hoping she would one day be able to return them to Anne.

After they were arrested, the people in hiding and two other helpers, Victor Kugler and Johannes Kleiman, were taken to the SD building on the Euterpestraat in Amsterdam-Zuid. After spending some time in a room with other prisoners, Kugler and Kleiman were taken to the Detention Centre on the Amstelveenseweg. It was the last time the people in hiding (except Otto Frank, who survived the war) saw their friends. The people in hiding were taken to the prison on Kleine-Gartmanplantsoen.

Deportation

On 8 August 1944 the eight people in hiding were taken from the secret annexe to Amsterdam Central Station and deported by train. In the afternoon the train arrived at its destination, camp Westerbork.

Because they had not volunteered for 'employment in Germany' (in reality: mass destruction) but had gone into hiding, they were put in the penal barracks. Prisoners in the penal barracks were given less food and had to work harder than other prisoners. Their work consisted of dismantling spent batteries in the work barracks of barrack 56.

On Sunday morning, 3 September 1944, approximately one thousand people were deported by train to the east. The evening before, a selection leader came to the punishment barracks, where he read out the names on his list. The people in hiding from the secret annexe were also on the list. It was the last train to leave Westerbork for Auschwitz.

On 5 September the train arrived at the Auschwitz-Birkenau extermination camp. The eight people in hiding passed the infamous selection for the gas chambers. Then the men were separated from the women. Otto Frank, Hermann van Pels, Peter van Pels and Fritz Pfeffer were deported to the nearby Auschwitz I camp. Anne, Margot, mother Edith and Auguste van Pels stayed behind in the women's camp at Birkenau. After some time Anne contracted scabies. She was put up in the so-called *Krätzeblock* (scabies block), which was separated from the rest of the camp by a high wall. Margot went with her.

Death

On 28 October 1944, a transport of 1308 women left Birkenau for Bergen-Belsen concentration camp. Anne and Margot were probably among them. Edith stayed behind and died on 6 January 1945. In Bergen-Belsen, Anne and Margot were very weak and were taken to the sick barracks, where they lay next to each other. They developed a high fever. Margot died in February 1945 and Anne died a few days later, probably from typhus. In that period an estimated 17,000 prisoners died in Bergen-Belsen. There was no camp administration at the time, so the exact dates of Anne's and Margot's deaths cannot be traced. The Red Cross assumed in 1954 (nine years after their death) that it must have been 'somewhere between 1 and 31 March'. The official death certificate from that same year states 31 March 1945. In *The Diary of Anne Frank*, historians David Barnouw and Gerrold van der Stroom wrote in 1986 that Anne and her sister Margot probably died in late February or early March 1945. They were based on Lientje Brilleslijper's written statement of 11 November 1945, in which she gave "around the end of February, beginning of March 1945" as their date of death. Lientje Brilleslijper and her sister Janny had witnessed Anne and Margot's final period in Bergen-Belsen. Documentary filmmaker Willy Lindwer (*De laatste zeven maanden*, 1988) who interviewed Janny Brilleslijper also assumed the end of February, beginning of March 1945, as did biographer Melissa Müller and other journalists and historians. Later research assumed that a death date earlier in February is more likely. Her mother Edith died in Auschwitz in January 1945, due to illness and debilitation. Of the eight people in hiding in the secret annexe, only Otto Frank survived the Holocaust.

Diary: The Secret Annexe

Anne Frank wrote her diary in the form of letters to a fictitious friend Kitty. She wrote: "I hope I will be able to confide everything to you, as I have never been able to confide in anyone before, and I hope you will be a great help to me.

After the writer and her family were betrayed and deported, assistant Miep Gies kept the diary papers. Only Anne's father Otto survived the extermination camp. After the war, Gies gave the diary to the writer's father. Otto Frank published the book in 1947 under the title *Het Achterhuis (The Secret Annexe)*. Not only does it contain Anne's rewritten version, but Otto also added Anne's original diary entries from 29 March 1944. He also sometimes added sections that Anne had left out of her rewritten version. Since then, The Secret Annexe has become one of the most widely read books in the world.

The Secret Annex is a book based on diary entries.

Other literary works

Besides *The Secret Annexe*, Anne Frank also wrote 34 short stories about her school days, events in the Secret Annexe and fairy tales she made up herself, which are published under the title *Verhaaltjes, en gebeurtenissen uit het Achterhuis [Tales, and events from the Secret Annexe]*.

In 2004 the *Mooie-zinnenboek (Beautiful Phrasebook)* appeared. On the advice of her father, Anne copied fragments from the many books she read at her hiding place (in a notebook). These were fragments and verses that made a special impression on her. The book contains facsimiles of Anne's original manuscript and the printed text. The manuscript has already been exhibited in the Anne Frank House and abroad, but has never appeared in print before.

Several of Anne's poems have appeared, but have not been collected. Also to her name is the book *Verhaaltjes, en gebeurtenissen uit het achterhuis*.

227

Memorial Centres

The memory of Anne Frank is kept alive by various foundations and museums. In 1963 Otto Frank established the Anne Frank Fund, based in Basel. The Fund administers the copyright to Anne Frank's writings and is responsible for publishing the diary in various languages. The Fund supports projects worldwide in the areas of human rights, racism, discrimination and anti-Semitism, and is involved in the Bildungsstätte Anne Frank in Frankfurt am Main. The Anne Frank Center for Mutual Respect is active in the United States, with its headquarters in New York.

Highlights

- On June 12, 1942, Anne Frank, in full Annelies Marie Frank, received a red-and-white plaid diary for her 13th birthday.
- Friends who searched the hiding place after the family's capture later gave Otto Frank the papers left behind by the Gestapo.
- Among them he found Anne's diary, which was published as Anne Frank: The Diary of a Young Girl (originally in Dutch, 1947).
- The Diary, which has been translated into more than 65 languages, is the most widely read diary of the Holocaust, and Anne is probably the best known of Holocaust victims.
- The Diary was also made into a play that premiered on Broadway in October 1955, and in 1956 it won both the Tony Award for best play and the Pulitzer Prize for best drama.

16 Influential Women

1. Benazir Bhutto (1953-2007)

Former Prime Minister of Pakistan

"You can imprison a man, but not an idea. You can exile a man, but not an idea. You can kill a man, but not an idea."

Benazir Bhutto or **Bhoetto** (Karachi, 21 June 1953 - Rawalpindi, 27 December 2007) was a Pakistani politician. She served as Prime Minister of the country from 1988 to 1990 and from 1993 to 1996.

She was the eldest daughter of former Prime Minister and ex-President Ali Bhutto executed on April 4, 1979 and was a fierce opponent of former Pakistani President, Pervez Musharraf.

Shortly after an election speech for Pakistan's 2008 elections, she died as an opposition leader after a suicide attack.

Background

Benazir Bhutto was born in Karachi in 1953. She was the eldest daughter of former Prime Minister Zulfikar Ali Bhutto, who was of Sindhi origin, and Begum Nusrat Ispahani, a Pakistani of Iranian-Kurdish origin.

Early career

230

Benazir Bhutto was initially home schooled, then studied at Harvard University and Oxford University. After completing her studies, she returned to Pakistan after eight years in 1977. In March 1978, her father was sentenced to death. From prison, Zulfaqar Ali urged his daughter to pursue his political career. After her father's death, she and her mother, Begum Nusrat Bhutto, assumed leadership of the Pakistan Peoples Party (PPP). Soon after, both women were put under house arrest by President Zia-ul-Haq. Zia was the one who had deposed Zulfaqar Ali Bhutto and later had him hanged.

In 1984, Benazir received permission to go to Britain for medical treatment. She had a chronic ear infection and had become deaf on one side.

Resistance

In 1986 she returned to Pakistan, where the situation had become unsettled and resistance against dictator Zia-ul-Haq was growing. Benazir and Nusrat assumed leadership of the resistance and free elections were held after Zia-ul-Haq's plane crash (August 1988). These elections were won by the centre-left (Islamic socialist) PPP, after which Benazir Bhutto became prime minister. This made her the first female prime minister of an Islamic republic. However, the regime was characterized by corruption and nepotism. In 1990 she was dismissed by President Ghulam Ishaq Khan.

Government

After Prime Minister Nawaz Sharif was sacked in 1993, for the same reasons as Bhutto, Bhutto again became Prime Minister.

Her second government (a coalition between the PPP and the Muslim League), was defeated in the 1997 elections by the Muslim League of former Prime Minister Nawaz Sharif.

Emancipation policy

Benazir Bhutto was known as an advocate for the rights of Muslim women in Pakistan. During her election campaigns, she voiced concern over the lack of women's rights and denounced discriminatory practices against Pakistani women. To improve the position of women, Bhutto announced plans to establish police stations, courts and development banks for women. Despite these plans, she never proposed legislative changes during her reign to improve women's welfare. During her election campaigns she also promised to roll back controversial women-unfriendly Sharia laws, but her party never managed to deliver on this promise due to strong opposition from opposition parties. In 2008 she was one of the seven winners of the United Nations Human Rights Prize.

Money laundering investigation

Swiss prosecutors, after some twenty million Swiss francs were found in Swiss bank accounts belonging to Bhutto and her family in 1998, had been investigating her and her husband's (Asif Ali Zardari) possible money laundering of kickbacks through Swiss banks for years. In 2003 the two had been convicted in absentia but, having appealed, the investigation was reopened in 2004. Bhutto has consistently denied the allegations and claimed that the issue had a political background. In 2007, the judicial investigation was terminated due to her death. This termination did not apply to her husband.

Exile

Bhutto settled in Dubai in 1999 to avoid prosecution. However, her husband Asif Ali Zardari was arrested and convicted of corruption. He was released on bail in December 2004 after eight years of imprisonment.

Bhutto and Sharif, incapable of any cooperation under democracy, regularly called for the resignation of President Musharraf and the holding of free elections in joint statements since 1999. Both former prime ministers had drafted a so-called "Charter of Democracy," which would become their handbook for the next elections.

In 2007, Musharraf dropped corruption charges, reportedly in exchange for Bhutto's party's support in the presidential election, after which Benazir Bhutto returned to Pakistan on October 18, 2007. Upon her arrival, she survived a severe attempt on her life that left over 140 people dead.

On 8 November 2007, Bhutto was placed under house arrest by President Musharraf, officially to ensure her safety. In practice, the house arrest was

to prevent her from organizing a protest march against incumbent
President Pervez Musharraf.

Attack

A month and a half later, on Thursday 27 December 2007, Benazir Bhutto
was killed in an attack at the age of 54 after delivering an election speech
at a political rally of the Pakistan Peoples Party in Rawalpindi.

After Bhutto got into her bulletproof car, she stood up to wave to the
crowd. At that moment, a man shot her with a firearm. Then a suspected
accomplice blew himself up, killing at least 20 more people. Bhutto was
taken to hospital in Rawalpindi immediately after the attack. A press officer
stated that her death, at 6:16pm local time, was due to damage to her
cervical vertebrae from an entering bullet.

The body of Benazir Bhutto was interred in the family grave in Garhi
Khuda Bakhsh on December 28, 2007.

Aftermath

Immediately after Bhutto's assassination, riots broke out in several
Pakistani cities by angry supporters of Bhutto accusing the Musharraf
government of negligence and attempts to cover up the attack. The
assassination attempt shocked many politicians around the world and was
condemned with horror. A day later, on 28 December, the Islamist terrorist
group Al-Qaeda claimed responsibility for the attack. According to
Pakistan's Interior Ministry in Islamabad, an intercepted phone call from Al
Qaida proves that Baitullah Mehsud was behind the attack. However, it
has not yet been established with certainty that al-Qaeda is actually
behind the attack. Her son Bilawal Bhutto Zardari succeeded her as
chairman of the Pakistan Peoples Party.

Highlights

- Benazir Bhutto is a Pakistani politician who became the first woman
  leader of a Muslim nation in modern history. She served two terms
  as prime minister of Pakistan, in 1988-1990 and in 1993-1996.
- After her father's execution in 1979 during the rule of the military
  dictator Mohammad Zia-ul-Haq, Bhutto became the titular head of

her father's party, the Pakistan People's Party (PPP), and endured frequent house arrest from 1979 to 1984.

- Legally separate and free from the restrictions brought upon the PPP by Bhutto's leadership, the PPPP participated in the 2002 elections, in which it proceeded to earn a strong vote. However, Bhutto's terms for cooperation with the military government-that all charges against her and against her husband be withdrawn-continued to be denied.

2. Betty Friedan (1921-2006)

American feminist writer and activist

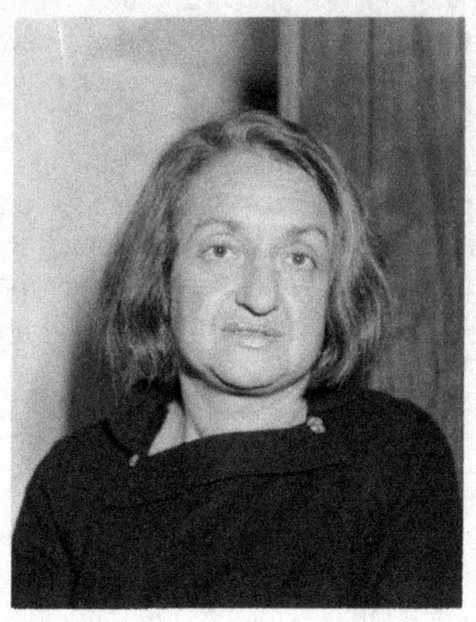

---

*"It is easier to live through someone else than to become
complete yourself."*

Betty Friedan, born *Bettye Naomi Goldstein* (Peoria (Illinois), February 4,
1921 - Washington D.C., February 4, 2006) was an American feminist,
social activist, and publicist.

Lifecycle

Friedan was an active Marxist and radical Jewish activist in her
adolescence. Even while on the campus of Smith College High School
where she was a student, she published her own newspaper. She studied
psychology at the University of Berkeley in California, but did not complete
that degree. Soon after, she became a journalist for leftist and union
newspapers. In 1947 she married Carl Friedan, whom she would divorce
in 1967. She died of a heart attack on her 85th birthday.

The Feminine Mystique

When she was pregnant with her second child in 1952, she was dismissed because of her pregnancy. In 1958 she met her former high school classmates at a reunion, whose life experiences she chronicled. Because she noticed how many of her female classmates' careers had ended prematurely, she wrote an article about them for a newspaper. She then decided to use the material as the basis for a book.

In 1963 she wrote that book, a seminal feminist work, *The Feminine Mystique*. The first printing reached 1.3 million copies and it became the best-selling book of that year. The book describes the role of the middle-class woman in industrial society: housewifery, and the numbing it brings, the *housewife syndrome*. This bestseller is widely regarded as the beginning of the Second feminist wave.

Activism

In 1966, Friedan founded the National Organization for Women (NOW) and in 1969, along with Bernard Nathanson and Larry Lader, the pressure group NARAL, which sought to eliminate the criminality of induced abortion in the United States.

Afterwards she remained active as a feminist until an advanced age, including as (co)founder and president of many women's organisations. Unlike Nathanson, she also remained active in the pro-abortion movement.

Highlights

- Bettye Goldstein graduated in 1942 from Smith College with a degree in psychology and, after a year of graduate work at the University of California, Berkeley, settled in New York City.
- The Feminine Mystique (1963), which explored the causes of the frustrations of modern women in traditional roles, was an immediate and controversial best seller and was translated into a number of foreign languages.
- A founding member of the National Women's Political Caucus (1971), she said it was organized "to make policy, not coffee."

- In 1976 Friedan published It Changed My Life: Writings on the Women's Movement and in 1981 The Second Stage, an assessment of the status of the women's movement.
- The Fountain of Age (1993) addressed the psychology of old age and urged a revision of society's view that aging means loss and depletion.

3. Grace Hopper (1906-1992)
Mathematician, computer scientist and naval officer

"Leadership is a two-way street, loyalty up and loyalty
down. Respect for one's superiors; care for one's crew."

Grace Brewster Murray Hopper (New York, December 9, 1906 -
Arlington (Virginia), January 1, 1992) was an American mathematician,
pioneering computer scientist, physicist, and officer (Rear Admiral) of the
United States Navy. Her credits include the first programs for the Mark I
Calculator and the first true compiler for a programming language.

Lifecycle

Hopper received her bachelor's degrees in mathematics and physics from
Vassar College in 1928; during her studies, she was inducted into the
academic society ΦBK (Phi-Beta-Kappa) because of her scientific talents.
She continued her studies at Yale and received her master's degree in the
same two directions in 1930. In 1934, she became the first woman in the
United States to receive a doctorate in mathematics. Her dissertation was

entitled *New Types of Irreducibility Criteria* and concerned hitherto unknown criteria of irreducibility. From 1931 Hopper also taught mathematics at Vassar; by 1941 she was associate professor there.

In 1943, she joined the U.S. Naval Reserve and was stationed in the computer applications research laboratory. There she worked with Howard Aiken on the Mark I Calculator. She was the first person ever to write a program for it. By the end of the war, she retired from the Navy, but continued to work on developing the Mark II and Mark III Calculator machines.

In 1949 she went to work for the Eckert-Mauchly Computer Corporation, coming on board just as the company was working on UNIVAC I. She was axed on that project. In the early 1950s, the company was acquired by the Remington Rand Corporation, and she was employed by them when she published her first work on compilers. Her compiler was called the A compiler, with the first version being A-0. Later editions were marketed under the names ARITH-MATIC, MATH-MATIC, and (especially) FLOW-MATIC.

Some time later she returned to the Navy, where she was employed to write validation software for the new COBOL programming language. The COBOL definition was established by the CODASYL committee, but was actually an extension of Hopper's FLOW-MATIC with some things from the COMTRAN language (IBM's FLOW-MATIC equivalent). Despite the wrapping up with committees and all sorts of other officialese, it is nevertheless certain that Hopper's idea was that a computer could be programmed in a language that resembled a natural language such as English and not in machine language or something very similar to it (such as the assemblers used at the time). It is certainly also defensible to say that COBOL was based entirely on her philosophy and insights.

Hopper swung back into the National Reserve in 1966, with the rank of commander. In August 1967, however, she was recalled to active duty for a period of six months - later converted to an indefinite assignment. In 1973, she was promoted to captain by Admiral Elmo R. Zumwalt Jr.

During the 1970s, she conducted research on standardized computer testing, primarily for programming languages and focusing (of course) on COBOL and FORTRAN. The Navy's testing program for the extent to which programs followed the standards in these languages led to a major

239

convergence of the various dialects of programming languages as offered by commercial parties. These test suites (as well as their management) were taken over in the 1980s by the National Bureau of Standards, now called NIST.

In March 1983, Hopper appeared on television on the program *60 Minutes*. There she was noticed by Philip Crane, a member of the U.S. House of Representatives. He filed a motion with the House to get President Ronald Reagan to promote her to Commodore, which was done by Special Order of Commander. In 1985, this rank was converted to Rear Admiral (lower half). In 1986 she (involuntarily) retired from the Navy.

She was then hired as a senior consultant at Digital Equipment Corporation, an appointment she kept for the rest of her life. Her primary activity in this job was as a kind of "goodwill ambassador." She was sent out on the lecture circuit and gave speeches about the early days of computers, her career, and what computer builders could do to make life easier for their users. She visited most of Digitals R&D facilities and normally received a standing ovation after her lecture. On these occasions she always appeared in uniform, in grand attire.

Grace Hopper died at the age of 85 on New Year's Day 1992 and was buried with military honors at Arlington National Cemetery. Until that time, she lived in Arlington, Virginia. On South Joyce Street, across from her home, is a small park now managed by Arlington County: the Grace Murray Hopper Park.

Highlights

- She became a lieutenant and was assigned to the Bureau of Ordnance's Computation Project at Harvard University (1944), where she worked on Mark I, the first large-scale automatic calculator and a precursor of electronic computers.
- She wrote the first computer manual, A Manual of Operation for the Automatic Sequence Controlled Calculator (1946), which described how to operate Mark I and was the first extensive treatment of how to program a computer.
- Grace Hopper's development of compilers for COBOL and her strong advocacy of the language led to its widespread use in the 1960s.

- Hopper retired from the navy with the rank of commander in 1966, but she was recalled to active duty the following year to help standardize the navy's computer languages.

4. Margaret Thatcher (1925-2013)

The first woman to become Prime Minister of the United Kingdom

When people are free to choose, they choose freedom

Baroness Margaret Hilda Thatcher, (Grantham, England, October 13, 1925 - London, England, April 8, 2013) was a British Conservative Party politician and the first female Prime Minister of the United Kingdom from 1979 to 1990.

Thatcher's father was a shopkeeper and mayor of Grantham in Lincolnshire. She trained as a chemist at Somerville College (Oxford University) and was a Member of the House of Commons from 1959 to 1992. From 1970 to 1974 she was Minister of Education and Science in the Heath cabinet. In 1975 Thatcher became the first female party leader of the Conservative Party and served as Leader of the Opposition in the House of Commons. In 1979 Thatcher won the election, defeating the incumbent Labour Party Prime Minister, James Callaghan. Thatcher thus became the first female Prime Minister of the United Kingdom. In the 1983 and 1987 elections, she was elected to a second and third term. In 1990

242

Thatcher resigned as party leader and Prime Minister and was succeeded by John Major.

In 1992 Thatcher was elevated to the rank of Baroness and thus became a member of the House of Lords.

Thatcher has been inducted into the following knighthoods in her lifetime: Member of Her Majesty's Honourable Privy Council - Member in the Order of Merit - Dame of Justice in the Order of St John - Dame Knight in the Order of the Garter.

Foreign Orders: Presidential Medal of Freedom - Grand Cross in the Order of Good Hope - Grand Ribbon in the Order of the Precious Crown - Grand Order of King Dimitar Zvonimir - Order of the White Lion, first class - Lady Grand Cross in the Royal Order of Francis I.

Origin

Margaret Thatcher was born Margaret Roberts in Grantham in the English county of Lincolnshire. Her father was Alfred Roberts and came from Northamptonshire. Her mother's name was Beatrice Ethel (born Stephenson) and came from Lincolnshire. She spent her childhood in Grantham, where her father had two grocery shops. Margaret and her older sister Muriel grew up in the apartment above the larger of these two. Her father was active in both local politics and the Christian church, where he served as an alderman (Alderman) and a Methodist lay preacher, respectively. Margaret was raised a strict Methodist. Her father came from a liberal family, but - as was common in local politics at the time - stood for election as an *independent*. He was mayor of Grantham in 1945-46. In 1952 he lost his position as councillor after the Labour Party gained a majority on Grantham Town Council.

High school and university

Roberts attended Huntingtower Road Primary School and won a scholarship to Kesteven and Grantham Girls' School. Her school reports showed that she worked hard and continuously improved; her extra-curricular activities included playing the piano, hockey, poetry recitals, swimming and walking. In 1942-1943, she was head girl (*headgirl*). In her senior year, she applied for a scholarship to study chemistry at Somerville

243

College, a women's college at Oxford University. At first she was rejected, but after another applicant dropped out, she was offered a place. She arrived in Oxford in the fall of 1943, where she earned a Bachelor of Science in chemistry in 1947 with Second Class Honours. In her final year she specialized in X-ray crystallography under the supervision of Dorothy Hodgkin. She was not in favor of admitting male students to Somerville College.

In 1946 Roberts became president of the Oxford University Conservative Association She was influenced at university by political works such as Friedrich von Hayek's *The Road to Serfdom* (1944), which condemned government intervention in the economy as a first step towards an authoritarian state.

Working life

After graduating, Roberts moved to Colchester, Essex, in 1947, where she joined BX Plastics as a research chemist. She became a member of the local Conservative Association. In 1948 she attended the party conference in Llandudno, representing the University Graduate Conservative Association.

Qualifying as a candidate for the House of Commons

One of her friends in Oxford was also a friend of the chairman of the Dartford Conservative Association in Kent. There, the Conservative Party was looking for candidates for the British House of Commons. Members of this Association were so impressed by Roberts' political views that they asked her to stand as a candidate. She was selected in January 1951.

Campaigns in Dartford

At a dinner after her formal acceptance as a candidate for Dartford in February 1951, she met Denis Thatcher, a successful, wealthy, divorced businessman, who dropped her off at the station to catch her train to Essex. In preparation for the election, Roberts moved to Dartford, where she supported herself by joining J. Lyon and Co. in Hammersmith as a research chemist. She was part of a team developing emulsifiers for ice creams.

In the February 1950 and October 1951 parliamentary elections to the House of Commons, she stood as a candidate in the Labour safe constituency of Dartford, where, as the youngest and only female candidate, she attracted media attention. Both times she lost to Norman Dodds, but managed to reduce the Labour majority by 6,000 votes in February 1950 and again by 1,000 in October 1951. During these campaigns she was supported by her future husband Denis Thatcher, whom she married in December 1951. Denis paid for his wife's studies to join the Bar; Thatcher qualified as a solicitor in 1953, specialising in tax law. That same year her twins, Carol and Mark, were born.

Member of the House of Commons

Following her experiences in Dartford, Thatcher went in search of a constituency in the mid-1950s where she was certain of a seat in the House of Commons. Roberts was narrowly rejected as a candidate for Orpington in 1955, but was selected for the Finchley constituency in April 1958. After a tough election campaign, she was elected to the House of Commons in 1959. Her maiden speech dealt with her bill ("Public Bodies (Admission to Meetings) Act 1960"), which required local authorities to hold their council meetings in public from now on. In 1961 she voted against the official Conservative Party position by voting for the reintroduction of "birching".

In October 1961 Thatcher rose in political prominence by being allowed to sit in the front row of the House of Commons from now on. She was appointed Parliamentary Secretary to the Department of Pensions and National Insurance in Harold Macmillan's government. After losing in the 1964 election she became spokeswoman for housing and land policy, promoting her party's policy of giving tenants the right to buy their housing association house. In 1966 she moved to the shadow Treasury team. As financial spokeswoman, she opposed Labour's compulsory price and income controls, arguing that these controls would produce unintended effects that would warp the economy.

Minister

In the cabinet of Prime Minister Edward Heath, she served as Minister for Education and Science from 1970 to 1974. As Education Minister she abolished the free supply of milk to primary school children. This earned her the nickname 'Thatcher the milk snatcher'.

245

Conservative Party Leader

In 1975 she challenged Heath as leader of the Conservative Party and won the leadership election. In 1979, as Leader of the Opposition, she won a vote of no confidence in the government of James Callaghan, who had made a pact with the Liberal Party, by a majority of 311 votes to 310. She won the subsequent general election and became Prime Minister. She was re-elected in 1983 and again in 1987. Since 1988 she has been the longest serving British Prime Minister since 1827. To be precise: she served eleven years, six months and 26 days. The United Kingdom was in bad economic shape when Thatcher took office. Industry was badly outdated, and ongoing labour disputes were preventing necessary renewal. Inflation was raging, and national self-confidence had fallen to a minimum. Her rigorous classical-liberal recovery policies, later named thatcherism after her, and consisting mainly of the privatisation of many state-owned enterprises, brought her into constant conflict with opposition leaders and Labour chairmen Michael Foot and Neil Kinnock.

Falklands War

Argentina, which had long laid claim to the Falkland Islands, attacked these British islands on 2 April 1982. Thatcher promptly answered the occupation with a counterattack. On 21 May 1982 the British landed at the settlement Port San Carlos. Seventy-two days later, the islands were recaptured. A total of 236 British and 655 Argentineans were killed. On the eve of the war Thatcher was the least popular British prime minister since the Second World War. Afterwards she was immensely popular. Thatcher took advantage of her popularity by bringing forward parliamentary elections, which she won in 1983.

Miners' strike

Emboldened, Thatcher began her plan to close dozens of loss-making coal mines. The miners' unions, led by the radical Arthur Scargill, organized a massive national strike in 1984. A winter of violent confrontations between strikers and police followed. Nine months later the mines closed.

IRA attack

Thatcher narrowly escaped an IRA bomb attack on 12 October 1984. At 02:54 that day a bomb was detonated at the Grand Hotel in Brighton, where she and many other leading figures in her party were staying in connection with the annual party conference in the city. At the time of the attack Thatcher was working in her first floor suite. Shortly before, she had left the bathroom, which was severely damaged in the blast. Five people were killed, but she and her husband were unharmed. Thatcher later indicated that if she had been in the bathroom when the bomb exploded, she would have suffered only cuts and bruises. Thatcher insisted that Congress would open at 9:30 that day as scheduled. In the afternoon at 14:30 she gave her speech.

Foreign policy

Although the United Kingdom had joined the European Communities, Thatcher was suspicious of any form of supranationalism and turned to the United States. She got on very well with the American president Ronald Reagan. She felt less at home in Europe. Her "I want my money back" led only after very tough negotiations to compensatory measures in the social field and in agricultural subsidies for Europe.

Thatcher's government supported the Khmer Rouge coalition after the Khmer Rouge was ousted by Vietnamese communist forces in 1979. During the Chino-Russian Conflict, the Vietnamese communists were on the side of the Soviet Union, while the Khmer Rouge was on the side of China. Support from the Thatcher government helped the Pol Pot coalition retain the official Cambodian seat in the United Nations. The Thatcher government also supported the Khmer Rouge coalition with money, food, and trainers. In 1991, the government acknowledged that the SAS had indeed trained some of the troops of the Khmer Rouge-led coalition. Officially, the British government supported only the non-communist parts of the coalition, but the Khmer Rouge benefited greatly from British support. Thatcher claimed that "*the more reasonable people of the Khmer Rouge will have to play some part in the future government.*" During its prior rule from 1975 to 1979, the Khmer Rouge killed an estimated two million people.

Poll tax

In 1990, riots broke out in the United Kingdom when Thatcher wanted to introduce an income-neutral tax, the poll *tax*. This led to her resignation: 247

the party wanted to get rid of her and several Conservatives challenged Thatcher for the leadership of the Conservative Party. In the first round of the elections for the presidency she won more votes than Michael Heseltine, who would become Deputy Prime Minister a few years later, but the difference was not large enough for her to be immediately re-elected. Thereupon Thatcher decided, partly on the advice of her husband, that stepping down was more honourable than being defeated. At her last cabinet meeting tears flowed in public for the second time: the first time was when her son Mark Thatcher went missing for six days during the famous Paris-Dakar car rally in Algeria. The leadership of the party and the premiership went to John Major, minister of finance under Thatcher.

After her political life

After her resignation Thatcher lectured all over the world. In 2001 she had to stop on doctor's advice. On 13 October 2005 she celebrated her 80th birthday with a lavish dinner for some 650 guests, including Queen Elizabeth II, Labour Prime Minister Tony Blair, singer Shirley Bassey and actress Joan Collins.

On December 7, 2005, she was hospitalized for one night for observation after she suddenly began feeling unwell at the hair salon. Her daughter Carol Thatcher announced that her mother's short-term memory was seriously deteriorating. Other sources reported that she might be suffering from Alzheimer's disease. This was confirmed in 2008 by her daughter Carol in her book: A Swim-On Part in the Goldfish Bowl: A Memoir'.

Following the death on 11 December 2006 of Pinochet, who had been politically instrumental in the Falklands War, she announced that she was saddened. In 2007 Thatcher was still sitting for the Conservative Party in the House of Lords as Baroness Thatcher of Kesteven.

In mid-2008 a controversy arose in the United Kingdom as to whether or not she would receive a state funeral after her death. Until now, this honor had only been reserved for Winston Churchill and members of the royal family.

On April 8, 2013, Thatcher died of a stroke at London's The Ritz hotel. She was offered a ceremonial funeral service with full military honours by the British government at St. Pauls Cathedral, which she herself had chosen as the venue. The funeral service on April 17 was accorded the

248

same status as that of Princess Diana in 1997 and that of Queen Mother Elizabeth in 2002. More than 2,300 guests attended the funeral service, including Queen Elizabeth II and her husband Prince Philip. A total of 170 countries were represented. Afterwards she was cremated privately.

Reactions to Thatcher's death, especially in the UK, were mixed. She was hailed as one of the finest leaders the UK had ever had, but there were also bitter reactions from working class and left wing critics who denounced her economic policies. Critics used a social media campaign to ensure that the song 'Ding-Dong! The Witch Is Dead' from The Wizard of Oz reached number two in the UK and number one in the Scottish charts. The action was termed tasteless and disrespectful by many, including Ruth Duccini and Jerry Maren who had sung the song in the original film. Thatcher supporters tried the same thing with the song 'I'm in Love with Margaret Thatcher' by the Notsensibles. The song reached 35th place.

In the very month of her death plans were announced to establish a museum and library in honour of Thatcher in London. The centre will be called *the Margaret Thatcher Centre* and will be housed at Buckingham University.

Highlights

- Margaret Thatcher led the Conservatives to a decisive electoral victory in 1979 following a series of major strikes during the previous winter (the so-called "Winter of Discontent") under the Labour Party government of James Callaghan.
- Thatcher entered office promising to curb the power of the unions, which had shown their ability to bring the country to a standstill during six weeks of strikes in the winter of 1978-1979.
- The second half of Thatcher's tenure was marked by an inextinguishable controversy over Britain's relationship with the European Community (EC). In 1984 Margaret Thatcher succeeded, amid fierce opposition, in drastically reducing Britain's contribution to the EC budget.

5. Kamala Harris (born 1964)

Vice President of the United States

---

*"I hope that by being a 'first,' I inspire young people to
pursue their dreams."*

Kamala Devi Harris (Oakland, California), October 20, 1964) is an
American politician and, since January 20, 2021, the 49th Vice President
of the United States. A member of the Democratic Party, she was the first
African-American, the first Asian-American, and the first female Vice
President at her inauguration. Previously, Harris served as San Francisco
prosecutor from 2004 to 2011, California attorney general from 2011 to
2017, and senator for California from 2017 to 2021.

Biography

Harris was born in Oakland on October 20, 1964. Her mother Shyamala
Gopalan, a Tamil, was a cancer researcher who had emigrated from India
to the United States in 1960. Her father Donald J. Harris migrated from
Jamaica in 1961. He taught economics at the University of California -
Berkeley. Harris identifies herself as Afro- and Indian-American.

Harris' parents separated when Kamala Harris was 7 years old, after
which Kamala and her younger sister Maya lived with their mother during
the week. They grew up in Berkeley. When Harris was 12, they moved to

Montreal, where their mother researched and taught. She attended school at Westmount High School until 1981.

Harris studied economics and political science at Howard University in Washington. As a student, she was active in debate club, student council and the African-American *sorority* Alpha Kappa Alpha. She demonstrated against apartheid and organized mentoring programs for local youth.

After graduating from Howard, Harris returned to California, where she earned a law degree from Hastings College of the Law in San Francisco in 1989. She was admitted to the bar and from 1990 to 1998 she served as a *deputy district attorney* in Alameda County. During that time, she was a couple with the 30-year-old Willie Brown, then the Speaker of the California State Assembly. Brown introduced Harris to his political network and twice assigned her to paid positions in 1994. In 1996, Brown became mayor of San Francisco and the couple broke up.

From 1998 to 2000, Harris worked for the San Francisco District Attorney (*District Attorney*), where she prosecuted serious crimes. From 2000 to 2003, Harris served as city attorney. In 2003, she ran to succeed her former boss as San Francisco's district attorney. Her campaign spent more than $600,000, more than ever before, and more than was legally allowed. After a turbulent campaign, Harris won the election with 56 percent of the vote. She was re-elected in 2007, as the only candidate.

California Attorney General (2011-2017)

In November 2008, Harris announced that she would run for attorney *general* of the State of California. She was supported by Senators Dianne Feinstein and Barbara Boxer and by Speaker of the House of Representatives Nancy Pelosi. In the primary she received 33.6 percent of the vote, the most of any candidate. In the general election, Harris ran against Republican Steve Cooley, then the Los Angeles District Attorney. She eventually won the election with 46.1 percent of the vote, 0.8 percent more than her opponent. On January 3, 2011, she succeeded Jerry Brown, who became governor. She ran for re-election in 2014 and stayed on until January 2017. She was succeeded by Xavier Becerra. Harris was both California's first female African-American and first Asian-American attorney general.

In September 2014, there was speculation that she was a candidate to succeed Eric Holder as *United States Attorney General*. Ultimately, President Barack Obama appointed Loretta Lynch to this post.

Senator (2017-2021)

When Barbara Boxer, a 24-year senator on behalf of California, announced she would not run for re-election in 2016, Harris was the first to run for successor. On January 13, 2015, her election campaign officially kicked off. Harris was immediately the frontrunner and received the support of both her party and the incumbent governor. She emerged strongest in the primaries and defeated her party colleague Loretta Sanchez in the general election in November 2016 with 63 percent of the vote.

Harris took the oath of office on January 3, 2017. In the Senate, she is affiliated with the Congressional Black Caucus, the Congressional Asian Pacific American Caucus, and the Congressional Caucus for Women's Issues. She serves on several committees, including the Budget Committee, Homeland Security and Governmental Affairs Committee, and the Judiciary Committee. In the first months of her tenure, Harris emerged in the Senate as an outspoken critic of Trump's policies and his ministerial choices. Harris did, however, support the decision to move the U.S. embassy to Jerusalem.

She stepped down as a senator on January 18, 2021.

Presidential Elections 2020

Shortly after Republican Donald Trump was elected president of the United States in the 2016 presidential election, there was speculation about a possible candidacy by Harris to defeat Trump in the next presidential election. In June 2018, she posted that she was "not ruling out" a candidacy. She would eventually officially announce her candidacy on January 21, 2019. In the first 24 hours after announcing her candidacy, Harris matched a 2016 Bernie Sanders record for most donations collected the day after an announcement. On January 27, 2019, more than 20,000 people attended her first campaign event in her hometown of Oakland, California.

With her candidacy, Harris became one of the candidates in the 2020 Democratic presidential primaries. During the first debate with other Democratic candidates, she blamed former vice president and favorite Joe Biden for "offensive remarks," referring to Biden's positions in the 1970s on busing, a way to combat segregation in schools. After the debate, Harris rose in the polls from 6 to 9 percent. Then in the second debate, which took place in August 2019, Harris faced criticism from fellow candidates Tulsi Gabbard and Biden over her policies as California's attorney general, after which her popularity in the polls dropped. In the following months, her score in polls continued to drop to a few percentage points. Indeed, at a time when progressives were increasingly critical of the excesses of criminal justice policy, she was criticized for her tough policies as California's attorney general. In 2014, for example, she was still defending the death penalty in California courts.

She also refused - unlike Sanders and Elizabeth Warren - to place conditions on U.S. military aid to Israel. Harris believes that the security of Israelis should not be used as a means of pressure.

On December 3, 2019, Harris dropped out of the Democratic race after her campaign failed to find sufficient funding. In March 2020, Harris endorsed Joe Biden as the Democratic Party's presidential candidate.

Vice presidential candidacy under Joe Biden (2020)

In May 2019, after both Harris and Biden launched their candidacies for president, some key members of the Congressional Black Caucus declared that a Biden-Harris candidacy would be the ideal combination to defeat President Trump and Vice President Mike Pence. Although Biden posted poor results in the first primaries, his candidacy got a second wind after his victory in the primaries in the state of South Carolina, where he enjoyed significant support from African-American voters. Some days later, Biden would also become the big winner of Super Tuesday, after which Biden would become the presumptive Democratic nominee for president. In March 2020, when only he and Bernie Sanders were still in the race for the Democratic nomination, Biden promised in a televised debate that he would choose a woman as his running mate.

On April 17, 2020, Harris responded to media speculation regarding a possible vice presidential candidacy. She stated that she would be honored if Biden asked her to become his running mate. After protests erupted in late May 2020 following the death of black man George Floyd, killed during a police arrest, Biden came under pressure to choose a black woman as a vice presidential candidate, increasing Harris' chances and also Val Demings'.

On June 12, 2020, *The New York Times released* the news that Harris was emerging as a top favorite to become Biden's running mate. Then on June 26, 2020, CNN released that Harris was one of the top favorites from a list of a dozen potential candidates, alongside Elizabeth Warren, Val Demings and Keisha Lance Bottoms.

Finally, on August 11, 2020, Biden announced that he chose Harris as a running mate and vice presidential candidate. In doing so, she became the first African-American and the first South Asian woman to be nominated by a major American party as a candidate for vice president.

Vice President (2021)

On January 20, 2021, she took the oath of office as the 49th Vice President of the United States. In doing so, she became the first African-American, the first Native American and the first female Vice President.

Highlights

- Kamala Harris served in the U.S. Senate (2017-2021) and as attorney general of California (2011-2017).
- Kamala Harris, in full Kamala Devi Harris, became a leading advocate for social-justice reform following the May 2020 death of George Floyd, an African American who had been in police custody.
- In November 2020, Kamala Harris became the first Black woman to be elected the 49th vice president of the United States (2021 -) in the Democratic administration of Pres. Joe Biden.

6. Sally Ride (1951-2012)

American astronaut

"It's easy to sleep floating around - it's very comfortable.
But you have to be careful that you don't float into
somebody or something!"

Sally Kristen Ride (Los Angeles, May 26, 1951 - La Jolla, July 23, 2012) was an American physicist and former astronaut for NASA. In 1983, she was the first American woman in space; to this day, she is the youngest American ever in space.

Young years

She was the oldest daughter in the family where her parents were active in the Presbyterian Church. Her father was a teacher at a school in Santa Monica and her mother volunteered at a women's prison. Her younger sister, Karen, became a pastor in that same faith community.

Ride attended Portola Middle School and Westlake School for Girls in Los Angeles (now the Harvard-Westlake School). In addition to having an interest in science, she was also an accomplished tennis player. She continued her education at Swarthmore College and Stanford University. She earned a bachelor's degree in English and physics, a master's degree
255

in physics, and a Ph.D.. During her studies, she conducted research on astrophysics and the free electron laser.

Career

Ride was one of 8,000 people who responded to a newspaper ad seeking volunteers for the U.S. space program. In 1978, she joined NASA. Early in her career at NASA, she was a member of the ground crew during the second and third Space Shuttle missions (STS-2 and STS-3). She also helped with the development of the Canadarm.

In 1983 she was chosen to participate in the STS-7 mission aboard the Challenger. Thus, on June 18, 1983, she became the first American woman ever in space. She was not the first woman ever in space; Russian cosmonauts Valentina Tereshkova and Svetlana Savitskaya preceded her. During the mission, during which the crew orbited two satellites and performed pharmaceutical experiments, Ride operated the Canadarm, which she helped design.

In 1984, Ride participated in a second mission, STS-41-G, also aboard the Challenger. In total she spent 343 hours in space. She would go on a third mission, for which she had been training for eight months. But after the Challenger exploded during launch in January 1986 her mission was scrapped. She was asked to join a committee to investigate the disaster. After the investigation was completed, Ride was transferred to NASA headquarters in Washington DC. There she engaged in strategic planning for future missions. She also helped establish NASA's Office of Exploration.

After NASA

In 1987, Ride left NASA to work at the Center for International Security and Arms Control at Stanford University. In 1989, she became professor of physics at the University of California - San Diego and head of the California Space Institute.

In 2003, she was approached to help investigate the Spaceshuttle Columbia disaster. In her final years, Ride was president and CEO of her own company, Sally Ride Science, which she founded in 2001. She was also a member of the Review of United States Human Space Flight Plans Committee.

Ride has written or helped write five books about space exploration. These books are all aimed at children.

In 1982, Ride married fellow astronaut Steven Hawley, but their marriage broke up in 1987. Since 1985 Ride was in a partnership with Tam O'Shaughnessy, an old friend from her childhood. This only became known after her death. Ride died at the age of 61 from pancreatic cancer.

Prizes and honours

Ride has received multiple awards in her lifetime, including the Jefferson Award for Public Service, the Von Braun Award, the Lindbergh Eagle, and the NCAA's Theodore Roosevelt Award.

She has been inducted into the National Women's Hall of Fame, and the Astronaut Hall of Fame. She has twice received the National Spaceflight Medal. In the United States, two elementary schools are named after her; Sally K. Ride Elementary School in The Woodlands, Texas, and Sally K. Ride Elementary School in Germantown, Maryland.

On December 6, 2006, Ride was inducted into the California Hall of Fame. In 2013, she posthumously received from President Barack Obama the Presidential Medal of Freedom the highest award given to citizens by the government of the United States of America.

Highlights

- Sally Ride showed great early promise as a tennis player, but she eventually gave up her plans to play professionally and attended Stanford University, where she earned bachelor's degrees in English and physics (1973).
- In 1978, as a doctoral candidate and teaching assistant in laser physics at Stanford, she was selected by the National Aeronautics and Space Administration (NASA) as one of six women astronaut candidates.
- Sally Ride received a Ph.D. in astrophysics and began her training and evaluation courses that same year.

257

- On June 18, 1983, Ride became the first American woman in space while rocketing into orbit aboard the shuttle orbiter Challenger.

7. Audrey Hepburn (1929-1993)
American actress

Audrey Hepburn, stage name of **Audrey Kathleen van Heemstra
Hepburn-Ruston**, (Ixelles, May 4, 1929 - Tolochenaz, January 20, 1993),
was a Belgian-born British actress, dancer (as she preferred to call herself
rather than actress), and special ambassador for the United Nations
Children's Fund (Unicef). In the 1950s and 1960s, she was a style icon.

She won an Oscar, a BAFTA Award and a Golden Globe in 1953 for her
female lead in *Roman Holiday*. This made Hepburn the first actress to
receive all three film awards for the same performance. In total, she was
awarded three BAFTAs, a record for women, and was nominated five
times for an Oscar. She is one of the few to receive an Oscar, a BAFTA,
an Emmy and a Tony Award. She also received the Cecil B. DeMille
Award, the Screen Actors Guild Life Achievement Award, the Special Tony
Ward and in 1992 a BAFTA Lifetime Achievement Award. She had well-
known leading roles in the films *Sabrina* (1954), *The Nun's Story* (1959),
Breakfast at Tiffany's (1961), *Charade* (1963), *My Fair Lady* (1964), *Wait
Until Dark* (1967) and others.

Youth in Belgium (1929-1935)

Hepburn was born Audrey Kathleen van Heemstra Ruston in Elsene, Belgium. She was a daughter of the British banker Joseph Anthony Ruston and the Dutch Ella Baroness van Heemstra. This gave her the British nationality.

Hepburn's father, Joseph Victor Anthony Ruston, was a son of an English father and a German mother born in Bohemia, Czech Republic, in 1889. During his marriage to Ella van Heemstra he changed his family name to that of Hepburn-Ruston. The children in the family were also given the name *Hepburn*.

Hepburn's mother was a daughter of Aarnoud van Heemstra, former mayor of Arnhem and governor of Surinam and descendant of a noble Frisian family. Hepburn had two half-brothers, Alexander and Ian Quarles van Ufford, from her mother's first marriage to the Dutch aristocrat Hendrik Gustaaf Adolf Quarles van Ufford.

Hepburn spent her early years at 48 Keienveldstraat in Ixelles. When she was almost two, the family moved briefly to 311 Elsensesteenweg and to 99 Bronstraat in Saint-Gilles. From January 1932 the family lived in a villa in rural Linkebeek (now Beukenstraat 129). During this Brussels childhood she sometimes went with her mother to ballets and concerts. At home she was called *Adriaantje*.

Years in England (1935-1940)

Her parents moved to London and joined the British Union of Fascists (BUF). Audrey and her brothers were left with their grandparents who lived in Velp in villa Beukenhof (Rozendaalselaan 32). Her father collected money for the BUF in London and her mother was an editor for the BUF party organ, *The Blackshirt*. In this capacity Ella van Heemstra attended the Reichsparteitag in Nuremberg in 1935, where she met Adolf Hitler.

After many arguments between her parents, during which Audrey developed asthma and suffered from anxiety attacks, they divorced in 1939. By then her mother had been living in the Netherlands for several years, while Audrey stayed with her father in London and was placed by her mother at a private school in Elham in Kent in 1937. She took ballet lessons in Folkstone.

Residence in the Netherlands during the Second World War (1940-1945)

After the invasion of Poland in September 1939 and the subsequent British declaration of war on Germany, Audrey was brought to the Netherlands by her mother in the expectation that the neutral Netherlands would stay out of the war and arranged for her to obtain Dutch nationality. Her father, by now an accomplished German secret agent, was watched by the British secret service MI5 and disappeared from sight.

Audrey, who was now registered at school as Edda van Heemstra by her mother, went to the 5th grade of the Public Primary School no. 21 in Arnhem and had difficulty adapting to the Dutch language and customs, but eventually she mastered them reasonably well.

In Arnhem the family first lived in a single-family house at Sickeszlaan 7, but soon moved to a spacious upstairs apartment at Jansbinnensingel 8a. Eventually, from 1942 Audrey lived with her grandparents at Villa Beukenhof at Rozendaalselaan 32 in Velp until the end of the war. Audrey lived through the winter of starvation in Velp and helped the local doctor Dr. Visser 't Hooft with the wounded. In this way she also came into contact with the Red Cross to which she later referred when she became an ambassador for Unicef.

In those days she also gave dancing lessons to Velp girls and living room performances. The proceeds were for 'the resistance' in which Velp general practitioners (a.o. Dr. Visser 't Hooft) and the hospital Velp played an important role.

She attended the Arnhem School of Music at Boulevard Heuvelink 2 from 1939 to 1945, where she took ballet lessons with Winja Marova. During the Second World War she gave several public ballet performances with her school. She refused to join the Nederlandsche Kultuurkamer, which excluded her from participation in public ballet performances.

Her mother no longer saw fit to hide her daughter behind the name Edda, so from then on she was allowed to bear the very English-sounding name Audrey Hepburn-Ruston.

About the war period, one of her biographers, Barry Paris, wrote that she was said to have performed courier duties and secretly danced for audiences to raise money for the resistance. The Airborne Museum in Oosterbeek concluded in 2016 that there was no evidence to support the claim that Hepburn had been active for the Resistance.

She experienced a number of V1's crashing on the village nearby, which caused relatively many casualties and heavy damage. Also all troop movements via the Hoofdweg, and in the second half of the war the establishment of various services from The Hague in confiscated villas around her house, the bomb and shell rains over the village, the continuous threat of confiscation of the house, the frequent need to flee to the shelter. She also witnessed, according to her own words, that a number of random citizens were 'put against the wall' (shot), while she and her fellow citizens had to watch on a closed part of the street. She was a victim of a raid in 1944, in which girls were rounded up by the Grüne Polizei to work in the German kitchens, but managed to escape, leaving her terrified to spend a month in the basement of her home. Hepburn's half-brother Ian Quarles van Ufford had also been rounded up in a raid and put to work in a German labour camp in Berlin.

After the landing of the Allies in Normandy on D-Day, living conditions became more difficult because Arnhem was hit hard by the fighting during Operation Market Garden. She experienced that Velp regularly came under heavy fire from the air on everything the British airmen saw as a target, where no distinction was made between Germans and civilians, and where she, according to her own account, once was pushed under a German tank and thus escaped a shower of bullets and death.

During the last year of the war, food aid, through distribution, came in from neutral Sweden, brought in by Swedish ships. Audrey Hepburn, however, was already so weak by then that she could no longer dance or give dance lessons. By her own account, she suffered during the Second World War from acute anaemia, respiratory problems and oedema, but by the end of the war she had recovered somewhat, partly thanks to her family who fed her more than they did.

After the Liberation, the trucks came with relief supplies. Hepburn said in an interview that she ate an entire can of condensed milk and became nauseous from her first meal of relief food because she had put too much sugar in her oatmeal. This experience later inspired her to work for Unicef.

Hepburn spent her war years making drawings, some of which have been published.

In late October 1945, at her mother's instigation, Hepburn moved with her to Amsterdam, where she was allowed to take ballet lessons with Sonia Gaskell and drama lessons with the English actor Felix Aylmer. Gaskell said in a later interview that she considered it her "duty to develop her technically without harming her personality: her own style must be maintained". After the death of Gaskell's husband, Hepburn lived with her for several months and produced her own programmes with her own music, choreography and costumes.

Elaboration of the war

In a television interview with Henk van der Meijden in 1983, when asked what memories she had of the war, she said: 'A lot; my whole life has been shaped by those memories'. These violent events shaped her way of responding to questions during interviews, in which she gave appropriate answers.

Start of career and breakthrough on Broadway (1945-1953)

After the war, at the age of eighteen, she played a role as a KLM stewardess in *Dutch in Seven Lessons*. The director of this 1948 Dutch film, Charles Huguenot van der Linden, would later claim to have been Hepburn's discoverer. He kept her under contract for six months, hoping to cast her in a major film. No such opportunity arose and Hepburn decided to leave Amsterdam for London.

Hepburn moved with her mother to London where she took ballet lessons. She always had a passion for ballet and wanted to make it in this world. But by no audition was she selected. It ended up with small roles in revues, movies and nightclubs. She then worked as a model and in 1951 started acting in feature films - in her own words just to pay the bills. She soon landed her first leading role in *Nous irons à Monte Carlo* (1952). During a shoot in the south of France she was noticed by the writer Colette, who wanted her to play the leading part in the play *Gigi, which she had* written.

Movie star in Hollywood (1953-1967)

263

After a successful run on Broadway, Hepburn auditioned for the film *Roman Holiday*. At first the role of princess was assigned to Elizabeth Taylor, but contractual problems forced her to give up the film. Hepburn's opponent, Gregory Peck, realized during the filming that he was up against a natural talent. He was right, because Hepburn immediately received an Oscar for best actress for this first Hollywood role. She would be nominated four more times during her career. The song *Moon River*, which she sang in the film *Breakfast at Tiffany's*, won an Oscar for best original song. The key was changed because of her limited singing abilities. Hepburn's singing voice in *My Fair Lady* was largely taken over by the American soprano Marni Nixon. Hepburn's mother played a supporting role in the film *Funny Face*, as a café customer.

One of Hollywood's most popular crowd-pleasers, Hepburn starred on the silver screen alongside the likes of Gregory Peck, Humphrey Bogart, William Holden, Mel Ferrer, Peter Fonda, Fred Astaire, Gary Cooper, Maurice Chevalier, Anthony Perkins, Peter Finch, Burt Lancaster, George Peppard, Cary Grant, Rex Harrison, Peter O'Toole, Albert Finney, Sean Connery, James Mason and Ben Gazzara.

Later years (1967-1993)

From 1967, after sixteen very successful years as an actress, Hepburn slowed down and appeared only occasionally in a feature film. Her last film was shot in 1988, just before she was appointed special ambassador for Unicef. According to her, she started working for Unicef out of gratitude for the emergency aid she had received from the predecessor of this UN organisation at the end of the Second World War. Another reason was her own hardships under the Nazis. She remained a goodwill ambassador until her death.

In 1992 Hepburn received the Presidential Medal of Freedom from U.S. President George H.W. Bush in recognition of her work for Unicef. She died at her home in Tolochenaz in the Swiss canton of Vaud from the disease Pseudomyxoma peritonei, a cancer of the wormy appendage thought to be due to nutritional deficiencies during World War II, and is also buried there. The Academy of Motion Picture Arts and Sciences posthumously awarded her the Jean Hersholt Humanitarian Award for her work in the humanitarian field.

Style icon

264

Hepburn was a world-famous style icon in the 1950s and 1960s, thanks in part to the creations of French couturier Hubert de Givenchy. She wore his gowns both in films and privately. Legendary in film and fashion circles is the black dress designed by de Givenchy that she wore in combination with a necklace by Roger Scemama during the opening scene of the film *Breakfast at Tiffany's*. The white dress she wore when visiting the horse races in the film *My Fair Lady* is also one of the most famous film gowns ever. Givenchy employed her to promote its perfumes. Hepburn is the first world-famous movie star to do such a thing and possibly the last one not to get paid for it.

Private

Hepburn was married twice. On 25 September 1954 she married the twelve years older American actor Mel Ferrer. For him it was his fourth marriage; with his first wife he married twice. On December 5, 1968 the divorce was pronounced. On January 18, 1969 Hepburn married nine years younger Italian psychiatrist Andrea Dotti. The marriage was dissolved in 1982. She had two sons, Sean Ferrer and Luca Dotti. Scottish writer A.J. Cronin was Sean's godfather. At the time of her death, she was the life partner of nine years younger Dutch former actor Robert Wolders, the widower of film star Merle Oberon. In 1952, she was engaged to James baron Hanson. Hepburn broke off the relationship in the same year. She argued that a marriage with him would be doomed to failure because they would see little of each other due to her work as an actress. Hepburn suffered four miscarriages in her lifetime, one of which occurred when she fell off a horse while shooting the film *The Unforgiven*.

Honors, naming, TV movie

Hepburn has a star on the Hollywood Walk of Fame, at 1652 Vine Street. KLM named a passenger plane after her: the McDonnell Douglas MD-11 with registration PH-KCE. The municipality of Arnhem named a square in the city centre after her, the Audrey Hepburnplein. A bust made by Kees Verkade has been on display on the Burgemeestersplein in Arnhem since 1994.

A statue of Audrey Hepburn as a young girl was unveiled in Velp on September 14, 2019. The statue stands in front of the apartment complex the Nieuwe Beukenhof, where her grandparental home, villa Beukenhof stood.

265

In Almere a street is named after her, in Doorn an avenue and in Arnhem a square. There is a plaque on Jansbinnensingel 8 in Arnhem, where she lived with her mother until the war.

In her birthplace of Ixelles, a brass plaque reading *Ici naquit le 4 mai 1929 la comédienne Audrey Hepburn* was attached to the birthplace by the Cercle d'Histore Locale d'Ixelles and a statue of her was planned there in 2017.

Part of her life was filmed for television in 2000 under the title *The Audrey Hepburn Story*. The role of Hepburn was played by Jennifer Love Hewitt, who also took on the production.

Highlights

- Although born in Belgium, Audrey had British citizenship through her father and attended school in England as a child.
- By the 1960s, Hepburn had outgrown her ingenue image and begun playing more sophisticated and worldly, albeit often still vulnerable, characters, including the effervescent and mysterious Holly Golightly in Breakfast at Tiffany's (1961), an adaptation of Truman Capote's novella; a chic young widow caught up in a suspenseful Charade (1963), costarring Cary Grant; and a free-spirited woman involved in a difficult marriage in Two for the Road (1967).
- Audrey Hepburn's most controversial role was perhaps that of Eliza Doolittle in the motion picture musical My Fair Lady (1964).
- After appearing in the thriller Wait Until Dark (1967), Hepburn went into semi-retirement. She did not return to acting until 1976, when she costarred in the nostalgic love story Robin and Marian.

8. Shirin Ebadi (born 1947)

The first Muslim and Iranian woman to receive the Noble Prize

"I maintain that nothing useful and lasting can emerge from violence."

Shirin Ebadi (Hamadan (Iran), 21 June 1947) is a well-known Iranian lawyer and human rights defender. In 2003 she was awarded the Nobel Peace Prize for her fight for the rights of women and children in Iran.

Nobel Prize

She was the first Muslim woman to be awarded this prize. When she was accepted on 10 December 2003, without mentioning the United States by name, she fiercely criticised "states that have been violating universal human rights since 11 September under the pretext of fighting international terrorism". On 26 November 2009, it was announced that the prize, along with other personal belongings of Ebadi, had been confiscated by the Iranian authorities.

Ebadi, who calls herself an Islamic feminist, was a judge in Iran. After the Iranian Revolution in 1979, she had to resign her position. Women were

267

no longer allowed to be judges because, according to the ayatollahs, they were too emotional for such positions. Ebadi became a law lecturer at Tehran University and became internationally known as a human rights lawyer. She was the unofficial spokesperson for the women who played a key role in the election of Mohammad Khatami as president in 1997.

In 2000 Ebadi was discharged and on 28 June 2000 she was taken into custody. She was later sentenced to 15 months' suspended imprisonment.

Shirin Ebadi expressed sharp criticism when the Iranian regime hanged two underage boys for homosexual acts. This execution caused worldwide outrage.

In late 2008, as the Islamic Republic prepared for the 30th anniversary of the Islamic Revolution, Ebadi's *Center for the Defence of Human Rights* was closed. A celebration was planned there to mark the 60th anniversary of the Universal Declaration of Human Rights. Just before the meeting, plainclothes security officers raided the Center, which was sealed due to 'missing permits'.

In early January 2009, Ebadi's home was damaged by protesters who called her "American." One of the protesters told the press that he was a member of the *Basij*, a paramilitary group linked to the Iranian Revolutionary Guard. Orderlies allowed the protesters to go about their business, even after a telephone call from Ebadi.

The next action against Ebadi was the January 14, 2009 arrest of her assistant Jinous Sobhani, a follower of the Bahá'í faith banned in Iran. Since Ebadi and her daughter took on the defense of seven Bahá'í leaders last summer, attacks against them have steadily increased.

Visiting the United States on February 2, 2009, Ebadi called on President Barack Obama's administration to establish direct diplomatic relations with Iran after three decades of enmity. Before a packed auditorium at the *Carnegie Endowment for International Peace* in Washington, Ebadi called for a broad dialogue between the two countries.

According to Ebadi, who herself is regularly at odds with the Iranian government, the international community should not hesitate to denounce the human rights situation in Iran. "The Iranian government has every right to talk about *human rights violations in the Palestinian Territories*," she
268

said. "Just as other governments are allowed to talk about *human rights violations in Iran*."

Highlights

- While serving as a judge, Shirin Ebadi also earned a doctorate in private law from the University of Tehrān (1971).
- After the 1978-1979 revolution and the establishment of an Islamic republic, women were deemed unsuitable to serve as judges because the new leaders believed that Islam forbids it.
- Ebadi wrote a number of books on the subject of human rights, including The Rights of the Child: A Study of Legal Aspects of Children's Rights in Iran (1994), History and Documentation of Human Rights in Iran (2000), and The Rights of Women (2002).
- Shirin Ebadi reflected on her own experiences in Iran Awakening: From Prison to Peace Prize, One Woman's Struggle at the Crossroads (2006; with Azadeh Moaveni; also published as Iran Awakening: A Memoir of Revolution and Hope) and Until We Are Free: My Fight for Human Rights in Iran (2016).

9. Vigdís Finnbogadóttir (born 1930)

The first female who was democratically elected as president

---

*"We are all, as citizens of the world, duty bound to
contribute to our utmost ability to the continuing progress
of the spirit of humanity."*

Vigdís Finnbogadóttir (Reykjavik, 15 April 1930) is a former Icelandic
politician.

Vigdís Finnbogadóttir was elected the fourth President of Iceland in 1980.
This made her not only the first female head of state in Iceland, but also
the first woman to be democratically elected as head of state.

After three re-elections in 1984, 1988 and 1992, she made way for Ólafur
Ragnar Grímsson in 1996.

In 1996, she was founder and first chair of the Council of Women World
Leaders at the John F. Kennedy School of Government at Harvard
University. In 1998 she was appointed president of the United Nations
Educational, Scientific and Cultural Organization World Commission on
the Ethics of Scientific Knowledge and Technology. The same year she
also accepted the position as UNESCO Goodwill Ambassador and in this
she was engaged in the promotion of linguistic diversity, women's rights,
education.

Highlights

270

- Vigdís Finnbogadóttir was born into a wealthy and well-connected family. Her mother chaired Iceland's national nurses association, and her father was a civil engineer.
- From 1972 to 1980 Vigdís Finnbogadóttir served as director of the Reykjavík Theatre Company (Leikfélag Reykjavíkur) and participated in an experimental theatre group.
- Vigdís Finnbogadóttir became a member of the Advisory Committee on Cultural Affairs in Nordic Countries in 1976 and was elected its chair in 1978.
- Although the Icelandic presidency is largely a ceremonial position, Finnbogadóttir took an active role in promoting the country as a cultural ambassador and enjoyed great popularity.

10. Sandra Day O'Connor (born 1930)

Justice of the United States Supreme Court

"Do the best you can in every task, no matter how unimportant it may seem at the time. No one learns more about a problem than the person at the bottom."

Sandra Day O'Connor (El Paso, Texas), March 26, 1930) is an American lawyer.

She served as a United States Supreme Court justice between 1981 and 2006. On 1 July 2005 she announced that she would resign as soon as her successor was appointed - President George W. Bush nominated Harriet Miers for the position on 3 October 2005, and after her withdrawal Samuel Alito, whose nomination was approved on 31 January 2006. *Forbes* magazine named O'Connor one of the most powerful women in the world in 2004.

Sandra Day was born in Texas, but her family moved to a ranch in Arizona soon after. In 1950 she graduated in economics from Stanford University, after which she also earned her bachelor's degree in law within two years; William Rehnquist was the only one in her year with higher grades.

Despite her college achievements, no law firm in California wanted to hire her, although she was offered a job as a secretary. Therefore, from 1954 to 1957, she worked as a prosecutor in Frankfurt, Germany. In 1958, she returned to the United States and worked for the Phoenix Department of Justice. In 1969 O'Connor was appointed a seat in the Arizona Senate, and two years later she was re-elected as a Republican. She became the first ever female list leader in America in 1973.

For the next several years, she worked as a judge in various courts until President Ronald Reagan nominated her to serve as a judge on the Federal Supreme Court in Washington D.C. in 1981. Her nomination was unanimously approved by the Senate. This also made her the first female judge on this court, and the only one until Ruth Bader-Ginsburg was nominated by Bill Clinton in 1993. During her judgeship, O'Connor was initially part of the conservatives, but in later years she moved to the center, often making her vote decisive. In general, O'Connor made her decisions in such a way that she could not be put in a particular ideological corner, so her vote could not be attributed to either party in advance.

After stepping down as a Supreme Court justice, O'Connor remained active. In 2009 she founded iCivics, a charitable organization that tries to stimulate and develop citizenship among American youth by means of interactive communication tools such as games. In 2016, for example, iCivics developed the game 'Race to the White House' about the (American) presidential elections.

Highlights

- Sandra Day O'Connor was the first woman to serve on the Supreme Court.
- In a series of rulings, O'Connor signaled a reluctance to support any decision that would deny women the right to choose a safe and legal abortion.
- Through her stewardship in Planned Parenthood of Southeastern Pennsylvania v. Casey (1992), the Court refashioned its position on the right to abortion.

11.   Yingluck Shinawatra (born 1967)
Prime Minister of Thailand

*"I am ready to fight according to the rules, and I ask for
the opportunity to prove myself. "*

Yingluck Shinawatra (San Kamphaeng, June 21, 1967) is a Thai
entrepreneur and politician. From 2011 to 2014, she served as Prime
Minister of Thailand. She is the current president of Bangkok-based real
estate developer SC Asset Co., Ltd. and the youngest sister of Thailand's
former Prime Minister Thaksin Shinawatra. In May 2011, Thailand's
opposition party, the Pheu Thai - which has close ties to the former prime
minister in exile - chose Yingluck as their presidential candidate for the 3
July 2011 elections. She campaigned on the issues of national
reconciliation, poverty eradication and corporate tax cuts. In this election
the party obtained an absolute majority. On 5 August 2011 she was
elected as the first female prime minister of Thailand.

She studied public administration. She received her Bachelor from Chiang
Mai University, and her Master from Kentucky State University.

On 7 May 2014, she was removed from office by the Constitutional Court for alleged abuse of power. According to the court, she had violated the Thai constitution by firing a top official and replacing him with a family member. She was arrested on 23 May following a military coup, taken away to a military camp and released two days later.

Shinawatra is Chinese Thai. Her jiaxiang is in Meizhou.

Highlights

- Yingluck Shinawatra, is a Thai businesswoman and politician who was prime minister of Thailand from 2011 to 2014.
- She was the younger sister of former prime minister Thaksin Shinawatra and the first woman in the country to hold that office.
- Thaksin was ousted from office in a bloodless military coup in September 2006.
- A warrant was issued for her arrest, but members of her party reported that she had fled the country to join her brother in Dubai.

12.   Gertrude B. Elion (1918-1999)
American biochemist and pharmacologist

Gertrude Belle Elion (New York, January 23, 1918 - Chapel Hill (North Carolina), February 21, 1999) was an American pharmacologist and known for her research on drugs. In 1988, she won the Nobel Prize in Physiology or Medicine, along with George H. Hitchings and James W. Black.

Biography

Gertrude Elion was born the daughter of Robert Elion (dentist) and Bertha Cohen, immigrants from Lithuania and Russia, respectively. She attended Walton High School until 1933. She then attended Hunter College, where she received her degree in chemistry in 1937. She then attended New York University, graduating in 1941. As a young woman in a male-dominated field, she had difficulty getting a job. Eventually she was able to work as a chemical analyst for a food company. During World War II she went to work (in 1944) at the Burroughs Wellcome Research Laboratories (now GlaxoSmithKline) until her retirement in 1983.

It was at this firm (among others, together with George Hitchings, who hired her as an assistant for $50 a week) that she would make her important discoveries: substances effective against leukaemia and *acyclovir*, the first drug effective against a virus. To do this, Elion and Hitchings introduced an entirely new way of developing drugs: imitation molecules. These molecules are so similar to the original that they confuse a cancer cell or pathogen so that it cannot exert its destructive effect. She received the Nobel Prize for Medicine in 1988 for this approach.

She and Hitchings also developed azathioprine to prevent rejection of transplanted organs and was used to treat severe rheumatoid arthritis, allopurinol to treat gout, pyrimenthamone for malaria and trimethoprim for bacterial infections. In 1988, Elion and Hitchings were awarded the Nobel Prize in Medicine.

In 1990 Elion was admitted to the National Academy of Sciences and in 1991 she was awarded the National Medal of Science by George W. Bush. The always unmarried Elion (she considered her medications her children) died in 1999 at the age of 81.

Highlights

- Gertrude B. Elion, in full Gertrude Belle Elion, graduated from Hunter College in New York City with a degree in biochemistry in 1937.
- Unable to devote herself to full-time studies, Elion never received a Ph.D.
- Elion and Hitchings developed an array of new drugs that were effective against leukemia, autoimmune disorders, urinary-tract infections, gout, malaria, and viral herpes.
- Though Elion officially retired in 1983, she helped oversee the development of azidothymidine (AZT), the first drug used in the treatment of AIDS.
- In 1991 she was awarded a National Medal of Science and was inducted into the National Women's Hall of Fame.

13.   Babe Didrikson Zaharias (1911-1956)

American athlete

---

*"Luck? Sure. But only after long practice and only with the
ability to think under pressure."*

Mildred Ella (Babe) Didriksen-Zaharias (Port Arthur, June 26, 1911 -
Galveston, September 27, 1956), born *Mildred Didriksen*, nicknamed *Babe
Zaharias*, was an American golf player and also a versatile athlete. In the
latter capacity, she competed in the Olympics once, winning two gold
medals and one silver.

Sports prodigy

Didriksen, who called herself Didrikson, grew up in Beaumont. She was
the sixth of seven children. Her parents had emigrated from Norway. She
was a sports prodigy, playing many sports such as: track and field, boxing,
tennis, baseball and softball.

Didriksen wrote that she was born in 1914, but her tombstone and
baptismal certificate read 1911. Her mother called her "Babe" from a
young age, but she herself boasted that she was named after Babe Ruth
after hitting five home runs in a baseball game.

Two golds and one silver

In 1932 Babe Didriksen participated in the Olympics in Los Angeles. Here she won gold in the javelin throw and the 80 m hurdles, setting the world record at 11.7 seconds in the latter event, together with her compatriot Evelyne Hall, who finished second. In the high jump there was an exciting battle between Didriksen and another compatriot, Jean Shiley. The two were evenly matched, because prior to the Games both had already shared first place with 1.60 m at the American Championships, which were also selection competitions for the Games. In Los Angeles they finished equal again, this time at the world record height of 1.65. This led to a jump-off at 1.67, where both jumped off three times. To come to a decision they had to jump off again, again over 1.65. Both jumped off again, after which the judges came to a very strange decision. They declared the jumps of Babe Didriksen invalid, because she had used the *Western Roll* technique, where first the head passed the bar. Didriksen did not understand this, because she had used this technique from the beginning, without any comments were made. Shiley was awarded the gold based on the decision of the jury, while Didriksen had to settle for the silver. That even the IAAF disagreed with the vision of the jury appeared later, because the 1.65 of both Shiley and Didriksen was recognized as a world record.
Didriksen would have had a chance at more medals if she had been allowed to compete in more events, but at that time women were only allowed to compete in three individual athletics events.

Golf

In 1935, Didriksen began playing golf as a late bloomer. In 1938, she competed in the Los Angeles Open, a men's PGA tournament. In this tournament, she teamed up with well-known professional wrestler George Zaharias. Eleven months later, on December 23, 1938, they married in Saint Louis.

In the 1940s and early 1950s, she was America's first top-ranked golfer. She obtained amateur status in 1942 and won the U.S. Amateur Golf Championship in 1946 and was the first American to win the British Women's Championship in 1947. She also won several open championships. In 1947, she became a professional golfer and dominated the WPGA and the LPGA. She won the LPGA Championship in 1947 and the U.S. Open Championship in 1948. She became a seventeen-time champion. By 1950, she had won every golf title there was to win.

Babe Zaharias was a golfing member of the *Employers' Casualty Co. Club*.

Highlights

- In 1950 Didrikson Zaharias helped found the Ladies Professional Golf Association, and she became the LPGA's star competitor.
- Not only did she attract interest in the women's game, she revolutionized the sport and was known for her powerful drives.
- Diagnosed with colon cancer, she underwent surgery in 1953. The following year, in one of sport's greatest comebacks, she captured her third U.S. Open. Although she wore a colostomy bag, Didrikson Zaharias dominated the event, winning by 12 strokes.
- She was posthumously awarded the Presidential Medal of Freedom in 2021.

14. Mother Teresa (1910-1997)
Albanian-Indian Roman Catholic nun and missionary

"Spread love everywhere you go. Let no one ever come to you without leaving happier. "

Mother Teresa, born *Agnes Gonxha Bojaxhiu* (Skopje, 26 August 1910 - Calcutta, 5 September 1997), was a Catholic nun, foundress of the Missionaries of Charity and Nobel Peace Prize winner. She worked among the poorest of the poor in India. The congregation she founded in 1950 had more than 4,500 members in 2012 with 300 homes and was active in 133 countries.

After her death, India declared a day of national mourning. She received a state funeral, an honour normally accorded in India only to the highest political leaders.

She was beatified in 2003 and was canonized on September 4, 2016.

Lifecycle

281

Agnes Gonxha Bojaxhiu was born in the then Ottoman Empire (now northern Macedonia) and grew up in a prominent Albanian-Catholic family. At the age of 17 she entered the Order of Our Lady of Loreto in Rathfarnham, Ireland. A year later she left for Calcutta, India where she became a teacher at a girls' school. There she chose the name *Mother Teresa* in reference to Therese of Lisieux.

Struck by the fate of the countless homeless sick and dying, wandering children, the hungry and the lepers, she decided to devote herself to these poorest of the poor. With the permission of Pius XII, she left her monastery and established in Calcutta a worldwide known work among the poor, which she led until shortly before her death. She founded the Order of the Missionaries of Charity, a religious order for nuns in Calcutta. Many nuns joined her. The organisation became so large that many orders were founded outside India as well. In 25 years 90 houses were founded all over the world and 1132 sisters worked there.

In 1979 she received the Nobel Peace Prize for her work.

Beatification and canonization

In 2002, the Vatican recognized the healing of a malignant tumor in the abdomen of Indian Monica Besra as a miracle. Monica Besra testified that when she went to Mass, upon entering the church she saw a picture of Mother Teresa and rays of light came out of her eyes. After this she felt dizzy and was put to bed by sisters. The sisters placed a medallion of Mary on her lump. Six hours later she was healed. To this end, 113 witnesses were interviewed and 35,000 pages of documentation collected. However, there is controversy over the veracity of these witnesses and documentation. Besra's doctors say that her cyst and tuberculosis were cured by their treatment.

Pope John Paul II beatified Mother Teresa on October 19, 2003. Present at the beatification in St Peter's Square in Vatican City were, among others, the French Prime Minister Raffarin, the French President Bernadette Chirac, Queen Fabiola of Belgium and President Rugova of Kosovo.

On September 4, 2016, nineteen years after her death, Mother Teresa was canonized by Pope Francis at a special Mass in St. Peter's Square.

Praise and criticism

Mother Teresa was both praised and criticized for her views on responsible parenthood and the protection of unborn life. Belgian atheist and philosopher Etienne Vermeersch wrote critically of Mother Teresa for speaking out against artificial contraception, but was in turn criticized by philosopher Herman De Dijn. Journalist Christopher Hitchens wrote a critical book about Mother Teresa: *The Missionary Position: Mother Teresa in Theory and Practice* (1995), to which the Belgian sinologist and man of letters Simon Leys responded in 1997. He first did so via the readers' section of the *New York Review of Books* and later in an elaborate essay *The Hall of Uselessness* (2011) in which he denounced Hitchens' lack of knowledge of the Christian tradition.

In a 2003 article, Hitchens claimed that Mother Teresa allegedly accepted stolen money from Haitian dictator Jean-Claude Duvalier (in exchange for which she allegedly praised his rule) and from Charles Keating, an American banker, who robbed thousands of Americans of their savings in 1989 through the bankruptcy of the *Lincoln Savings and Loan* savings bank.

Researchers at the University of Montreal analyzed 300 documents and found details in them that they believe contradict Mother Teresa's positive image.

Namesake

As a tribute, many things have been named after Mother Teresa, especially in the Albanian world, including Tirana Airport and the Sheshi Nënë Tereza in Tirana, the Bulevardi Nënë Tereza in Pristina, the Rruga Nënë Tereza in Pejë (Kosovo) and the Rruga Nënë Tereza in Gjakovë, also in Kosovo. The cathedral of the diocese of Sapë in the northern Albanian town of Vau i Dejës is also called the Mother Teresa Cathedral.

Trivia

In 1969 Malcolm Muggeridge made a documentary for the BBC entitled *Something beautiful for God*. Muggeridge became impressed with the work of Mother Teresa, who was filmed for this documentary. For this documentary they shot in a building where Mother Teresa worked, called

The House of the Dying. The cameraman, Ken McMillan, used a new type of Kodak film, which he had never used before, to film the inside of the house. Back in England they looked at the footage and noticed that the footage taken in The House of the *Dying* was of very good quality and every detail was visible. The cameraman said that he found this amazing and extraordinary and went on to explain that the quality was due to the new Kodak film. Muggeridge stated that this was divine light. He was convinced that he had witnessed a miracle and testified about it to the media.

Highlights

- Mother Teresa, in full St. Teresa of Calcutta, also called St. Mother Teresa, original name Agnes Gonxha Bojaxhiu, was the recipient of numerous honors, including the 1979 Nobel Prize for Peace.
- In her later years Mother Teresa spoke out against divorce, contraception, and abortion.
- A worsening heart condition forced her retirement, and the order chose the Indian-born Sister Nirmala as her successor in 1997.
- Although Mother Teresa displayed cheerfulness and a deep commitment to God in her daily work, her letters (which were collected and published in 2007) indicate that she did not feel God's presence in her soul during the last 50 years of her life.

15. Angela Merkel (born 1954)
First female Chancellor of Germany

"I never underestimated myself. And I never saw anything wrong with ambition."

Angela Dorothea Merkel, born **Kasner**, (Hamburg, 17 July 1954) has been Chancellor of Germany since 22 November 2005. She is the country's first female head of government and also the first female party leader of the Christian Democratic CDU.

Private life

Merkel is the daughter of Lutheran pastor Horst Kasner, whose father was from Poland, and his wife Herlind Kasner-Jentzsch. The family moved in the fall of 1954 from Hamburg to Brandenburg's Quitzow in the GDR, where the father took over the leadership of a Lutheran Evangelical congregation. In 1957 the family moved permanently to the small town of Templin, where the father was jointly responsible for the development of an interdenominational training centre. There Kasner was involved in the Pastoral Council of the Evangelical Lutheran Church, which worked closely with the SED authorities. This allowed the Kasner family, among other things, the privilege of free travel to 'non-socialist' countries,

285

including the USA and Italy. The family could also easily receive packages from relatives in the West, and Angela would later admit that she never wore 'GDR clothes'. Moreover, father Kasner had a service car and a private vehicle. However, Angela's mother, Herlind Kasner-Jentzsch, was not allowed by the SED government to become a teacher. In this way she could fully devote herself to the education of her three children.

In 1961 Angela became a student at the Polytechnic High School in Templin. Her fellow students and her teachers describe her as rather inconspicuous, yet socially well integrated. Although she was not considered a "striver", she did very well at school with very good results in languages (including Russian), mathematics and natural sciences. With her class she did not participate in the ordination of youth customary in the GDR; however, in May 1970 she was accepted as a member of the Evangelical Lutheran Church ("die Konfirmation"). During her school years she was a member of scout organization Ernst Thälmann and later of the FDJ (Freie Deutsche Jugend). In 1973 she graduated from the 'Erweiterte Oberschule' in Templin.

During her school years, Angela had already decided to study physics. By choosing to study the exact sciences, she was able to largely avoid too pronounced social engagement. In 1973 she began her studies at the then Karl-Marx-Universität in Leipzig. In 1977 Angela Kasner married her fellow physics student, Ulrich Merkel; although the marriage was dissolved in 1982, Angela retained her first husband's name. After completing her thesis (Magisterarbeit) in June 1978 with the mention 'very good' and being refused a position at the technical college Ilmenau, Angela left with her husband for East Berlin. She did doctoral research at the Zentralinstitut für physikalische Chemie (ZIPC) of the Academy of Sciences of the GDR in Berlin-Adlershof. She was awarded the doctorate in 1986 with a thesis on quantum chemistry, after which she continued working as a researcher at the same institute until 1990 and published several papers. Also from 1978 to 1990 she was secretary of culture of the FDJ. In this position she was responsible for Agitprop ('agitation and propaganda') and also made training trips to the Soviet Union.

In 1978 she actively refused to work for the Stasi, however, according to other information she was said to be "IM (Informeller Mitarbeiter) *Erika*". Her Stasi file includes her GDR-critical attitude and her sympathy for the Polish Solidarność. She is also known to have been friends with the writer Rainer Kunze, who was critical of the regime, and to have read works by

Rudolph Bahro, Andrei Sakharov and Alexander Solzhenitsyn, all three well-known dissidents, among others. In the 1980s, Merkel lived in a squat in Berlin on several occasions. In December 1998 she married Berlin chemistry professor Joachim Sauer. Angela Merkel has no children; Sauer has two adult children.

GDR

In late 1989, Angela Merkel herself became politically active: she joined the GDR citizens' movement Demokratischer Aufbruch (DA), which was absorbed into the East German CDU in August 1990. Even before German reunification, she became vice-president of the last East German government under CDU member and GDR prime minister Lothar de Maizière.

Federal Minister (1991-1998)

In the first Bundestag elections for the whole of Germany in December 1990, Angela Merkel was elected to the German Bundestag by direct mandate from Stralsund-Rügen. She will always represent this most north-eastern district.

Chancellor Helmut Kohl (CDU) immediately brought her into his cabinet in January 1991 as Minister for Women and Youth Affairs. She quickly earned a great deal of respect for her expertise and knowledge of the dossier. Another advantage will have been that she was East German, a woman, Protestant and young. She was soon labelled a 'Kohl's Mädchen', a label that stuck to her until the end of 1999.

After the 1994 elections she succeeded Klaus Töpfer as Minister for the Environment, Nature Conservation and Reactor Safety.

In December 1991 she was also elected one of the vice-presidents of the CDU. From June 1993 to May 2000 she was also CDU President of Mecklenburg-Western Pomerania.

CDU President (1998-2005)

The 1998 Bundestag elections were lost to the CDU. In November 1998, party chairman Wolfgang Schäuble put Merkel forward as Secretary

General of the CDU. During the scandal that hit the CDU concerning illegal party financing in the period 1999-2002, she distanced herself early on from her protector Kohl. On 22 December 1999, she wrote an open letter to her own party in the Frankfurter Allgemeine Zeitung . When Wolfgang Schäuble also became controversial and resigned as party chairman, she was elected party chairman on 10 April 2000 with 96 percent of the votes.

Some unrest arose before the 2002 elections, when the CSU put forward Edmund Stoiber as its candidate for chancellor, even before the CDU had settled on its own candidate. Merkel knew she did not yet have enough support within the party to take on Stoiber internally, and Stoiber was also outperforming her in the polls. After a communal breakfast in Wolfratshausen she agreed to Stoiber's candidacy. After the red-green coalition narrowly won the election, Merkel maneuvered Friedrich Merz out of the position of group chairman and thus captured the political power needed to become the Union chancellor candidate in the next election.

The CDU's successive victories in elections in various Länder strengthened its position considerably. The majority of the federal states came into Union hands, enabling it to influence or block all laws to be voted on in the Federal Council. Furthermore, its personal candidate for the office of Federal President, Horst Köhler, was elected by the Federal Assembly in spring 2004.

On 22 May 2005, the SPD lost the state elections in North Rhine-Westphalia. Immediately after this hard blow, Gerhard Schröder announced new elections to the Bundestag. On May 30, the CDU officially nominated Merkel as a chancellor candidate. As the first female chancellor candidate in history, she took on the incumbent coalition of SPD and Bündnis 90/Die Grünen with Schröder as chancellor candidate in the September 2005 elections.

Chancellor (since 2005)

On October 10, 2005, it was announced that Angela Merkel would become Germany's new Chancellor if coalition talks with the SPD succeeded. On November 11, negotiations between the Union and SPD ended with the signing of the coalition agreement, giving Germany a "grand coalition" for only the second time in history. On 22 November Merkel was elected Chancellor by the Bundestag, as the first woman in the history of

288

Germany. She succeeded Gerhard Schröder. The Merkel I cabinet ruled until 27 October 2009.

The 2009 Bundestag elections turned out well for Chancellor Merkel. Although her own party lost slightly, the FDP won so many seats that Merkel was able to form a CDU/CSU-FDP coalition, which she had favoured back in 2005. The Merkel II cabinet was installed on 28 October 2009. As leader of the largest economy in Europe, Merkel played an important role within the European Union in combating the credit crisis.

In December 2012, Merkel was overwhelmingly re-elected as party leader of the CDU. She received 97.94 percent of the vote, the highest vote percentage since she became party leader in 2000. At the congress, Merkel called her government with the liberal FDP "the most successful government since German reunification. "We led Germany out of the credit crisis and Germany is now in a better position," she declared.

On 22 September 2013, Merkel once again participated in the Bundestag elections on behalf of the CDU/CSU. Her party gained more than 41% of the votes and thus became the largest party again. However, her coalition partner FDP lost so much that the incumbent coalition did not retain a majority. As in her first term as chancellor, Merkel had to team up with the SPD again. A coalition agreement was reached in late November 2013, which was subsequently approved by both the CDU and SPD. On 17 December 2013 the new cabinet was installed and Merkel began her third term.

During her third administration, Merkel received increasing praise for her international policies. The New York Times called her "the last defender of the free world" because of the rise of populism. Merkel was also praised for her role during the Euro crisis.

In 2015, Merkel decided to allow a large group of refugees into Germany. She reinforced this position with her famous statement *Wir schaffen das*. In the time that followed, Merkel continued to stress that refugees have a right to protection. Internationally, Merkel received praise for her approach to the refugee crisis, but at home dissatisfaction grew and protests broke out. Many Germans felt that Merkel allowed too many refugees. Partly because of this, some within the CDU/CSU have seen her as too left-wing in recent years. It was the AfD that took advantage of this. Later, however, Merkel tightened the immigration rules.

289

Also in the Bundestag elections of 24 September 2017, Merkel drew the list on behalf of the CDU/CSU. Her party received just under 33 percent of the vote, a loss of 8 percent but once again remained the largest party. It was almost certain before the election that Merkel would continue to govern. Her main opposing candidate, SPD member Martin Schulz, had - always supported Merkel's policy as president of the European Parliament and, despite his verbal qualities, was no longer able to present himself as a convincing alternative. Moreover, the German economy grew substantially under Merkel, and unemployment fell. Because of her policies, Merkel also enjoyed a lot of popularity among the German people, despite much criticism.

The government negotiations for the Merkel IV cabinet, in which the SPD initially refused to return to the table, were very difficult. Eventually, the various attempts did result in a new GroKo, a German grand coalition. Only in February 2018 was a coalition agreement reached, which was then submitted to the members of the CDU, CSU and SPD for approval. On March 14, 2018, the new Merkel cabinet was installed and Merkel began her fourth term.

In June 2018, refugee policy led to another disagreement, this time between Merkel and Foreign Minister Horst Seehofer. This was because Seehofer wanted to refuse asylum seekers entry to Germany if they were previously registered in another European country, while Merkel wanted to accept asylum seekers in Germany. This led to a government crisis, which Merkel ended in July 2018 with an agreement on closed transit centers in Germany, where the status of asylum seekers will be reviewed. Rejected asylum seekers will then have to return to the European country where they made their initial application.

On 29 October 2018, Merkel announced that she would not stand for a new term as president of the CDU at the congress in December 2018. This was the result of the state elections in Hesse and Bavaria that year, in which the CDU had to lose heavily. A fight will erupt in her party for the succession, not only as president, but possibly also as Chancellor.

Although Merkel's popularity and authority was waning in 2019, her popularity suddenly soared in 2020 during Germany's Corona crisis. Indeed, the Chancellor has been praised internationally for her handling of the crisis. In a televised speech on March 18, 2020, Merkel called the corona virus "the greatest challenge since World War II.

290

Relationship with the United States

The relationship between the EU and the United States took a dent on 23 October 2013 when it emerged that Merkel's mobile phone had been tapped by the NSA for years.A friendly bond grew between Merkel and President Barack Obama, but relations with his successor Donald Trump are extremely frosty. The import tariffs on aluminum and steel that Trump declared in 2018, and his fierce criticism of Merkel's refugee policy and the German contribution to NATO have contributed to this, among other things.

Positions

Within the CDU, the protestant, East German Merkel is regarded as pragmatic. In February 2003 she supported the American-British intervention in Iraq. Merkel opposes Turkey's accession to the European Union, but offers that country a privileged partnership on behalf of her party. During the German Presidency of the European Union, in the first half of 2007, she declared herself in favour of further development of the European Constitution, which had previously failed in referendums. Following the Fukushima nuclear disaster, Merkel decided that Germany should eventually abandon nuclear power and switch to renewable energy sources, the Energiewende.

Awards

Merkel was awarded the Order of Merit of the Republic of Italy in 2006, the Grand Cross of the Royal Norwegian Order of Merit in 2007, Grand Crosses of the Order of Merit of the Federal Republic of Germany and the Peruvian Order of the Sun in 2008, the Grand Cross of the Order of the Infant Dom Henrique in 2009, the Order of the Stara Planina in 2010, from the hands of President Obama the Presidential Medal of Freedom in 2011 and the Grand Gold Medal of Merit for the Republic of Austria in 2015.

She was laureate of the International Charlemagne Prize Aachen in 2008, of the German Media Prize in 2009 and of the Freedom Medal in the Four Freedoms Award series in 2016.

She became Doctor honoris causa of the Hebrew University of Jerusalem in 2007, of the University of Leipzig in 2008, of The New School and the

University of Bern in 2009 and of Babeș-Bolyai University in 2010.
Radboud University Nijmegen honored her in 2013, Comenius University
Bratislava in 2014, University of Szeged in 2015 and University of Nanking
in 2016. [2]Merkel received a joint honorary doctorate from UGent and KU
Leuven in 2017. Both universities appreciated *her diplomatic and political
efforts to build Europe's political strength, and defend the values that allow
our continent to find unity in diversity yet.*

Highlights

- In the first postreunification election, in December 1990, Angela
  Merkel won a seat in the Bundestag (lower house of parliament)
  representing Stralsund-Rügen-Grimmen.
- Merkel was appointed minister for women and youth by Chancellor
  Helmut Kohl in January 1991.
- Merkel's second term was largely characterized by her personal role
  in the response to the euro-zone debt crisis.
- More than one million migrants entered Germany in 2015, and
  Merkel's party paid a steep political price for her stance on refugees.

16. Tsai Ing-wen (born 1956)
First female president of Taiwan

"Taiwan is the Republic of China, the Republic of China is Taiwan."

Tsai Ing-wen (Fangshan, Pingtung, 1956) is a Taiwanese politician. She was sworn in as President of Taiwan (Republic of China) on May 20, 2016.

Tsai trained as a lawyer, but later became a politician for the DPP. On January 16, 2016, her party won the absolute majority. As a result, she was sworn in as Taiwan's - first female - president on May 20, 2016.

More than her predecessor, Ma Ying-jeou, Tsai advocates Taiwan's independent course from the People's Republic of China. She believes China should respect Taiwan's choice of democracy. In 2016, China cut all official ties with Taiwan after she was elected.

In November 2018, the DPP lost heavily in local elections. The Kuomintang, the DPP's conservative rival, won and this party stands for rapprochement and cooperation with China. On the island, a minority is in favour of an actual secession from China. The voters are dissatisfied with its economic policy and support the party that wants to stimulate the economy by strengthening ties with China.

293

On January 2, 2019, Chinese President Xi Jinping delivered a speech marking 40 years since China ceased shelling a number of Taiwanese islands off the Chinese coast on January 1, 1979. Xi said he wants a peaceful reunification with Taiwan but does not rule out violence. He said Taiwan "must and will" rejoin China. These statements are more threatening than usual and Tsai Ing-wen has said in a response that Taiwan will not become part of one big China.

In January 2020, she was re-elected. She received 57% of the vote, a record 8.2 million votes and 1.3 million more than she obtained in 2016. She thus remained far ahead of her opponent Han Kuo-yu, of the Kuomintang. Han received 39% of the vote. Tsai Ing-wen did not soften her stance on China, and in her acceptance speech she once again called on China not to forcibly draw Taiwan back to China. Han does want to improve relations mainly for economic reasons.

Highlights

- Tsai Ing-wen spent her early childhood in coastal southern Taiwan before going to Taipei, where she completed her education.
- In December 2016, the delicate balance of Taiwan-China relations was disturbed when Tsai placed a telephone call to U.S. President-elect Donald Trump, who overturned several decades of diplomatic protocol by becoming the first U.S. chief executive to speak with his Taiwanese counterpart since 1979.
- Although Tsai Ing-wen and Trump would later say that their call did not indicate a policy shift, by 2019 the Trump administration had committed to major arms sales to Taiwan that included, tanks, missiles, and jet fighters.
- Having championed unpopular reforms to Taiwan's energy and pension policies, Tsai Ing-wen witnessed a considerable drop in her popularity as the 2020 presidential election approached.

16 Black Women

1. Bessie Coleman (1893-1926)

First African American female aviator

*"If I can create the minimum of my plans and desires,
there shall be no regrets."*

Bessie Coleman (Atlanta (USA), January 26, 1892 - Jacksonville (USA), April 30, 1926) was one of the first American pilots in civil aviation. She was the first woman of African-American descent and also the first person of Native American (or American Indian) descent to hold a pilot's license. Coleman obtained her pilot's license from the *Fédération Aéronautique Internationale* on June 15, 1921, and she was the first person of color to obtain an international pilot's license.

Coleman, born into a family of sharecroppers in Texas, was in the cotton fields from an early age and also attended education in a small segregated school. She then attended one semester of college classes at Langston University. She developed an interest in flying at an early age, but African Americans, Native Americans, and women did not have opportunities for pilot training in the United States. Therefore, Bessie saved money and received financial assistance to go to France for pilot training. She became a prominent pilot in notoriously dangerous flying shows in the United States. Bessie was known to the public as *Queen Bess* and *Brave Bessie*, and she hoped to establish a school for African-American pilots. Coleman
296

was killed in a plane crash in 1926 when she was testing a new airplane. Her pioneering role was an inspiration to budding pilots and to the African-American and Native American communities.

Early years

Bessie Coleman (sometimes called Elizabeth) was born on January 26, 1892 in Atlanta, Texas, the tenth child of George Coleman, whose parents belonged to the Cherokee people and Susan Coleman who was African American. Nine children survived infancy which was typical for that time. When Coleman was two years old her family moved to Waxahachie, Texas where they lived as sharecroppers. Coleman attended school in Waxahachie from the age of six. She walked six miles every day to her segregated school which consisted of one classroom. Coleman loved to read at school and she developed as an excellent student in mathematics. She completed elementary education at this school.

Each year Coleman's rhythm of school, chores, and church services was interrupted by the cotton harvest. In 1901, George Coleman left his family. He returned to Oklahoma, or Indian Territory as it was then called, for better opportunities, but his wife and children did not follow him. At the age of twelve, Bessie was admitted to *Missionary Baptist Church School* on a scholarship. When she turned eighteen, she took her savings and enrolled at *Oklahoma Colored Agricultural and Normal University* in Langston, Oklahoma (now known as Langston University). She finished one semester before her money ran out and then returned home.

Career

When Coleman was 23, she moved to Chicago, Illinois, where she went to live with her brothers. In Chicago, Coleman worked as a manicurist at the *White Sox Barber Shop*. There she heard stories about wartime flying from pilots who had returned from World War I. She took a second job in a shop to save money in hopes of becoming a pilot. American flight schools did not admit women or African-Americans, so Robert S. Abbott, founder and publisher of the African-American newspaper *Chicago Defender*, encouraged her to train abroad. Abbott published Coleman's quest in his newspaper, and she received financial support from banker Jesse Binga and the *Defender*.

France

Bessie Coleman took French lessons at the Berlitz Language Schools in Chicago, and she traveled to Paris on November 20, 1920, where she was able to train to get her pilot's license.

She learned to fly in a World War I French military reconnaissance aircraft, the Nieuport 564, a biplane with "a steering system that consisted of a vertical control stick as thick as a baseball bat in front of the pilot and a rudder pedal under the pilot's feet." On June 15, 1921, Coleman became the first African American woman and the first Native American to obtain a pilot's license and also the first African American person and the first Native American person to obtain an international pilot's license from the *Fédération Aéronautique Internationale*. For the next two months, Coleman took lessons from a top French pilot near Paris to improve her flying skills. In September 1921, she took the boat to America. When Coleman returned to America, she became a media sensation.

Flight Shows

The sky is the only place free of prejudice. I knew we had no pilots, male or female, and I knew the African-American people needed to be represented in this most important area, so I felt it was my duty to risk my life to learn to fly

Because the era of commercial flight would be a decade or more away, Coleman realized she would have to become a stunt pilot in "traveling air shows" in order to make money as a civilian pilot. As a stunt pilot, she would have to perform dangerous stunts for paying audiences at a time when aircraft technology was in its infancy. But to be successful in this highly competitive world, she would have to take additional classes and expand her repertoire. Back in Chicago, Coleman couldn't find anyone willing to teach her, so she left for Europe again by boat in February 1922. She spent the next two months in France, completing an advanced flying course. She then traveled to the Netherlands to meet Anthony Fokker, one of the world's most famous aircraft designers. Coleman also traveled to Germany where she visited aircraft manufacturer Fokker and received additional training from one of the company's chief pilots. She then returned to the United States to begin her career in stunt flying.

"Queen Bess," as she was also known, was a very popular crowd pleaser for the next five years. Bessie was admired by African-American and white Americans alike. She was invited to important events and interviewed many times for newspapers. Bessie flew primarily in biplanes of the Curtiss JN- 4 "Jenny" model and other aircraft left over from the war by the military. On September 3, 1922, she made her first appearance in a U.S. air show at an event honoring veterans of the African-American 369th Infantry Regiment from World War I. The event was held at Curtiss Field. The event was held at Curtiss Field on Long Island near New York City and was sponsored by her friend Abbott and the *Chicago Defender* newspaper. Posters for the air show advertised Coleman as "the best female pilot in the world" . The air show featured flying skills by eight other top American pilots and a jump by African-American skydiver Hubert Julian. Six weeks later, Coleman returned to Chicago for a stunning demonstration of reckless aerial acrobatics including eights, loops, and drops to near the ground before a large and enthusiastic audience at the Checkerboard Airdrome (now the site of the *Hines Veterans Administration Medical Center*, Hines, Illinois, *Loyola Hospital*, Maywood, and the nearby Cook County Forest Preserve).

The excitement of stunt flying and the admiration of cheering crowds were only part of Coleman's dream. Coleman never forgot the promise she had made during her youth to one day "achieve something." As a professional aviator, Coleman was often criticized by the press for her opportunistic nature and the flamboyant style she reflected in her stunts. But she also quickly built a reputation as a skilled and courageous pilot who would stop at nothing to perform a difficult stunt. During an air show in Los Angeles on February 22, 1923, she broke a leg and three ribs when her plane stalled and crashed.

Aiming to promote aviation and combat racism, Coleman addressed audiences across the country about promoting aviation and pursuing causes for African-Americans. She resolutely refused to participate in aviation events where the presence of African-Americans was prohibited.

In the 1920s in Orlando, Florida, Coleman met pastor Hezakiah Hill and his wife Viola, community activists, who invited her to stay with them at the parsonage of the *Mount Zion Missionary Baptist Church* on Washington Street in the Parramore neighborhood. In 2013, a street there was renamed "Bessie Coleman Street" in her honor. The couple, who considered her a daughter, persuaded her to stay in Orlando. Coleman

299

opened a beauty salon there to earn extra money so she could buy her own plane.

Through her media contacts, she was offered a role in a feature film titled *Shadow and Sunshine* that would be financed by the African American Seminole Film Producing Company. She gladly accepted the role, hoping that the publicity would further her career and that the role would provide her with the money she needed to establish her own flight school. But when she learned that the first film scene required her to appear in rags with a cane and a backpack on her back, she refused to move forward. "It was clear that Bessie's leaving the set was a statement of principle. Although she was opportunistic regarding her career, she never was when it came to race. She had no intention of validating the derogatory image most white people had of most African-Americans," wrote actress Doris Rich.

It is tempting to draw parallels between me and Mrs. Coleman . . .[but] I point to Bessie Coleman and say that this is a woman, a being, who is the model for all humanity, the definition of strength, dignity, courage, integrity, and beauty. - Mae Jemison (the first African-American female astronaut)

Coleman would not live long enough to establish a school for young African-American pilots, but her groundbreaking accomplishments served as an inspiration to a generation of African-American men and women. "Through Bessie Coleman we have overcome that which was worse than racial barriers," wrote Lieutenant William J. Powell in *Black Wings* (1934), dedicated to Coleman. We overcame the barriers within ourselves and dared to dream." Powell served in a segregated Army unit during World War I and tirelessly promoted the importance of African-American aviation through his book, his diaries, and the Bessie Coleman Aero Club he founded in 1929.

Death

On April 30, 1926, Coleman was in Jacksonville, Florida. She had recently purchased an airplane, a Curtiss JN-4 (Jenny), in Dallas. Her mechanic and publicity agent, 24-year-old William D. Wills, was flying the plane from Dallas to Florida in preparation for an air show, but he had to make three emergency landings along the way because the plane was so poorly maintained. Upon hearing this, Coleman's friends and family did not think the plane was safe and begged her not to fly it. During takeoff, Wills was

piloting the plane and Coleman was in the passenger seat. She had not
fastened her seat belt because she was planning to do a parachute jump
the next day, and she wanted to look over the edge of the cockpit to
explore the area.

About ten minutes after takeoff, the plane unexpectedly made a nose dive
and then hit a spin at an altitude of 900 feet. Coleman was ejected from
the plane at an altitude of 610 feet and was instantly dead when she hit
the ground. William Wills was unable to regain control of the aircraft and it
crashed. Wills was killed instantly and the plane exploded and caught fire.
Although the wreckage of the plane was badly burned, it was later
discovered that a wrench used to service the engine had blocked the
controls. Coleman was 34 years old.

The funeral took place in Florida after which her body was taken to
Chicago. Although there was little mention of it in most of the media, her
death received much attention in the African-American press and 10,000
people attended memorial services in Chicago led by activist Ida B. Wells.

Highlights

- One of 13 children, Bessie Coleman grew up in Waxahatchie, Texas,
  where her mathematical aptitude freed her from working in the
  cotton fields.
- Discrimination thwarted Coleman's attempts to enter aviation
  schools in the United States. Undaunted, she learned French and in
  1920 was accepted at the Caudron Brothers School of Aviation in Le
  Crotoy, France.
- In further training in France, she specialized in stunt flying and
  parachuting; her exploits were captured on newsreel films.
- She returned to the United States, where racial and gender biases
  precluded her becoming a commercial pilot. Stunt flying, or
  barnstorming, was her only career option.

2. Miriam Makeba (1932-2008)

South African singer and the first African to receive a Grammy award

Miriam Makeba, nicknamed *Mama Africa* (Prospect Township near
Johannesburg, 4 March 1932 - Caserta, Italy, 10 November 2008), was a
South African singer and anti-apartheid activist. She was one of the first to
introduce African music to a Western audience. Her biggest hit was the
song *Pata Pata* (1967). Her fame paved the way for African artists such as
Fela Kuti, King Sunny Adé, Youssou N'Dour and Salif Keita. Makeba was
an active opponent of South Africa's apartheid policy and lived in exile for
thirty years after the South African government refused her an entry visa.

Lifecycle

At the age of twenty she already became a national celebrity in South Africa as the lead singer of the Manhattan Brothers. In the 1950s Makeba broke through as a singer with a South African version of jazz. In 1959 the black jazz opera *King Kong premiered* in Johannesburg. Besides Makeba, trumpeter Hugh Masekela, whom she later married, and Letta Mbulu, among others, participated in this performance. Afterwards *King Kong* went on tour in Europe. In the same year Makeba appeared in the documentary *Come back, Africa* (1959) by the American Lionel Rogosin (1924-2000). This film was an indictment of South Africa's apartheid policy. These performances meant a breakthrough for Makeba in Europe and the United States.

When she wanted to return to South Africa in 1960 for her mother's funeral, the South African government refused her an entry visa. Later, her citizenship was also revoked. In the early 1960s Makeba went to live in the United States. Her political activism brought her to the United Nations in 1963, where she called for an international boycott of South Africa. After this, her records were banned in South Africa.

In the United States she was discovered by singer and human rights activist Harry Belafonte. With him she recorded several albums in the sixties in a mixture of traditional styles, before world music became a concept. With *An Evening With Belafonte/Makeba* in 1966 Makeba was the first African woman to win a Grammy Award. A year later she scored a worldwide hit with the song *Pata Pata*, sung in Xhosa, a language with characteristic click and thud sounds.

Makeba married five times, the first time at the age of 17. On 22 December 1950 she gave birth to her first and only child, daughter Bongi. Bongi died in childbirth after giving birth to a daughter. Other husbands included singer Sonny Pillay, whom she both married and divorced in 1959, and trumpeter Hugh Masekela (1964-1966). To Black Power activist Stokely Carmichael, Makeba was married from 1968 to 1978. This marriage led to controversy in the United States. Major record companies like RCA and Reprise cancelled their record contracts. Scheduled concerts were cancelled. The couple moved to Guinea. After the marriage was dissolved Makeba remained in Guinea, where she married Bageot Bah, who worked for a Belgian airline. Also in Guinea, Makeba continued to speak out against South Africa's apartheid regime. During this period she also became Guinea's delegate to the United Nations.

In 1985 she moved to Brussels. In 1987 Makeba participated in Paul Simon's *Graceland tour*. Two years later her records were allowed to be sold again in South Africa. In December 1990, after thirty years of exile, she returned to her native South Africa at the invitation of Nelson Mandela, who had just been released from prison.

In 2005 she toured to end her career. On 10 November 2008, Miriam Makeba died of a heart attack at the age of 76, following an anti-mafia concert in Castel Volturno in support of death-threatened anti-mafia writer Roberto Saviano.

Besides prizes for her music, Makeba received the Dag Hammerskjøld Peace Prize and the Otto Hahn Peace Medal for her fight against inequality.

Highlights

- By the late 1950s Miriam Makeba's singing and recording had made her well known in South Africa, and her appearance in the documentary film Come Back, Africa (1959) attracted the interest of Harry Belafonte and other American performers.
- In 1960 Makeba was denied reentry into South Africa, and she lived in exile for three decades thereafter.
- In 1990 the South African Black activist Nelson Mandela, who had just been released from his extended imprisonment, encouraged Makeba to return to South Africa, and she performed there in 1991 for the first time since her exile.
- Miriam Makeba made 30 original albums, in addition to 19 compilation albums and appearances on the recordings of several other musicians.

3. Marian Anderson (1897-1993)

The first African American to perform with the New York Metropolitan Opera

"Fear is a disease that eats away at logic and makes man inhuman."

Marian Anderson (Philadelphia, February 27, 1897 - Portland, April 8, 1993) was an American contralto and one of the most renowned singers of the twentieth century. Music critic Alan Blyth said, "Her voice was a lively, rich contralto of an intrinsic beauty." Her former home in Philadelphia is now a museum, the Marian Anderson House.

Biography

She spent most of her career giving concerts with well-known orchestras, in the major venues in the United States and Europe between 1925 and 1965. Although she was offered several roles in major European operas, Anderson always turned them down because she had no training in acting. She preferred giving concerts. However, she did sing arias from operas during her concerts. She made many recordings, which together give an idea of her broad repertoire: from concert works, German songs and opera to traditional American songs and spirituals. Between 1940 and 1965 the German-American pianist Franz Rupp was her regular accompanist.

Anderson was a key figure in the struggle of dark-skinned artists to overcome racist prejudice in the United States during the mid-twentieth century. In 1939, the *Daughters of the American Revolution (DAR)* refused to allow Anderson to sing for a mixed audience at the DAR Constitution Hall. The incident placed Anderson in the limelight of the international community in a way that was unusual for a classical musician. With the help of first lady Eleanor Roosevelt and her husband Franklin D. Roosevelt, Anderson gave a well-received outdoor concert on April 9, 1939, on the steps of the Lincoln Memorial in Washington, D.C. She sang before an audience of more than 75,000 and a radio audience of millions, and a film was also made of the concert. Anderson continued to break down barriers for dark-skinned artists in the United States, and was the first dark-skinned artist to perform at the Metropolitan Opera in New York, on January 7, 1955. Her performance as Ulrica in Giuseppe Verdi's Un ballo in maschera was the only time she played an opera role on stage.

Anderson worked for several years as a delegate to the United Nations Human Rights Committee and as a goodwill ambassador for the United States Department of State, giving concerts around the world. She participated in the civil rights movement in the 1960s and sang at the March on Washington for Jobs and Freedom in 1963. She has received many awards and honors, including the Presidential Medal of Freedom in 1963, the Kennedy Center Honors in 1978, the National Medal of Arts in 1986, and a Grammy Lifetime Achievement Award in 1991.

Highlights

- Anderson displayed vocal talent as a child, but her family could not afford to pay for formal training. From the age of six, she was tutored in the choir of the Union Baptist Church, where she sang parts written for bass, alto, tenor, and soprano voices.
- On January 7, 1955, she became the first African American singer to perform as a member of the Metropolitan Opera in New York City.
- In 1977 her 75th birthday was marked by a gala concert at Carnegie Hall.
- Among her myriad honors and awards were the National Medal of Arts in 1986 and the U.S. music industry's Grammy Award for Lifetime Achievement in 1991.

4. Maya Angelou (1928-2014)
African American poet, playwright, and performer

"I've learned that people will forget what you said, people will forget what you did, but people will never forget how you made them feel. "

Maya Angelou, actually Margueritte Johnson (Saint Louis, Missouri, April 4, 1928 - Winston-Salem, North Carolina, May 28, 2014), was an American writer, poet, singer, dancer, civil rights activist, and professor of American Studies. She acted, wrote and produced films, soundtracks and directed.

Angelou made her name with her first novel *I know why the caged bird sings*, in which she described her tumultuous youth in the segregated south of America and, later, in California. This bestseller was made into a film. In her autobiographical novels she portrays an energetic, adventurous (growing up) African-American woman who will stop at nothing. In her youth she was raped, and this subject frequently recurs in her books. Her book *Just give me a cool drink of water 'fore I die* was nominated for the Pulitzer Prize. For the audiobook *A song flung up to heaven* she received a Grammy in 2003. She also received a Grammy in 1993 and 1995.

In 1981 she became professor of American Studies in Winston-Salem. She was involved in the Civil Rights Movement, where she worked with Martin Luther King and Malcolm X.

She spoke several times on official occasions of the United States government. At President Clinton's inauguration, she read her poem *On the Pulse of Morning* at his request. In June 1995, she recited her poem *A brave and startling truth* at the 50th anniversary of the United Nations. In 2013, she performed the poem *His day is gone*, about the life of Nelson Mandela, in a United States Department of State video on behalf of the American people.

In 2000, she received the National Medal of Arts. In 2010, she was awarded the Presidential Medal of Freedom. She received honorary doctorates from Smith College, Howard University, Tufts University, University of Southern California, Lafayette College, Hope College and the University of Illinois at Urbana-Champaign, among others.

Highlights

- Maya Angelou's poetry, collected in such volumes as Just Give Me a Cool Drink of Water 'fore I Diiie (1971), And Still I Rise (1978), Now Sheba Sings the Song (1987), and I Shall Not Be Moved (1990), drew heavily on her personal history but employed the points of view of various personae.
- She also wrote a book of meditations, Wouldn't Take Nothing for My Journey Now (1993), and children's books that include My Painted House, My Friendly Chicken and Me (1994), Life Doesn't Frighten Me (1998), and the Maya's World series, which was published in 2004-05 and featured stories of children from various parts of the world.
- She celebrated the 50th anniversary of the United Nations in the poem "A Brave and Startling Truth" (1995) and elegized Nelson Mandela in the poem "His Day Is Done" (2013), which was commissioned by the U.S. State Department and released in the wake of the South African leader's death.
- In 2011 Angelou was awarded the Presidential Medal of Freedom.

5. Ellen Johnson Sirleaf (born 1938)

The first elected female head of state in Africa

> *"The size of your dreams must always exceed your current capacity to achieve them. If your dreams do not scare you, they are not big enough."*

Ellen Johnson Sirleaf (Monrovia, October 29, 1938) is a Liberian politician who served as the first female president of Liberia between 2006 and 2018. She is also the first woman in history to be elected head of state of an African country. In 2011, she was awarded the Nobel Peace Prize along with Leymah Gbowee and Tawakkul Karman.

Johnson Sirleaf was elected president in the 2005 Liberian presidential election, at the expense of her opponent George Weah. In 1997 she lost the election to Charles Taylor.

Sirleaf studied accountancy and economics in the United States from 1964 to 1971. Since 1972 she has held various offices for her country and for the United Nations.

Family background

309

Ellen Johnson was born in Monrovia, the capital of Liberia into a family of Americo-Liberians (former African slaves from the Americas, who on their return to Liberia enslaved the local people themselves). Ellen Johnson Sirleaf, however, denies that she belonged to the elite: 'If such a class existed, it has faded in recent years through marriages and social integration'.

Her ethnicity is ½ Gola on her father's side and ¼ German (grandfather) and ¼ Kru (grandmother) on her mother's side.

Training

From 1948 to 1955, Ellen Johnson studied accounting and economics at the College of West Africa in Monrovia. She married James Sirleaf when she was 17 and traveled to the United States in 1961 where she received her degree from the University of Colorado. From 1969 to 1971, she continued her studies at Harvard, where she earned her master's degree in Public Administration. Then she returned to Liberia and began working for William Tolbert's government.

Start of political career

Sirleaf was assistant minister of finance (1972-73) under William Tolbert and minister of finance (1980-85) during Samuel Does military regime. She had run-ins with both heads of state: twice during Does' rule she was imprisoned and narrowly escaped the death penalty. During the 1985 national elections, she openly criticized the government and was sentenced to ten years in prison.After a short time she was released and fled to Kenya. For the next twelve years she lived and worked in Kenya and the United States where she became an influential economist at the World Bank, Citibank and other financial institutions. From 1992 to 1997 she was Director of the Africa Department for the UN Development Programme.

Political career

During her exile, Liberia was embroiled in a constant civil war. President Samuel Doe was assassinated and several rebel groups fought for control of the country. At first, Sirleaf supported Taylor's rebel group by helping him raise funds, but later she turned against him. In 1996, African peacekeepers ended the war and Sirleaf returned to Liberia to campaign against Taylor in the presidential election. She finished second and again had to go into exile when she was charged with treason.

In 1999 Liberia was again embroiled in a civil war and there were allegations that Taylor was involved in arms trafficking and that he was involved in the war in neighbouring Sierra Leone. He was indicted for war crimes by the United Nations and in 2003 he succumbed to the pressure and fled to Nigeria. Sirleaf then returned to head the Commission on Good Governance, which monitored preparations for democratic elections.

In 2005 she stood for re-election as president with the main campaign points being an end to conflict and corruption, creating unity and repairing the infrastructure. Her rival was the well-known ex-footballer George Weah from whom she won with 59% of the votes. On November 23, 2005 it was announced that she had won the election and she was inaugurated on January 16 as President of Liberia and Africa's first female head of state.

Sirleaf's challenges were immense. Liberia's public services were minimal, the roads, schools and medical facilities barely functioned and there was much distrust among the population as a result of the civil wars. Ellen Johnson Sirleaf invested a lot in education, partly because she saw it as a way to convey norms and values. When asked if there would still be war if all world leaders were women, she said: 'No, it would be a better, safer and more productive world. A woman would bring an extra dimension to that task, namely a sensitivity to humanity. That's because of being a mother.' In March 2012, Ellen Johnson Sirleaf was challenged by a journalist from The Guardian over her refusal to lift the criminality of homosexual acts. Active homosexuals can be punished by one year in prison in Liberia, but according to Sirleaf, the law has not been applied recently. That homosexuals can be prosecuted in Liberia is a traditional view that deserves to be maintained, according to the Nobel laureate.

After a 12-year presidency, she was succeeded by George Weah in January 2018.

Awards

1988: Four Freedoms Award for freedom of speech

2012: Honorary doctorate from Tilburg University.

311

Highlights

- With more than 15,000 United Nations peacekeepers in the country and unemployment running at 80 percent, Johnson Sirleaf faced serious challenges.
- By late 2010 Liberia's entire debt had been erased, and Johnson Sirleaf had secured millions of dollars of foreign investment in the country.
- Though Johnson Sirleaf was reelected with slightly more than 90 percent of the vote, her victory was clouded by Tubman's withdrawal and low voter turnout, which was less than half that of the first round.
- Johnson Sirleaf was one of three recipients, along with Leymah Gbowee and Tawakkul Karmān, of the 2011 Nobel Prize for Peace for their efforts to further women's rights.

6. Coretta Scott King (1927-2006)
American author and civil rights movement leader

---

*"It doesn't matter how strong your opinions are. If you
don't use your power for positive change, you are, indeed,
part of the problem."*

Coretta Scott King (Marion (Alabama), April 27, 1927 - Rosarito
(Mexico), January 30, 2006) was an American activist. Like her husband
and many others, including Mahalia Jackson and Rosa Parks, she spent
her life standing up for the rights of the so-called black community. In
addition to the civil rights struggle, she devoted herself to human rights
worldwide. She protested against American support of the apartheid
regime in South Africa and spoke out against the Iraq war. She was the
widow of the well-known American preacher Martin Luther King and leader
of the American civil rights movement. After his death, she continued his

work with the help of the *Martin Luther King Jr. Center for Social Change* in Atlanta.

In August 2005, she suffered a mild heart attack and stroke. Coretta Scott King died in early 2006 at the age of 78 and was buried on February 7. On May 15, 2007, one of their four children, Yolanda King, died of a heart attack in Santa Monica at the age of 51.

Coretta Scott King had been a strict vegan since 1995.

Awards

In 1983, she received the Four Freedoms Award for religious freedom.

Highlights

- Following the assassination of Coretta Scott King's husband in 1968 and the conviction of James Earl Ray for the murder, she continued to be active in the civil rights movement.
- She founded in Atlanta the Martin Luther King, Jr., Center for Nonviolent Social Change (commonly known as the King Center), which was led at the turn of the 21st century by her son Dexter.
- Coretta Scott King wrote a memoir, My Life with Martin Luther King, Jr. (1969), and edited, with her son Dexter, The Martin Luther King, Jr., Companion: Quotations from the Speeches, Essays, and Books of Martin Luther King, Jr. (1998).
- In 1969 Coretta Scott King established an annual Coretta Scott King Award to honor an African American author of an outstanding text for children, and in 1979 a similar award was added to honor an outstanding African American illustrator.

7. Hattie McDaniel (1895-1952)

The first African American actress to win an Oscar

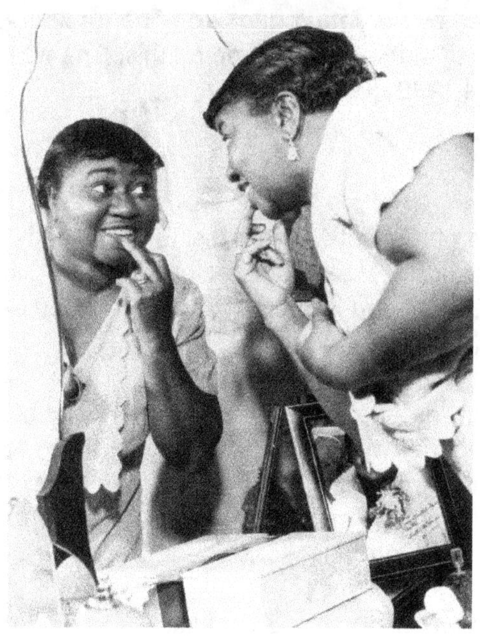

"To you young people who are aspiring to succeed in some line of endeavor, in spite of the troubles that many of us have experienced, let me say this: There is still room at the top."

Hattie McDaniel (Wichita, June 10, 1895 - Los Angeles, October 26, 1952) was an American actress. She was the first African American to win an Oscar.

Youth

McDaniel was born in Wichita, the daughter of Henry McDaniel and Susan Holbert. Her father was a preacher and her mother sang religious songs. Her grandmother was a slave, working as a cook in Virginia. Because of this, McDaniel's father was born a slave. He fought in the American Civil War.

315

McDaniel was the youngest of thirteen children. In 1910 she received a medal for a poem she wrote. Since then, she knew she wanted to be an entertainer. She dropped out of school and traveled with a group of performers founded by her father and two of her brothers, Otis and Sam. After Otis died in 1916, they stopped doing this. She was not employed as an entertainer until 1920.

Career

McDaniel was one of the first women to sing on the radio. In 1925, she sang regularly for a radio station out of Denver: KOA. Since she also wrote songs, she sometimes sang them too. She got noticed and was allowed to sing in theaters in big cities.

In 1931 she left for Los Angeles, where some of her siblings were already living. She could not get work in the film industry here, so she worked temporarily as a maid and as a cook. At the time, her brother Sam worked for a radio program called *The Optimistic Do-Nut Hour* and arranged for her to have her own program.

From 1932 McDaniel got small roles in films. Here she often played a maid or a singer in a choir. She was criticized for playing a maid over and over again, but often replied, "I'd rather play a maid than be one."

Her first major role in a film came in 1934. She then starred in *Judge Priest*, directed by John Ford. She soon became friends with the biggest stars, such as Joan Crawford, Bette Davis, Shirley Temple, Henry Fonda, Ronald Reagan, Olivia de Havilland and Clark Gable.

Gone with the Wind

McDaniel became popular as an actress although criticism of her choice of roles persisted and there was also opposition from racist quarters. Nevertheless, in 1939 she received an Oscar for best supporting actress for her role in one of the most popular films of the time: *Gone with the Wind*. She was the first African-American to win an Oscar. Many people were against this. They didn't think McDaniel was suitable for a role in such an important movie anyway. They thought she wasn't good enough.

During the premiere of *Gone with the Wind,* McDaniel did not attend. She told the director of the film, Victor Fleming, that she was ill but in reality didn't show up because she was afraid of the racists. When Clark Gable heard this, he tried to persuade her to come anyway; without success, by the way.

Due to all the backlash McDaniel faced from racists, her career was put on hold. Her last film was released in 1949. However, she was still active on radio and television.

McDaniel has two stars on the Hollywood Walk of Fame: one for her work in radio and one for her movies. Since 29 January 2006 there is also a stamp with her face on it.

Personal life

McDaniel was married four times. In 1922, she married George Langford, who, however, was killed with a gun shortly after the wedding. In 1938, she was briefly married to Howard Hickman. From 1941 through 1945, James Lloyd Crawford was her husband. She was the wife of Larry Williams from 1949 to 1950.

In 1945 she announced through columnist Hedda Hopper that she was expecting. She was very happy and was already buying clothes for her child. However, it turned out to be a false pregnancy and she became depressed.

Death

McDaniel died of breast cancer on October 26, 1952 at the age of 57 in Woodland Hills. It was her wish to be buried with her colleagues in Hollywood Cemetery, but her body was refused because of her skin color. Therefore, she was buried in Angelus-Rosedale Cemetery, her second choice.

When Hollywood Cemetery (now called Hollywood Forever Cemetery) got a new owner in 1999, he offered to rebury McDaniel's body here. Because her family didn't want to disturb her grave, they declined the offer. Instead, the cemetery erected a cenotaph for her. This is a much-visited spot today.

Highlights

- Hattie McDaniel left school in 1910 to become a performer in several traveling minstrel groups and later became one of the first Black women to be broadcast over American radio.
- She performed at a club for more than a year until she left for Los Angeles, where her brother found her a small role on a local radio show, The Optimistic Do-Nuts; known as Hi-Hat Hattie, Hattie McDaniel became the show's main attraction before long.
- Two years after her film debut in 1932, Hattie McDaniel landed her first major part in John Ford's Judge Priest (1934), in which she had an opportunity to sing a duet with humorist Will Rogers.
- Hattie McDaniel's role as a happy Southern servant in The Little Colonel (1935) made her a controversial figure in the liberal Black community, which sought to end Hollywood's stereotyping.

8. Fannie Lou Hamer (1917-1977)

American civil rights activist

"When I liberate myself, I liberate others. If you don't speak out ain't nobody going to speak out for you. "

Fannie Lou Hamer, born **Fannie Lou Townsend**, (Montgomery County (Mississippi), October 6, 1917 - Mound Bayou, March 14, 1977) was an American activist for African-American civil rights and women's rights. She became widely known for her testimony at the 1964 Democratic National Convention, describing the racism and discrimination she had faced after trying to register to vote. Because of her simultaneous struggle for equal rights for men and women, she is also credited with *black feminism*.

Young years

Hamer was born in Montgomery County, Mississippi state, the youngest in a family of twenty children. In 1919, the family moved to Sunflower County, where father James Lee Townsend and mother Lou Ella Bramlett Townsend went to work as sharecroppers on a cotton plantation. Hamer's

319

father also worked as a minister in a Baptist church and her mother as a housekeeper. Sometimes her mother helped slaughter pigs, some of which she took as food for the family. The family lived in a wooden shack held together with a tin roof, where they slept on beds of dry grass and corn husks. There was no working toilet or running water. Fannie Lou recalled that she didn't get her first shoes until she was very old and had gone hungry a lot. She regularly had nightly dreams about food. She also became infected with polio, which weakened her throughout her life. Hamer later described her childhood as 'worse than hard'.

At the age of six Hamer started working on the plantation. The devious way in which she was induced to do this, she considered afterwards as her fate as well as betrayal. When she was playing as a child, the landowner came by. He spoke to the young, hungry Hammer and offered a reward of sardines and cheese, among other things, if she would pick thirty pounds of cotton. After a week she was ready and collected her reward. She realized very quickly, however, that this method of working was designed to get her started on the plantation from which she would never leave because of the never-ending dependency and continuing debts.

Because of the work on the plantation Hamer could only attend school outside harvest time, from December to March. She had a mostly good school time and learned well. She was known to spell well and was interested in poetry. When she was twelve years old, she had to stop school because of the economic situation.

She had a loving mother, who prayed daily that her children might reach adulthood. She also walked mostly in worn clothing to save money for materials to repair her children's clothing. Fannie Lou watched her mother come off the land daily. Taking in what conditions they were living in while white people seemed to be living a life without work pressure, hunger and miserable living conditions, one day Fannie Lou asked her mother why they were not white. She responded by urging Fannie Lou to respect herself as a black woman, stating that if she respected herself others should eventually respect her as well. Hammer would later use her mother's combination of self-sacrifice and self-respect as inspiration for the position and attitude of African Americans.

Development and family formation

320

Hamer was a woman of faith, and her participation in Bible studies caused her to develop her language skills beyond her limited schooling. When W.D. Marlow, the owner of a plantation near Ruleville, realized that Hamer could read and write at a high level, he offered her the opportunity to work on his plantation as a sharecropper and bookkeeper in 1944. It is possibly no coincidence that it was on this plantation that she found work and met her future husband, Perry Hamer. Perry, called 'Dad' by Hamer, had started work on this plantation in 1932 as a sharecropper, tractor driver and mechanic. In addition, he had started a juke joint where black sharecroppers gathered to dance, drink and listen to music. It was here that Fannie Lou may have met Perry earlier. Although Fannie Lou himself did not say a word about it, there are sources that mention that Fannie Lou was already married and therefore the relationship with Perry was an extramarital one. It is certain that Fannie Lou and Perry married in 1945. As an accountant, Fannie Lou also proved to be an excellent mathematician, and she was respected by landowners and sharecroppers alike. From 1951, Hammer's mother Lou Ella moved in with Fannie Lou and Perry, where she continued to live until her death in 1961.

After several attempts by Fannie Lou and Perry to get pregnant failed, they adopted two girls in 1954, 9-year-old Dorothy Jean and five-month-old Virgie Ree. Their own families could not adequately care for these girls, in Virgie Ree's case partly because of the high cost of care for burns. In 1961, Hamer was sterilized in a minor operation without her knowledge and consent. This "procedure," which was common and known as "Mississippi appendectomy," was used on about 6 out of 10 black women attending the hospital in North Sunflower County, according to her. This was an important reason for Hamer to publicly stand up for the rights of African-American people.

The oldest of the adopted daughters died after giving birth to two children of her own, and her husband returned wounded from the Vietnam War. Following this, Fannie Lou and Perry also adopted these two granddaughters in 1969.

First attempt at vote registration

In August 1962, Hamer attended a meeting on voting rights convened at a church in Ruleville by the Student Nonviolent Coordinating Committee (SNCC), which included James Forman. Until that moment, the forty-four-year-old Hamer had not considered that the black community also had the

321

right to vote. When asked who would join her the next day to register, she resolutely raised her hand. She did realize that this could have consequences and in the worst case even death, but she felt that she had been made to 'die a little' all her life. She had always been aware of the poverty and injustice that black people faced, and she was determined to depose administrators who did nothing about that situation through her vote.

The following day, on August 31, 1962, she and seventeen others went on a bus to Indianola, the county seat, to register to vote. However, the entire group failed the literacy test. On the way back, the bus driver was arrested because, in the officers' opinion, the color of the bus was too close to school bus yellow, making the distinction insufficiently clear. However, this had never posed a problem in its frequent use for transporting cotton pickers. The driver was fined $100, but was unable to pay it. The travelling party did not understand what was going on, but did not have the amount either. Since the officers were not eager to arrest the entire group, the fine was reduced to $30, which the travelers paid.

Upon returning home, Hamer heard from landowner Marlow that she should withdraw her registration because, in his opinion, Mississippi was not ready for the black community to vote. She responded with: "*I didn't go down there to register for you. I went down to register for myself.*" (I didn't go down there to register for you. I went down there to register for myself. She would often repeat these sentences in her speeches. Marlow fired Hamer immediately after she had worked on the plantation for eighteen years. Because she was aware of the possible reprisals from people in the area, she decided to temporarily move in with friends. Ten days later there was a shower of bullets at the safe house, and another house in Ruleville was also shot at. In the time that followed she sought shelter at various other addresses.

Field secretary and custody

After several attempts, Hamer passed the literacy test in January 1963, making her a registered voter. She went to work as *Field secretary* at the SNCC. As such, she participated in a course on voting registrations conducted by Annell Ponder, *Field supervisor* of the Southern Christian Leadership Conference (SCLC). On June 3 of that year, she traveled by bus with a group to Charleston to attend a training for voice registration teachers. This covered specific difficulties in the process, such as the literacy test.

On the return trip on June 9, the group felt less and less at ease. This was mainly because the bus driver stopped in every small town to make a phone call. The group stopped for a break at an eating place. Because of the limited time for the stop, six of them, including Hammer, remained on the bus. In addition to the need to eat, the group members who went inside also felt the urge to engage in social confrontation; in particular, they wanted to check whether the Interstate Commerce Commission's ban on segregated bus terminals was being enforced. Ponder was well aware of the changes regarding Jim Crow laws, and after refusing to serve the group food, altercations followed. A tipped off police officer and *highway patrol officer* intervened. Not following the newly instituted rules in their actions, the group members began writing down identities and license plate numbers. When the officers noticed this, they became furious. The entire group that had gone inside with them was arrested. Hamer had largely kept his distance and was on the bus at the time of the arrest. Because the group members had agreed in advance to be lenient with each other, Hamer got off the bus to ask the group for permission to continue the trip back to Greenwood with the other people remaining on the bus. However, she was then also arrested.

The group was taken to prison in Winona. Here followed what Hamer later called the most horrific moment of her life. For hours, one by one, the group members were severely beaten in solitary confinement. Officers forced other black inmates to beat Hamer with a truncheon and abused her. After the beatings, her face and back were so painful and swollen that she could not lie down. In addition, she could hardly move her hands because of the swelling and she developed a fever.

On June 11, in court in Winona, all seven inmates were pleaded not guilty. On June 13, the group was released from prison thanks to SNCC and SCLC staff, including Andrew Young. Interestingly, the group was imprisoned during three important events in the civil rights history of the United States: the Stand in the Schoolhouse Door action on June 11, 200 miles east of Winona, the televised speech on the same day by U.S. President John F. Kennedy encouraging civil rights activists, and the assassination of student activist Medgar Evers on June 12, just 100 miles south of Winona.

Hammer was immediately taken to a nearby hospital in Greenwood. However, her injuries were so severe that she was taken (at SCLC's expense) to a hospital in Atlanta. Here she stayed for several weeks. After that she avoided contact with her children and husband for a while, because she didn't want to confront them with her disfigured face. Only her sister Laura was allowed to see her during this time; she later said that she hardly recognized Fannie Lou. Hammer never fully recovered from the injuries.

In the trial of the agents, all seven group participants, the FBI agents involved, and the two inmates who had been forcibly caned testified. A doctor wrote testimony about his examination of Hammer and Ponder's injuries. The agents involved were acquitted. The jury was composed entirely of white males from Mississippi.

Democratic National Convention (1964)

In 1964, Hamer co-founded the Mississippi Freedom Democratic Party (MFDP) with Ella Baker and Bob Moses. In March, after some struggles, she became the first African-American woman in Mississippi to run for the U.S. Congress. Representing the party, she testified in August of that year at the Democratic National Convention in Atlantic City, New Jersey, a convention that was televised live and also attended by Martin Luther King. The purpose of the attendance was to advocate for a mixed Mississippi delegation, in view of the fact that due to continuous voting discrimination, the existing all-white delegation was not representative of the people of Mississippi. As Hamer had just begun her story, word reached the media that President Lyndon B. Johnson was holding a press conference at the same time. Since the media assumed that the new vice president would be announced, they immediately switched to the White House in Washington D.C. In the press conference, however, Johnson only paid attention to the fact that nine months earlier the assassination attempt on President Kennedy had taken place. Special attention was given to Governor John Connally, who had also been shot during the assassination attempt, but who had survived and remained in office as governor. When the press conference was over, Hamer had also finished her testimony. Because of this coincidence and special occasion for a press conference, the siege was seen by many as a deliberate move by the president to divert attention from Hamer's testimony. Following this, however, the media broadcast Hamer's testimony primetime and several times, which brought all the more attention to her story.

324

After sharing the horrors inflicted on her and others who wished to register, Hamer concluded emotionally:

All of this is on account of we want to register, to become first-class citizens. And if the Freedom Democratic Party is not seated now, I question America. Is this America, the land of the free and the home of the brave, where we have to sleep with our telephones off the hooks because our lives be threatened daily, because we want to live as decent human beings, in America?
Thank you.

(Translation: This is all because we want to register to vote, to become a first-class citizen. If the Freedom Caucus doesn't get a seat now, I doubt America. Is this America, the land of free and brave people, where we have to sleep with the phone on the hook because our lives are threatened daily because we want to live like decent people in America?
Thank you.)

Later years

In 1965, Hamer acted as a creditor in a lawsuit that resulted in the U.S. Court of Appeals for the 5th Circuit overruling the results of local elections in Moorhead and Sunflower the following year on the grounds that it had made it difficult or impossible for a substantial portion of the black population to vote.

From 1968 to 1971, Hamer was a member of the Democratic National Committee. In 1969 she founded the Freedom Farms Corporation. Hamer was convinced that the provision of food stamps, money or food was only a short-term solution in which, moreover, the poor remained constantly uncertain about their future. On a trip to Africa, Hamer was inspired by the many black people who were able to provide for themselves. The *Freedom Farm* made it possible for families to take care of themselves permanently. The farm served about 650 families.

In 1971, Hamer co-founded the National Women's Political Caucus (NWPC). At the founding conference, she sought sponsorship for her election campaign for the Mississippi senatorship; in turn, the NWPC benefited from association with a black, female civil rights activist. Younger black women blamed Hamer for allowing herself to be used by the NWPC, believing that the organization of white feminists benefited more from the collaboration than Hamer herself.

Hamer contributed to the National Council of Negro Women and various charitable organizations to improve the position of disadvantaged minorities. This organization established the *Fannie Lou Hamer Day Care Center* in 1970, of which Hamer became president. She gave several lectures, many of which she donated the proceeds. She also went to court, even when she was already seriously ill, to speak up for single mothers who, as "bad examples," could not get jobs in public schools.

Hammer was obese and had high blood pressure. She was eventually diagnosed with breast cancer, from which she died on March 14, 1977.

Tribute and memory

Several colleges and universities awarded Hamer honorary doctorates during her lifetime. In 1993, Hamer was inducted into the American National Women's Hall of Fame. A monument to her has been erected in Ruleville, her home for many years. Her epitaph reads "*I am sick and tired of being sick and tired*," a phrase Hamer had often uttered in her life.

Highlights

- Fannie Lou Hamer, née Townsend, was the youngest of 20 children, Fannie Lou was working the fields with her sharecropper parents at the age of six.
- Amid poverty and racial exploitation, she received only a sixth-grade education.
- Fired for her attempt to register to vote (Fannie Lou Hamer failed a literacy test), she became a field secretary for the SNCC; Fannie Lou Hamer finally became a registered voter in 1963.
- In 1964 Hamer cofounded and became vice-chairperson of the Mississippi Freedom Democratic Party (MFDP), established after unsuccessful attempts by African Americans to work with the all-white and pro-segregation Mississippi Democratic Party.
- As a member of the Democratic National Committee for Mississippi (1968-71) and the Policy Council of the National Women's Political

Caucus (1971-77), Hamer actively opposed the Vietnam War and worked to improve economic conditions in Mississippi.

9. Wangari Maathai (1940-2011)

Kenyan politician and environmental activist

"The generation that destroys the environment is not the generation that pays the price. That is the problem."

Dr **Wangari Muta Maathai** (Ihithe (Nyeri), 1 April 1940 - Nairobi, 25 September 2011) was a Kenyan environmental and political activist. She founded the environmental organization Green Belt Movement, served as a Member of Parliament in 2003-2005, and was Deputy Minister of Environment and Natural Resources. In 2004, she was the first African woman to receive the Nobel Peace Prize for her contribution to sustainable development, democracy and peace.

Youth

Maathai was born in Nyeri district and belonged to the Kikuyu, one of the many African ethnic groups.In her autobiography *Unbowed: A Memoir* she describes in detail what life was like for the Kikuyu before the British came and how life changed after their arrival. Before the arrival of the Christian Westerners, the Kikuyu believed that God lived on Mount Kirinyaga, later renamed Mount Kenya by the British. The second highest mountain in Africa was therefore a very sacred place for the various tribes that lived

around it. In everything the Kikuyu did they turned to the holy mountain:
'as long as the mountain stood there, they knew that God was with them
and that they would want for nothing'.
 With the arrival of the British, many of the rituals and customs
disappeared and Christianity now usually plays the leading role in the lives
of the Kikuyu. But not only religion changed under the influence of the
Westerners; for example, instead of the goats, mburi, in which the Kikuyu
normally traded, money was introduced as a standard means of trade.

In the early years of Maathai's life, therefore, much had changed for the
Kikuyu people. Maathai's father belonged to *the first generation of men in
Kenya who left home and hearth to find a job and earn money'*. He left for
the farm of a white pioneer. Maathai's father had a total of four wives and
ten children. He had his own house on the piece of land, which was *'the
domain of the men, the boys and the male visitors'*. Also, his four wives,
including Maathai's mother, all had their own homes, which was the
domain of the wife and her children.

In her autobiography, Maathai also describes her relationship with her
father and mother. She says that her father was always the dominant
figure in their family and that she, like her siblings, kept a certain distance
from her father. She does not have many personal memories of her father.
With her mother, on the other hand, she has always had a strong bond.
When Maathai was eight years old, she moved with her mother to Nyeri,
where she went to school for the first time. Maathai was already a very
eager learner at that young age. She loved learning to read and write. She
was also very interested in nature even then; she had her own vegetable
garden where she could spend hours looking at the emerging plants and
could often be found in the woods.

Education

After a few years her mother decided to send her to St. Cecilia, a boarding
school of the Mathari Catholic Mission. The main purpose of St.-Cecilia
was actually the spreading of Christianity and the training of girls to
become nuns, although Maathai herself did not realize this at first. She
enjoyed it very much, although the conditions at the boarding school could
be called 'Spartan' according to her. She was still very eager to learn and
moreover she made friends there for life.

However, there were also less pleasant things at the boarding school; the pupils were only allowed to speak English and if they did speak in their mother tongue, they were punished. This not only gave them the feeling that their own language and culture was inferior, but often also created a big gap between the students and their parents. Fortunately, this never happened to Maathai herself; she never lost her urge to speak Kikuyu.
 While Maathai was at the boarding school, the Mau Mau uprising against the British government broke out: the movement consisted of dissatisfied members from the Kikuyu, Meru and Embu community who felt betrayed by the British. Maathai did not experience much of the conflict himself, but at the boarding school the students were indoctrinated to believe that the Mau Mau was a terrorist movement. One evening, when shots were fired near the boarding school, they had to pray and everyone prayed for the Mau Mau members to be arrested: 'I did not understand that the Mau Mau movement was fighting for our freedom.

In 1956 Maathai passed her exams at St Cecilia's as best of her class. After this, she was admitted to the Loreto Girls' High School in Limuru, near Nairobi. It was at this school that her interest in science subjects would be awakened. After she graduated in 1959 she decided to continue her studies. This was not common at that time; girls went into nursing or teaching, if they studied at all.

University

As Kenya eventually headed toward independence, many highly educated men and women were needed to fill important positions in government and society. As a result, promising students were offered scholarships that would allow them to pursue higher education in the United States. Maathai was also offered such a scholarship. She went to the Mount St. Scholastica College in Atchison (Kansas). Here she took many different subjects, but her major was biology. Maathai always felt at home at Mount St.-Scholastica College and made many friends.

After passing her candidature exam in science in 1964, Maathai studied biology at the University of Pittsburgh. Here she was commissioned by Prof. Charles Ralph to study the pineal gland of the Japanese quail, which later became her thesis research with which she became a PhD student in biology.Maathai says in her autobiography that she learned a lot from America: *'It made me the person I am today. The country has taught me to take every opportunity and do what you can, and there is a lot to do. The*

330

*feeling of freedom and unlimited possibilities that America had awakened
in me made me want the same for Kenya, and it was with this feeling that I
left home'.*

When Maathai completed her research in 1965, Kenya had been
independent for two years, and the Kenyan government was looking for
personnel to fill vacancies. Maathai was approached by the University of
Nairobi, which wanted her as a research assistant to a professor of
zoology.
 In 1966 she returned to Kenya and to her family for the first time in five
and a half years. Here, however, she was told that the professor had given
the job to someone else: someone of his own ethnicity and gender. After
months of searching for something else, she came across Rheinhold
Hofmann, a professor at the University of Giessen in Germany, in Nairobi.
He had the task of setting up a department of Veterinary Anatomy within
the Faculty of Veterinary Medicine at the University of Nairobi and he
needed an assistant in the field of microanatomy. This enabled Maathai to
work at the University of Nairobi.
 Later she would also do doctoral research in Germany. She would also
eventually be allowed to teach herself.

Maathai worked at the University of Nairobi from 1966 to 1981.

In 2001 she was asked by James Gustave Speth, the former head of the
UNDP, to teach at the School of Forestry and Environmental Sciences at
Yale University. Here she and another person delivered a curriculum on
sustainable development that focused on the work of the Green Belt
Movement. She also spoke on many panels on the environment, Africa,
and women's issues.
 In 2004, Yale awarded her an honorary doctorate in humanities.

Marriage

In 1966, Maathai met the man she was to marry: Mwangi Mathai. The
marriage had to be postponed because Maathai went to Germany for
twenty months to work on her research, but they eventually married in May
1969. By that time, Mwangi Mathai had also put herself forward as a
candidate for a parliamentary seat, so in addition to her research and
teaching, Maathai was also busy campaigning.

331

Maathai tells in her autobiography that her husband risked losing votes because his wife was so highly educated. Many people felt she would not be African enough. Yet, because she never forgot her own language and culture, Maathai managed to surprise many opponents when they visited.Mwangi and Maathai had a total of three children: Waweru, Wanjira and Muta.In the end, the marriage did not last, mainly because Maathai was such a successful woman. Mwangi probably felt intimidated by a woman who made it this far in a male-dominated world. The divorce led to a big court case, which Maathai lost. After that, she had a few days in jail because she called the judge corrupt. She was also not allowed to keep the surname of Mwangi, so in protest she added an extra *A* and was now called Wangari Muta Maathai.

In her autobiography, she says that her children still maintained a good relationship with both parents, which she is very happy about.However, the divorce did make things very difficult for Maathai, especially at the political level. For example, many men did not want their wives to vote for her because of her marital status.

Green Belt Movement

The Green Belt Movement is an environmental organization that plants trees to stop deforestation. Maathai describes the idea behind this as follows: '*The planting of trees is the planting of ideas. By starting with the simple act of planting a tree, we give hope to ourselves and to future generations'*. It is also a women's organisation fighting for human rights, good governance and peaceful democratic change through environmental protection. Their mission is to empower communities around the world to protect the environment. Also, through environmental protection, they involve women in sustainable management of scarce resources such as water, economic development, good governance and ultimately peace.

Origin

According to Maathai, the emergence of the Green Belt Movement is due to several reasons. As she says in her autobiography, "essentially *it comes down to my reaction to a series of problems and what could be done about them.* A big part has been her fight for women's rights. This arose largely while she was working at the University of Nairobi. Even when she was allowed to work as a research assistant for the professor of zoology, she encountered discrimination against women: the professor decided he would rather have a male research assistant after all. In the years that followed, Maathai also found out that men and women did not have equal rights. The few women who worked at the university, for example, earned considerably less than their male colleagues and also received many more bonuses and benefits. In the end, Maathai and Verstistine Mbaya, one of her female colleagues, succeeded in gaining equal rights. However, Maathai was not satisfied yet, because she wanted other women to have the same rights. She gets involved in a number of organizations, including the Kenya Association of University Women.

Besides her fight for women's rights, Maathai was also involved in nature for a long time. She was part of the local board of the Environment Liaison Centre, an environmental organisation that focuses on environmental issues.Everywhere around her, Maathai sees that nature is being neglected and she also sees that this has major consequences. There is much famine and malnutrition in areas that used to be very fertile. This is partly because nowadays, instead of food for their own use, farmers mainly grow coffee and tea for the international market. There was also very little firewood as a result of deforestation.
 Maathai found out that deforestation was becoming a very big problem and that it had many consequences. She heard many women complain about the lack of wood for stoking fires or making fences. Maathai realised that 'everything they lacked depended on the environment'. Gradually, the idea arose to plant trees. In this way, the women would not only be provided with firewood and wood for fences again, but the trees would also protect watersheds, 'keep the soil together, and provide food if they were fruitful'. All in all, in this way the vitality of the earth could be restored.

Before founding the Green Belt Movement, she tried a number of other things, many of which were not as great a success as she had hoped. For example, she decided to set up the company Envirocare Ltd, a company that employed poor people from Mwangi's constituency to keep the richer people from that area happy. However, she did not get much support in this, so the project failed.
 Yet she did not give up and she started a new venture: Save the Land Harambee, an initiative of the Women's Council. With this she wanted to plant trees together with poor and rich Kenyans to protect the land against desertification. The initiative started on Kenya's World Environment Day in 1977 with the planting of seven trees, the beginning of the green belt. Eventually Save the Land Harambee turned into the Green Belt

Movement. This name was chosen because the trees hold the soil like a belt, restoring the environment and making the landscape attractive again.

Purpose

The Green Belt Movement has several goals. Firstly, by planting trees it tries to stop deforestation and the problems it causes. Furthermore, the organisation involves poor women, who in this way can ensure that the land is no longer affected by deforestation. Moreover, the Green Belt Movement ensures that they can create their own income by, for example, selling seeds. The movement has also taught thousands of women about afforestation and created approximately 3,000 part-time jobs. Furthermore, the organization promotes good governance and democracy.

Performance

Currently, the Green Belt Movement has planted over forty million trees across Africa. This has reduced soil erosion in critical watersheds, restored and protected thousands of acres of forest. It has also helped hundreds of thousands of women and their families stand up for their rights and those of their communities. This has helped them lead healthier and more productive lives.

Still, they are not satisfied and continue to fight for the environment and human rights. Their goal for the future is to plant one billion plants worldwide and there are many other countries that see a lot in Maathai's initiative and have set up similar organizations.

Women's Council

After already being active in the National Women's Council of Kenya for a few years, Maathai decided to run for the presidency in 1979. However, she lost by three votes, according to her because of an ethnic strategy of President Danial arap Moi, who wanted to limit Kikuyu influence. President Moi belongs to the Kalenjin people and wanted, among other things, to curb the influence of the Kikuyu people. Nevertheless, she was overwhelmingly elected as vice president, making her the president's closest aide.
When Maathai ran for re-election in 1980, the struggle became even more difficult for her. Many cases were used against her; in particular her

divorce was revived. Still, she managed to win the elections. After that she was elected president every year until she withdrew in 1987.

Politics

In 1982, Maathai decided to get involved in politics by running for a seat in the Kenya African National Union (KANU), the only ruling party at the time. For this she had to quit her job at the university. The authorities came up with a reason why she would not be allowed to run and therefore she could not put herself forward as a candidate. She was still president of the National Women's Council of Kenya and still worked for the Green Belt Movement.
 For the next few years Maathai was mainly involved in developing the Green Belt Movement, but in the run-up to the 1997 elections she was encouraged to run not only for parliament but also for president. For one thing, Maathai needed a party that would enact her. In 2002, Maathai tried to run again on behalf of the Tetu constituency in Nyeri County. This time she did win the most votes and was elected to represent Tetu district as a candidate for NARC. This time she managed to win the elections.

In January 2003, she was appointed Deputy Minister of Environment and Natural Resources.

Nobel Prize

In 2004, Maathai was awarded the Nobel Peace Prize for her contribution to sustainable development, democracy and peace.According to the Nobel Commission, protecting the environment is very important when striving for peace on earth. According to them, Maathai promotes social, economic and cultural development in an environmentally friendly manner. They also recognize her fight against the former oppressive regime in Kenya: *'Her unique forms of action have contributed to drawing attention to political oppression - nationally and internationally'.* Moreover, she was, and is, an inspiration to other women, and they call her commitment to a better environment admirable. They say Maathai is not just trying to protect the environment, but is protecting and strengthening the basis for sustainable energy.

Maathai is the first African woman to be awarded a Nobel Prize. She is also the first African from the area between South Africa and Egypt to

335

have been awarded this prize. According to some, however, awarding the Nobel Prize to Maathai was a political choice.

Highlights

- Wangari Maathai's work was often considered both unwelcome and subversive in her own country, where her outspokenness constituted stepping far outside traditional gender roles.
- In 1971 Maathai received a Ph.D. at the University of Nairobi, effectively becoming the first woman in either East or Central Africa to earn a doctorate.
- While working with the National Council of Women of Kenya, Wangari Maathai developed the idea that village women could improve the environment by planting trees to provide a fuel source and to slow the processes of deforestation and desertification.
- The Green Belt Movement, an organization Wangari Maathai founded in 1977, had by the early 21st century planted some 30 million trees.
- When Wangari Maathai won the Nobel Prize in 2004, the committee commended her "holistic approach to sustainable development that embraces democracy, human rights, and women's rights in particular."

10.   Shirley Chisholm (1924-2005)

The first African American woman elected to the United States Congress

"You don't make progress by standing on the sidelines, whimpering and complaining. You make progress by implementing ideas."

Shirley Anita St. Hill Chisholm (New York, November 30, 1924 - Ormond Beach, January 1, 2005) was the first female federal parliamentarian of African-American origin in the United States. From 1969 to 1982, she represented Brooklyn as a Democrat in the House of Representatives.

On January 23, 1972, she became the first African-American candidate of a major party for President of the United States. She gained 152 delegates behind her. She eventually lost the nomination to Senator George McGovern. She received support from several ethnic groups and the National Organization of Women (NOW). In May 1972, she made a startling hospital visit to politician George Wallace, known to be racist, shortly after he was shot.

337

Chisholm championed civil rights for blacks, the poor and women and the African-American civil rights movement. She criticized the politico-legal system and was in favor of more controls on gun ownership.

She was married to Conrad Chisholm from 1949 to 1977. She then married Arthur Hardwick Jr. who died in 1986.

Highlights

- Shirley Anita St. Hill was the daughter of immigrants; her father was from British Guiana (now Guyana) and her mother from Barbados. Chisholm grew up in Barbados and in her native Brooklyn, New York, and graduated from Brooklyn College (B.A., 1946).
- An education consultant for New York City's day-care division, Shirley Chisholm was also active with community and political groups, including the National Association for the Advancement of Colored People (NAACP) and her district's Unity Democratic Club.
- In 1968 Chisholm was elected to the U.S. House of Representatives. In Congress she quickly became known as a strong liberal who opposed weapons development and the war in Vietnam and favoured full-employment proposals.
- Chisholm, a founder of the National Women's Political Caucus, supported the Equal Rights Amendment and legalized abortions throughout her congressional career, which lasted from 1969 to 1983.

11.   Mary McLeod Bethune (1875-1955)

Educator that opened one of the first schools for African American girls

"Without faith nothing is possible. With it, nothing is impossible."

Mary McLeod Bethune (July 10, 1875 - May 18, 1955) was an American educator, writer, and civil rights activist. She became known as the founder of a school for African-American students in Daytona Beach, Florida, the predecessor of Bethune-Cookman University, and as an advisor to President Franklin Delano Roosevelt.

Bethune was born in South Carolina as the daughter of former slaves. At a young age, she became interested in her own education. Thanks to the support of some sponsors, Bethune went to a Christian school for higher education, hoping to become a missionary in Africa. When that didn't work out, she started her own school for African-American girls in Daytona Beach. The school grew rapidly and merged with a similar boys' school to form the Bethune-Cookman School. The educational quality of the school exceeded the standards for other African-American schools and reached the level of white schools. Mary McLeod Bethune did everything in her power to obtain funds. Using her school as an example, Bethune demonstrated what educated African-Americans were capable of. She was president of the school from 1923 to 1942 and from 1946 to 1947, making her one of the few female heads of an institution of higher education.

Mary McLeod Bethune was also active in women's clubs. Through her leadership in such clubs, Bethune became known throughout the country. In 1932 she worked for Franklin D. Roosevelt's election campaign and thereafter was a member of Roosevelt's *Black Cabinet*. As such, she briefed the president on the concerns of the black community and shared Roosevelt's messages with her constituents, who traditionally voted for the Republican Party.

Highlights

- In 1904 Bethune moved to the east coast of Florida, where a large African American population had grown up at the time of the construction of the Florida East Coast Railway, and in Daytona Beach, in October, she opened a school of her own, the Daytona Normal and Industrial Institute for Negro Girls.
- In 1923 the school was merged with the Cookman Institute for Men, then in Jacksonville, Florida, to form what was known from 1929 as Bethune-Cookman College in Daytona Beach.
- In 1935 she founded the National Council of Negro Women, of which she remained president until 1949, and she was vice president of the National Association for the Advancement of Colored People from 1940 to 1955.
- She was an adviser to Roosevelt on minority affairs and assisted the secretary of war in selecting officer candidates for the U.S. Women's Army Corps (WAC).

12.   Toni Morrison (1931-2019)

African American author

*"Freeing yourself was one thing, claiming ownership of
that freed self was another."*

Toni Morrison (Lorain (Ohio), February 18, 1931 - New York, August 5,
2019) was an American writer.

In 1993 she received the Nobel Prize in Literature for her work. In 2012,
she received America's highest civilian award: the Presidential Medal of
Freedom. Several of her books are considered classics of American
literature, including *The Bluest Eye*, *Beloved* (for which she won a Pulitzer
Prize), and *Song of Solomon*. Her style is distinguished by themes of epic
proportions, vivid dialogue, and detailed African-American characters.

Early years

She was born the second in a family of four children to Chloe Anthony
Wofford in Lorain, Ohio. She was an avid reader, and her father told her
many folk tales from his culture.

She studied literature at Howard University in Washington and it was
there, that she changed her name to "Toni", after her baptismal name

341

"Anthony", with the reason that people found it difficult to pronounce *Chloe*. She received her BA in English in 1953 and then studied for her MA at Cornell University.

Teaching positions

After graduation, she taught English at Texas Southern University in Houston and then returned to Howard to teach. In 1958, she married Harold Morrison. They had two children, but divorced in 1964. After her divorce, she moved to Syracuse, New York, where she worked as an editor. As an editor for Random House, she played an important role in bringing African-American literature to the attention of the public.

She also taught at the State University of New York. In 1984 she was awarded an Albert Schweitzer Chair at the University at Albany in New York. From 1989, she was the Robert F. Goheen Professor of Literature at Princeton University for a long time. She retired in May 2006. In 2005 she received an honorary doctorate from the University of Oxford.

In April 2006 she was a guest at the PEN *World Voices* in New York, a festival organized annually by the chairman of PEN America, Salman Rushdie. Among the invitees, besides Morrison, were authors David Grossman, Jeanette Winterson, Margaret Atwood, Anne Provoost and Orhan Pamuk.

Books

The Bluest Eye (1970)

The main character of the book is Pecola Breedlove, a young black woman who prays every night that she wants to become a blue-eyed beauty, just like Shirley Temple. Her family has various problems, and she thinks that everything would be fine if only she had blue eyes. The book is controversial, not only for its subject matter, but also for its structure. Morrison uses a non-chronological structure and multiple narrators to create a fragmented and multifaceted approach.

Sula (1973)

Sula is about two black friends, Sula and Nel, and their lives in Medallion, Ohio. A mother there sets her junkie son on fire with kerosene. The book was nominated for the National Book Award.

Song of Solomon (1977)

Her third book, *Song of Solomon*, brought her into the spotlight. The book was one of the choices in the American "Book-of-the-Month" club - this was the first time an African-American writer was chosen for this after Richard Wright's *Native Son* in 1940. The book follows the life of Macon "Milkman" Dead III, from his birth to his death, in a town somewhere in Michigan. The book won the National Book Critics Circle Award.

Tar Baby (1981)

Tar Baby is set in the large Caribbean home of a white millionaire. Themes in the book are racial identity, sexuality, class, and family relationships.

Beloved (1987)

Beloved is loosely based on the life and trial of Margaret Garner. Sethe is a former slave who, during her escape, kills *Beloved*, her two-year-old daughter, so that she does not have to spend her life in slavery. The daughter nevertheless plays a role in the story. The book follows the tradition of slave stories, but also talks about the painful and taboo subjects such as sexual and other violence.

The book received the Pulitzer Prize for fiction and was filmed in 1998, with Oprah Winfrey and Danny Glover. Morrison reused the Margaret Garner story for the opera *Margaret Garner*. In May 2006, the *New York Times* awarded the book as the best American novel of the last 25 years.

Jazz (1992)

This book uses an unusual narrative style to mimic the improvisation so common in jazz music. The story is about an aging couple who lose love for each other. The man finally shoots his mistress. During the funeral his wife cuts up the corpse with a knife.

Paradise (1998)

This is the first book she released after receiving the Nobel Prize. It recounts the history and social upheaval in a small all-black town, from the time of its creation, to the sexual and social revolution in the mid-20th century. The chapters in the book are named after the female protagonists. This book was banned from American prisons because of its seditious nature.

Love (2003)

Love is the story of Bill Cosey, a fascinating, though deceased, hotel owner. It's really about the people around him, who continue to be influenced by him long after his death. The main characters are Christine, his grandchild, and Heed, his widow. The two are the same age, and were once friends, but 40 years after Cosey's death they are sworn enemies, although they still live in the same house. Morrison again used the fragmentary narrative style, and the story doesn't come together completely until the end.

A Mercy (2008)

In *A Mercy*, a 17th-century American settler enriches himself in the rum trade, then builds a gaudy house, which then serves as the backdrop for the story in this novel by Toni Morrison, which exposes the *"primal sins"* of American culture: slavery and the near-extinction of *American Natives* (*"Indians"*).

Highlights

- Toni Morrison, original name Chloe Anthony Wofford, grew up in the American Midwest in a family that possessed an intense love of and appreciation for Black culture. She received the Nobel Prize for Literature in 1993.
- Many of Morrison's essays and speeches were collected in What Moves at the Margin: Selected Nonfiction (2008; edited by Carolyn C. Denard) and The Source of Self-Regard: Selected Essays, Speeches, and Meditations (2019).

- She and her son, Slade Morrison, cowrote a number of children's books, including the Who's Got Game? series, The Book About Mean People (2002), and Please, Louise (2014).
- Toni Morrison penned Remember (2004), which chronicles the hardships of Black students during the integration of the American public school system; aimed at children, it uses archival photographs juxtaposed with captions speculating on the thoughts of their subjects.

13. Ida B. Wells-Barnett (1862-1931)

African American journalist and civil rights advocate

*"It is extremely rough to follow through with my goals,
but I felt a responsibility to show the world what the
African Americans are facing through this rough patch."*

Ida Wells (Holly Springs, July 16, 1862 - Chicago, March 25, 1931) was an African-American civil rights activist whose main effort was to make lynching of blacks - particularly in the southern United States - a thing of the past.

Wells was born in Mississippi. In 1884, she refused to leave a segregated train compartment in Memphis. After the train company forcibly removed her from the compartment, she sued the company. She won, but in 1887 the Tennessee State Supreme Court overturned the ruling.

Beginning in 1889, she was an editor of an anti-segregation magazine in Memphis. Her book on lynching, *A Red Record*, was published in 1895. In 1909, Wells was present when the National Association for the Advancement of Colored People (NAACP) was founded in New York. One of the first black women, she ran for the Illinois House of Representatives in 1930.

Wells died in Chicago in 1931. A new housing development in that city was later named after her, and in San Francisco there is a high school that bears her name.

Highlights

- Ida Wells was born into slavery, and educated at Rust University, a freedmen's school in her native Holly Springs, Mississippi, and at age 14 began teaching in a country school.
- In 1887 the Tennessee Supreme Court, reversing a Circuit Court decision, ruled against Wells in a suit she had brought against the Chesapeake & Ohio Railroad for having been forcibly removed from her seat after she had refused to give it up for one in a "colored only" car.
- Using the pen name Iola, Wells in 1891 also wrote some newspaper articles critical of the education available to African American children.
- In 1892, after three friends of hers had been lynched by a mob, Wells began an editorial campaign against lynching that quickly led to the sacking of her newspaper's office.

 # Venus Williams (born 1980)
African American tennis player

---

*"You have to believe in yourself when no one else does
that's what makes you a winner"*

Venus Ebony Starr Williams (Lynwood, June 17, 1980) is a professional
tennis player from the United States. She is the older sister of Serena
Williams. Venus has won Wimbledon singles five times and the US Open
twice to date, and is also a four-time Olympic champion (she won both the
singles and doubles in 2000, and the doubles in 2008 and 2012). In the
doubles (always together with her sister) she has won all grand slam
tournaments several times: four times the Australian Open, twice Roland
Garros, six times Wimbledon and twice the US Open. In mixed doubles,
she won the 1998 Australian Open and Roland Garros with her compatriot
Justin Gimelstob. From 1999-2016 and 2018, Williams was part of the US
Fed Cup team - she achieved a win-loss balance of 25-4 there. In 1999,
she went home with the cup. Despite a career with many injuries and other
medical woes, she is considered one of the best tennis players ever.

Career

348

Venus Williams made her debut on November 1, 1994 at the WTA Tournament in Oakland. She won in the first round in two sets (6-3, 6-4) from her 26-year-old compatriot Shaun Stafford. Williams made her first final appearance at the 1997 US Open, where she lost to Martina Hingis of Switzerland. In 1998 Williams captured her first WTA title, at the Oklahoma tournament, by defeating South African Joannette Kruger.

In 2000 Venus won gold at the Summer Olympics in Sydney: in the final she defeated Russian Jelena Dementjeva 6-2, 6-4. In Sydney, Venus and her sister Serena also won gold in the doubles: they defeated the Dutch duo Miriam Oremans and Kristie Boogert in a one-sided final (6-1, 6-1). At the 2007 US Open Venus Williams set a record for the women's serve: she hit a serve at 207,6 kilometres per hour. The sisters also won the gold medal at the 2008 Summer Olympics in Beijing: they defeated the Spanish duo Anabel Medina Garrigues and Virginia Ruano Pascual in an equally one-sided final (6-2, 6-0). At the conclusion of 2008 Venus won the WTA Championships in Doha, allowing her to call herself unofficial world champion of women's tennis for a year.

In the autumn of 2011 she was diagnosed with the autoimmune disease Sjögren's syndrome. She was out of action for months. It was even uncertain whether she would ever return to her old level, but after months of rehabilitation she managed to return to the top.

At the 2012 Summer Olympics in London, Venus and Serena Williams won gold for the third time: in the final, they defeated Czech pair Andrea Hlaváčková and Lucie Hradecká twice 6-4.

In singles, Venus won Olympic gold once, seven grand slam tournament titles, the year-end championship once, plus 40 other WTA titles. Her highest position on the WTA rankings is first place, which she reached in February 2002 and held for 11 weeks before being dethroned by her sister Serena.

In the doubles, Venus won three Olympic gold medals, fourteen grand slam tournaments and five other WTA titles, all without exception with her sister Serena. Her highest position on the WTA rankings is again first place, which she reached in June 2010 and held for eight weeks before being dethroned by compatriot Liezel Huber.

In mixed doubles, Venus won two grand slam titles, plus a silver medal at the Rio de Janeiro Olympics.

Highlights

- Like her sister Serena, Venus was introduced to tennis on the public courts in Los Angeles by her father, who early on recognized her talent and oversaw her development.
- Venus Williams turned professional in 1994 and soon attracted attention for her powerful serves and ground strokes.
- In 2000 Williams won both Wimbledon and the U.S. Open, and she successfully defended her titles in 2001.
- At the 2000 Olympic Games in Sydney, she captured the gold medal in the singles competition and claimed a gold medal with her sister in the doubles event.
- In 2008 Venus Williams defeated Serena for a fifth career Wimbledon title, placing her fifth all-time in women's Wimbledon singles championships.

15.   Zora Neale Hurston (1891-1960)

African American writer, folklorist, and anthropologist

"If you are silent about your pain, they'll kill you and say
you enjoyed it."

Zora Neale Hurston (Notasulga, January 7, 1891- Fort Pierce, Florida, January 28, 1960) was an American writer, anthropologist, and folklorist. She is considered an important representative of the Harlem Renaissance.

Life and work

Neale Hurston was born into a traditionally African-American environment. Her mother died when she was nine, when she was fourteen she left the parental home, and later in life, between 1918 and 1927, she went off to study on her own, first at Howard University in Washington DC and then anthropology at Barnard College in New York, where she was the only African-American student.

In New York she came into contact with writers of the *Harlem Renaissance*, such as Langston Hughes, and published her first stories and a play. In addition, after her studies she started collecting folkloric material (stories, songs, prayers, etc. of the black population), first in Florida and Alabama, after 1930 also in the Bahamas and in New Orleans. After the publication of her anthropological work *Mules and Men,* she received an official research assignment that took her to Jamaica and Haiti. At the end of the 1930s she worked for the WPA in Florida.

Neale Hurston was a multifaceted woman who, as an anthropologist for Columbia University, conducted field research on voodoo in Haiti and on the living conditions of black Americans in the rural South. But she ultimately went down in history primarily as a literary writer. In the 1930s she was considered one of the most important figures in African-American literature. In her stories and novels she describes experiences and memories of the life of blacks in rural America at the beginning of the twentieth century. In doing so, she emphatically refrains from the stereotyping of 'the respectable black' that was common at the time, a characteristic feature of the writers of the *Harlem Renaissance*. Her work has the South as its setting; *Jonah's Gourd Vine* (1934) was followed by her most important work, *Their Eyes Were Watching God* (1937). In this novel, the use of language is extremely evocative and lyrical, especially the dialogues in vernacular. It focuses on a woman who succeeds in shaping her own life without apologizing for it.

In the 1950s Neale Hurston fell into oblivion and hardly any work was published. Eventually she even ended up in relative poverty. In 1959 she suffered a stroke and had to accept social assistance. Zora Neale Hurston eventually died of heart failure in 1960.

In 2018, she posthumously published *Barracoon: The Story of the Last 'Black Cargo'*, her book on the Trans-Atlantic slave trade based on the story of survivor Cudjoe Lewis, which she had chronicled in 1927.

Highlights

- In 1930 Zora Neale Hurston collaborated with Hughes on a play titled Mule Bone: A Comedy of Negro Life in Three Acts (published posthumously 1991).

- For a number of years Zora Neale Hurston was on the faculty of North Carolina College for Negroes (now North Carolina Central University) in Durham.
- Despite Zora Neale Hurston's early promise, by the time of her death, she was little remembered by the general reading public, but there was a resurgence of interest in her work in the late 20th century.
- In addition to Mule Bone, several other collections were also published posthumously; these included Spunk: The Selected Stories (1985), The Complete Stories (1995), and Every Tongue Got to Confess (2001), a collection of folktales from the South.

16.   Mahalia Jackson (1911-1972)

African American gospel singer

"Faith and prayer are the vitamins of the soul; man cannot live in health without them."

Mahalia Jackson (New Orleans, October 26, 1911 - Chicago, January 27, 1972) was an American singer and was called 'the queen of gospel'. Her first record in 1934, *God Gonna Separate the Wheat from the Tares*, became especially populiar in the southern United States. The highlight of her singing career was probably on August 28 1963 during a mass demonstration against racial discrimination at the Lincoln Memorial in Washington. In front of a crowd of more than 250,000 people she sang *I've been buked and I've been scorned* at the request of Martin Luther King and *How I got over*. Through her financial support and her participation in the demonstrations organized by Martin Luther King, she certainly made a great contribution to the struggle for the emancipation of African-Americans, hand in hand with great figures and advocates against apartheid such as the Reverend Martin Luther King, a member of the same Baptist church, his wife Coretta Scott King and Rosa Parks. The great merits of Mahalia Jackson in the field of emancipation of African-Americans have not yet been sufficiently highlighted; she became known mainly as a singer.

Lifecycle

Jackson was born in New Orleans, the birthplace of jazz. She was a Baptist and sang as a gospel singer in the church of which she was a member. In 1927 she moved to Chicago, earned a living as a worker and sang in the choir of the Greater Salem Baptist Church. Soon she formed a group with the Johnson Singers. Later she collaborated with Thomas Dorsey, who composed the gospel song *Precious Lord, take my hand*, Martin Luther King's favorite song, which she also sang at his funeral in April 1968. From the money she saved she started a flower shop and a beauty salon. In 1945 she broke through with the white public by recording *I will move on up a little higher*, of which 2 million copies were sold. It was not until the 1950s that she became known in Europe, where she performed in 1952, 1961, 1964, 1968 and 1971. In 1971 she ended her foreign performances with a final concert in Munich. She had appearances at the White House and was received in private audience by Pope John XXIII in 1961. She died on January 27, 1972 in Chicago of heart failure and complications of diabetes mellitus. Several biographies have been written about her life.

Gospel music

The gospel songs of Jackson and many others constitute gospel-inspired religious music. They have the original rhythm of the African music of slaves imported to America. Jackson never sang blues or jazz. In 1958 she sang the *Come Sunday* in Duke Ellington's Black Brown and Beige Suite, after long insistence and only because the lyrics were religious. Under pressure from CBS she did record Christian songs that were not her style and were close to kitsch. She never crossed the line between blues and jazz. In 1978 she was posthumously inducted into the Gospel Music Hall of Fame.

Highlights

- Mahalia Jackson first came to wide public attention in the 1930s, when she participated in a cross-country gospel tour singing such songs as "He's Got the Whole World in His Hands" and "I Can Put My Trust in Jesus."
- Mahalia Jackson sang on the radio and on television and, starting in 1950, performed to overflow audiences in annual concerts at Carnegie Hall in New York City.
- Eight of Jackson's records sold more than a million copies each.
- In the 1950s and '60s Mahalia Jackson was active in the civil rights movement.